CW01594656

HISTORY IN THE MAKING
Series Editor: John Jones

1 The Ancient World

HISTORY IN THE MAKING

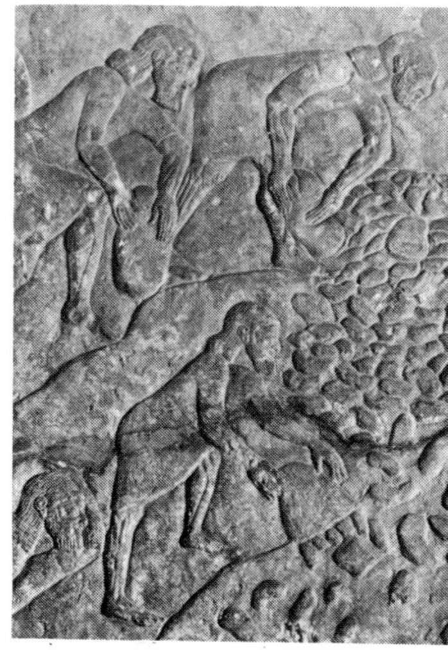

Martin Roberts
Headmaster,
The Cherwell School
Oxford

1 The Ancient World

Nelson

Thomas Nelson and Sons Ltd
Nelson House Mayfield Road
Walton-on-Thames Surrey
KT12 5PL UK

51 York Place
Edinburgh
EH1 3JD UK

Thomas Nelson (Hong Kong) Ltd
Toppan Building 10/F
22A Westlands Road
Quarry Bay Hong Kong

Thomas Nelson Australia
102 Dodds Street
South Melbourne
Victoria 3205 Australia

Nelson Canada
1120 Birchmount Road
Scarborough Ontario
M1K 5G4 Canada

First published by Macmillan Education Ltd 1979
(under ISBN 0-333-22383-7)

This edition published by Thomas Nelson and Sons Ltd 1992

ISBN 0-17-435068-6
NPN 9 8 7 6 5 4

Printed in Hong Kong.

Series preface

Changes in the teaching of History over the last decade have raised many problems, to which there are no easy solutions. The classification of objectives, the presentation of material in varied and appropriate language, the use and abuse of evidence and the reconsideration of assessment techniques are four of the more important. Many teachers are now encouraging their pupils individually or in groups to participate in the processes and skills of the professional historian. Moreover such developments are being discussed increasingly in the context of mixed ability classes and the need to provide suitable teaching approaches for them.

History in the Making is a new course for secondary schools intended for pupils of average ability. It is a contribution to the current debate, and provides one possible way forward. It accepts many of the proven virtues of traditional courses: the fascination of the good tale, the drama of human life, individual and collective, the need to provide a visual stimulus to support the written word.

But it has built on to these some of the key features of the 'new history' so that teachers can explore, within the framework of a text book, many of the 'new' approaches and techniques.

To this end each chapter in this volume has four major components.

1 **The text** This provides the basic framework of the chapters, and although the approach is essentially factual, it is intended to arouse and sustain the interest of the reader of average ability.

2 **The illustrations** These have been carefully selected to stand beside the written pieces of evidence in the chapter, and to provide (so far as is possible) an authentic visual image of the period/topic. Photographs, artwork and maps are all used to clarify and support the text, and to develop the pupil's powers of observation.

3 **Using the evidence** This is a detailed study of the evidence on one particular aspect of the chapter. Did the Walls of Jericho really come tumbling down? Was the death of William Rufus in the New Forest really an accident? What was the background to the torpedoing of the *Lusitania*? These are the sort of questions which are asked, to give the pupil the opportunity to consider not only the problems facing the historian, but also those facing the characters of history. Different forms of documentary evidence are considered, as well as archaeological, architectural, statistical, and other kinds of source material; the intention is to give the pupil a genuine, if modest, insight into the making of history.

4 **Questions and further work** These are intended to test and develop the pupil's reading of the chapter, in particular the *Using the Evidence* section. Particular attention is paid to the development of historical skills, through the examination and interpretation of evidence. The differences between primary and secondary sources, for example, are explored, and concepts such as bias in evidence introduced through specific examples. Some comprehension questions are included, but the emphasis is very much on involving pupils with the materials, and

helping them to develop a critical awareness of different kinds of evidence and its limitations. By applying the skills which they have developed, pupils may then be able to formulate at a suitable level and in appropriate language, ideas and hypotheses of their own.

History in the Making is a complete course in five volumes, to meet the needs of pupils between the ages of 11 and 16 (in other words up to and including the first public examination). However each volume stands by itself and may be used independently of the others; given the variety of syllabuses in use in schools today this flexibility is likely to be welcomed by many teachers. *The Ancient World* and *The Medieval World* are intended primarily for 11–13-year-old pupils, *The Early Modern World, 1450–1700* for 12–14-year-old pupils, *Britain, Europe and Beyond, 1700–1900* for pre-CSE pupils and *The Twentieth Century* for CSE examination candidates.

It is our hope that pupils will be encouraged, within the main topics and themes of British, European and World History, to experience for themselves the stimulus and challenge, the pleasure and frustration, the vitality and humanity that are an essential part of History in the Making.

J.A.P. Jones

Contents

The Greeks

The Romans

List of maps

Timecharts

1470 Man 2 500 000 years ago

Ice Ages 600 000 years ago

Peking Man 400 000 years ago

Swanscombe Man 250 000 years ago

Neanderthal Man 200 000 years ago

Modern Man 35 000 years ago

Invention of writing 5000 years ago

Man has been able to write for 5000 years.
1470 Man chipped stones beside Lake Turkana 500 × 5000 years ago.

Date BC	Technology/ inventions	Mesopotamia	Egypt	Eastern Mediterranean	Greece	Rome	India	China	The Americas	Britain
8000	farming weaving pottery copper-smelting						hunting continues	hunting continues	hunting continues	hunting continues
		farming c.6000		farming c.6000	farming c.6000	farming c.6000			some plant-growing in Mexico	
		beginnings of Sumerian civilisation	farming c.5500					some farming in the north c.5000		Stone Age farmers arrive c.3500
3000	writing the wheel bronze		Egypt united by Menes							
2900										
2800			Pyramid-building pharaohs							Megalith tombs
2700	365-day calendar Egypt							farming spreads		
2600										
2500				Phoenician and Cretan trading begins to prosper			Indus civilisation begins			
2400										
2300		Sargon the Great		Troy prospers						
2200									civilisations in Peru	
2100										
2000			Middle Kingdom begins Thebes the capital							Grimes Graves flint mines
1900				Minoan civilisations Crete						
1800		Hammurabi	end of Middle Kingdom	Hittite Empire			Aryan invasions			Stonehenge

Date	Technology/ inventions	Mesopotamia	Egypt	Eastern Mediterranean	Greece	Rome	India	China	The Americas	Britain
1700 BC		Mari an important city	Hyksos invades						Olmecs (Mexico)	
1600					rise of Mycenae					
1500	alphabet		Hyksos driven out New Kingdom	disasters in Crete				Shang Empire		
1400			Ikhnaton Tutankhamen				rise of Hindu religion			
1300			Rameses II	Hebrews conquer Palestine	Trojan War?					
1200		rise of Assyria								
1100		Tiglath-Pileser I								
1000	iron weapons and tools			Phoenicians set up colonies	emergence of Ionian and Dorian Greeks			Chou Empire		
900				Golden age of Hebrews						
800				Foundation of Carthage	Homer					
700		Sennacherib end of Assyria	Assyrian conquest			foundation of city				
600	spread and improvements in the use of iron	Nebuchadnezzar of Babylon		Tyre conquered by Babylon	rise of city-states	Etruscans powerful				
500		Cyrus of Persia Persian Empire	Persian conquest	Persian conquest	Persian Wars Peloponnesian Wars	Etruscan king driven off	Buddha	Confucius		
400		Greek conquest	Greek conquest	Greek conquest	rise of Macedon Alexander the Great					
300						Punic Wars expansion in the East	Mauryan Empire	Shih Huang Ti		Celtic invasions
200								Han Empire begins		
100				Roman conquest	Roman conquest	end of the republic		Emperor Wu		
AD O		Parthian Empire	Roman conquest	Jesus Christ		Augustus further expansion				Julius Caesar invades
100	paper in China			spread of Christianity		Golden Age of Roman Empire				Claudian invasion Hadrian's Wall
200		Sassanid Empire				Marcus Aurelius beginnings of barbarian attacks	Gupta Empire	Han Empire declines	Teotihuacan prospers	
300	decimal system of mathematics in India				Constantine makes Byzantium his capital	Diocletian Constantine				Barbarian attacks begin
400						end of Empire in the West			beginnings of Maya civilisation	
					Byzantine Empire continues until 1453					Anglo-Saxon conquest

Introduction

The Great Train Robbery

At 3 a.m. on 8 August 1964, the mail train from Scotland to London was stopped at the lonely Sears Crossing near Cheddington in Buckinghamshire and robbed of mailbags containing £2 517 975. It was the largest robbery in British history.

Who were these train robbers? The engine-driver and guard could not tell, since the gang had worn balaclava helmets and boiler suits. A huge police investigation began, which included detectives from London's Flying Squad, headed by Detective Chief Superintendent Butler.

Not far from Sears Crossing they found a farm, which though deserted had clearly been used only a few days before. In the farmyard stood a lorry and two Land-Rovers. In the remains of a bonfire were traces of mailbags and banknote wrappings.

Every part of the farm was then checked over for further *evidence*. The robbers had washed things off, but rather carelessly. On the vehicles, on the side of a cat's dish, in the bathroom, and on a bottle of tomato ketchup were the finger and palm prints of several different people.

When these prints were checked in London against the prints of known criminals, eight men were identified and the hunt for them began. Two were discovered buying cars with five-pound notes, some

Leatherslade Farmhouse – the robbers' hideout. Not far from the main railway line but well away from other homes.

of which had definitely come from the mail train. They also had £155 000 in their possession which they could not explain. Another was picked up carrying £131 in notes, including some which the National Commercial Bank of Inverness had sent on the mail train. He had another £12 000 in his possession which he said had been won by a friend gambling. He was, however, unable to produce this friend.

Seven men were eventually brought to trial at Aylesbury in Buckinghamshire in 1964, charged with robbery while armed with offensive weapons.

Using the evidence discovered by the police detectives, the prosecuting counsel set out to prove to the jury that the seven men had robbed the mail train, the defence counsel that they had not. The prosecution evidence was good enough. The jury decided that beyond all reasonable doubt the seven were guilty of the robbery. They were sentenced to thirty years' imprisonment.

Evidence is information, signs and indications from which conclusions can be reached. The bonfire, the vehicles and the position of the deserted farm were all signs to the detectives that it had been the robbers' base at the time of the crime. The fingerprints, palmprints and money found in their possession were clear indications that the seven men had been at the farmhouse and received the stolen money – and therefore that they were the ones who had carried out the robbery.

Inside the farmhouse kitchen – the stove as detectives found it. How can one tell that the robbers left in a hurry?

Edward Thompson at Chichen Itza

The historian acts in ways similar to a detective and to a prosecuting counsel in a trial. Take, for example, the mystery of the seventy-five metre wide water-filled hole near the extraordinary ruins of Chichen Itza in the Mexican jungle. Since a straight stone causeway connects it to the main temple area the inhabitants must have used it for something. But what? In this case the historian/detective/prosecuting counsel was an American, Edward Thompson, who carried out his investigations between 1904 and 1907.

His first *clue* was an old Indian story handed on to the Spanish when they conquered the area in the sixteenth century. In times of drought the priests of Chichen Itza used to kill human beings and throw their gold and jewelled bodies into the waterhole, hoping to persuade the gods to send rain. Such a story might have been completely untrue, no more than a fairy tale. Thompson, however, thought that there was enough in it to be worth following up. He bought a farmhouse near the waterhole and, with the help of a hand-powered grab, began exploring the mud at the bottom of the hole. For months he found nothing but foul-smelling slime, decaying tree stumps and a few animal bones. Then some more interesting things came up. First were balls of a gluey sweet-smelling sap. Thompson remembered from the Indian stories that these were burnt during the ceremonies at which the human victims were sacrificed (i.e. killed to please the gods). Then appeared ornaments of bronze, necklaces of jade and little gold bells which looked as if they had been designed to fit the human ankle.

Thompson, now most excited, got himself an old diving suit and, at the risk of his life, explored the murky waters at the bottom of the pool. There he found many more objects, including beautiful small gold crowns designed in the shape of serpents – and human bones!

Thompson the detective now had his evidence. First there was the Indian story and the position of the waterhole, near and linked to the temples. Then he had the balls of sweet-smelling sap, the precious jewellery and above all the human bones. The waterhole must be what the Indian story had said all along, the Sacred Well in which the priests of Chichen Itza had sacrificed to the gods. Thompson then became the prosecuting counsel. He wrote about his investigations and his explanation of the mystery in a book called *The People of the Serpent* which became a bestseller. His jury (first the experts in the history of Central America and then the general public) were convinced. He had proved his case about the Sacred Well beyond reasonable doubt.

Chichen Itza – the main temple area with the waterhole in the left foreground

Searching for evidence – the importance of layers (strata) at Pataliputra

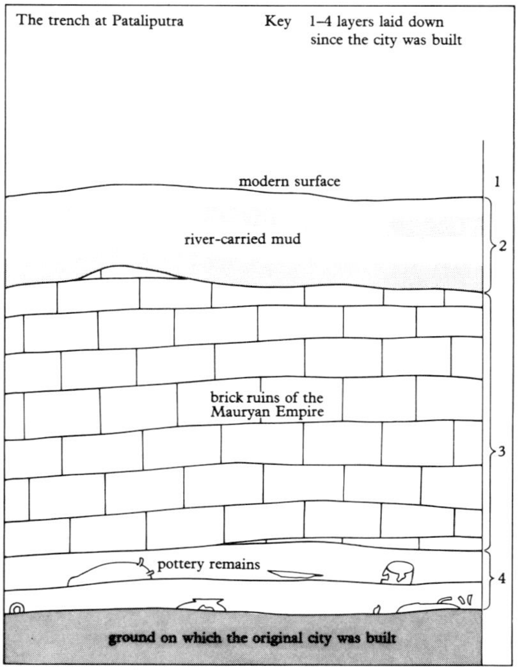

In every dig, the archaeologist must make a careful note of the layer in which each piece of evidence was found. The evidence can then be linked to the right group of people and the correct period of time. (See the Using the evidence section, chapter 1.)

Searching for evidence – by digging (excavation). These ruins, which are more than 2000 years old, were found by archaeologists digging the trench. They are of Pataliputra, the capital of the Mauryan Empire (see page 98). The present surface of the ground is nearly a metre higher than the highest part of the ruined walls. How do you think this has come about? Clue: the large River Ganges flows nearby.

Note also the pottery which has been found in the ruins. Pieces of pottery are found in almost all excavations and are a most important type of evidence.

History and evidence

The evidence about the ancient world is of two main types. First, objects which have been left behind by our ancestors and which can be seen, touched and measured. This is usually described as *archaeological evidence*. Secondly, there are the written records of the ancient civilisations, usually the historian's responsibility. However, the work of historians and archaeologists overlaps, especially in the task of finding out what really happened in the ancient world, when written records tell us much less than in later civilisations.

Using the evidence

This book has two main aims. The first is to introduce some of the most important events which historians are now sure beyond reasonable doubt took place in the ancient world. The second is to show you some of the pieces of evidence which (like Detective Chief Superintendent Butler and Edward Thompson) they have used to find the answers to some important questions. Each chapter contains a Using the evidence section based on a question which historians have not found easy to answer. Sometimes you will be asked to be the detective, to fit the pieces of evidence together to get to what you believe to be the truth; sometimes the prosecuting counsel, to present your case in a clear and persuasive way so that the jury will agree with you; and sometimes the jury when you will have to decide whether the case put forward by a particular archaeologist or historian can be regarded as proved beyond all reasonable doubt.

Sorting out the evidence – this archaeologist is piecing together the pieces of pottery she has found in a dig like that at Pataliputra. When she has finished, its size, shape and the way it was made will give her some idea of its age and who made it.

Understanding the evidence – an expert on ancient writing copies out the Egyptian hieroglyphic writing carved on pieces of stone which archaeologists have dug up. Open in front of him is a dictionary of hieroglyphics. Thanks to the work of Champollion and others (see chapter 3), many ancient languages can now be read.

Searching for written evidence – these historians are working in the Public Records Office in London. They are studying documents. One may be finding out about King John, another about people living in an Oxfordshire village in AD 1086. Expert staff will bring documents for them which date from past centuries and which may contain the evidence which they are looking for. The Public Records Office has many documents of the English Middle Ages.

Scientific help – this scientist is carrying out radio-carbon tests which will help date fragments of evidence found in an excavation.

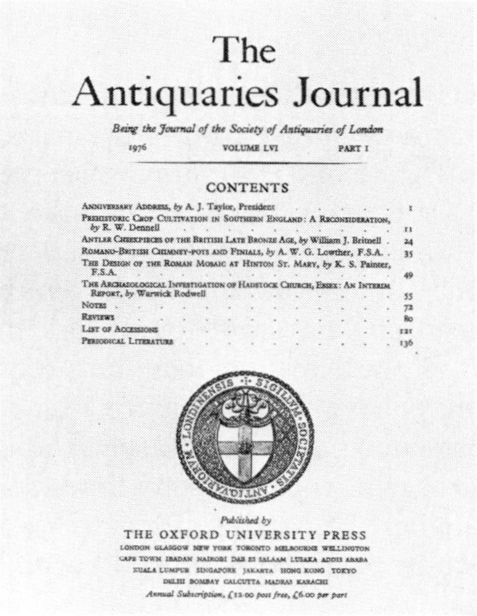

The
Antiquaries Journal

Being the Journal of the Society of Antiquaries of London

1976 VOLUME LVI PART I

CONTENTS

Anniversary Address, *by* A. J. Taylor, President	1
Prehistoric Crop Cultivation in Southern England: A Reconsideration, *by* R. W. Dennell	11
Antler Cheekpieces of the British Late Bronze Age, *by* William J. Britnell	24
Romano-British Chimney-pots and Finials, *by* A. W. G. Lowther, F.S.A.	35
The Design of the Roman Mosaic at Hinton St. Mary, *by* K. S. Painter, F.S.A.	49
The Archaeological Investigation of Hadstock Church, Essex: An Interim Report, *by* Warwick Rodwell	55
Notes	72
Reviews	80
List of Accessions	121
Periodical Literature	136

SIGILLVM · SOCIETATIS · ANTIQVARIORVM · LONDINENSIS

Published by
THE OXFORD UNIVERSITY PRESS
LONDON GLASGOW NEW YORK TORONTO MELBOURNE WELLINGTON
CAPE TOWN IBADAN NAIROBI DAR ES SALAAM LUSAKA ADDIS ABABA
KUALA LUMPUR SINGAPORE JAKARTA HONG KONG TOKYO
DELHI BOMBAY CALCUTTA MADRAS KARACHI
Annual Subscription, £12.00 post free, £6.00 per part

Presenting the evidence – in magazines such as this and in books, archaeologists and historians use evidence to explain their theories. They try to persuade the jury of other archaeologists and historians that they have found out the truth about something in the past. (In the same way, the prosecuting lawyer at Aylesbury convinced the jury that the train robbers were guilty.)

The Beginning of History

1 Early Man

Richard Leakey and 1470 Man

In 1967 a young archaeologist, Richard Leakey, was working on a dig in Ethiopia. As he flew home to Kenya, bad weather forced his plane off course.

Looking down, he saw the eastern shores of Lake Turkana (opposite page). Was this more than just a fine view, he wondered. Were these rocks the kind formed in the course of millions of years by the rise and fall of the waters of the lake? If so, they might well be full of fossil bones.

Fossils are the most important evidence which we have for earliest man. Imagine that a man dies beside a lake. Animals pick the flesh off his bones which then become covered by dust and sand. In some cases, as at Lake Turkana, minerals in the soil harden the bones into fossils. These fossilised bones will then survive for millions of years.

As soon as he could, Leakey got a helicopter to land him on the lake shore. He saw straight away that the soil was right for fossils. Although he did not find any bones, he found a pebble chipped as if to make a cutting tool. He felt certain that some of man's earliest ancestors must have lived on the shore of this ancient lake.

Leakey came to search the shores in 1968 and again in 1972. He spent much of his time in 1972 at the Nairobi Museum but a team of expert African fossil hunters inspected the lakeside. One of this sharp-eyed team noticed a tiny fragment of bone, close by another, then another. Were they human remains? Leakey, called by radio, came at once from Nairobi. He identified the pieces as parts of a fossil human skull which was certainly very old. The spot where the first fragment was found was clearly marked, then the earth from a large area around it was raised and sieved. Every piece of bone so found was brought to the main camp. There Mrs Leakey began the complicated job of piecing together all the fragments into the original shape of the skull.

Scientists applied various tests to the skull. They calculated that it was between 2 600 000 and 3 000 000 years old.

This ichthyosaurus is far older than the oldest fossil man. It died more than 100 million years ago. Yet its bones are perfectly fossilised from beak to tail and it is possible to work out how it must have looked when alive.

Lake Turkana

The skull Mrs Leakey put together is now in the Kenya National Museum. In the museum catalogue it is number 1470. For this reason it is known simply as 1470 Man.

Note the main types of evidence which Richard Leakey used. First he found a stone tool on the lake shore, then fragments of a fossil skull. Almost all our knowledge of early man is based on similar evidence.

Man the Hunter

Man is different from animals like the apes in a number of ways. He can walk upright. He can grip objects strongly and precisely. He has a larger brain. Because of these three advantages he became a maker of tools, and he was able to change his way of life to fit in with different climates and geographical conditions. The 1470 Man could walk upright. Almost certainly he could make and use stone tools. His brain was about 800 cc, half-way in size between the modern ape and modern man. For these reasons many experts believe him to be our ancestor and the earliest man yet discovered.

In 1927, at Choukoutien near Peking in China, the remains of about forty man-like creatures were found. These included an almost complete human skull. Peking Man dates from about 400 000 BC. He was the same height as 1470 Man, about one and a half metres, but his brain was bigger, his teeth smaller and his jaw less ape-like. Experts gave him the Latin name *Homo erectus* (Upright Man).

Upright Man was a tremendous hunter. Deer, antelope, horse, wild pig, bison, water-buffalo, rhinoceros and monkey were all among his victims. So too were other men. Because large and savage animals were successfully hunted, Upright Man must have hunted in groups. As

Peking Man in action. Has the artist got him right?

successful group hunting meant some simple kind of speech, almost certainly he could talk.

He could also make a fire. How he learned, we do not know. Perhaps a bush fire started by a flash of lightning was used to start another fire to warm the cave. Perhaps a chance spark struck from a flint set alight a dry leaf.

Soon he could also cook, a skill which may also have been learned by accident. It is easy to imagine a piece of raw meat falling into a fire; when it was pulled out it tasted better. The more he ate cooked food, the less he needed powerful jaws and large teeth.

Lastly, Upright Man made better tools than 1470 Man. Roughly chipped pebbles with a single cutting edge were not good enough. He used a sharply pointed hand-axe with two cutting edges, both for skinning animals and carving up meat.

The skull of Swanscombe Man (actually a woman)

Parts of a skull found at Swanscombe in Kent mark the next step towards modern man. Swanscombe Man lived about 250 000 years ago. Because his skull was considerably rounder and his brain larger than that of Upright Man, he and others like him have been named *Homo sapiens* or Wise Man. Then appeared another man-like creature who, because his first remains were found in the valley of the Neander river in Germany, is called Neanderthal Man. We would find him quite frightening to look at because he has a jutting-out lower jaw, an overhanging brow and large teeth. However, he had a larger brain than we have and made excellent stone tools.

The Neanderthals buried their dead in graves, and often placed tools and food beside the bodies. In a Swiss cave which they used for burials, a stone box was filled with the skulls of bears. Other bear bones were placed carefully round the cave walls. Perhaps to them the bear was a sacred animal whose bones might protect them in the life to come.

Neanderthal Man died out about 35 000 years ago. At much the same time an improved version of Wise Man appeared, who is technically known as *Homo sapiens sapiens*. His skull had grown rounder, his teeth smaller, his chin more clearly developed. Physically he was almost the same as us. He made his tools in a new way, striking long flakes from the flint with a wooden punch. He used many different kinds of stone tools and also tried new materials like ivory, bone and wood. He wore clothes of skin (sewn together with bone needles and thread of animal sinew) and decorations of shells, deer teeth and clay beads.

A stone hand-axe as it would have been held. See how the flint has had flakes hammered off to give two cutting-edges meeting at a point.

These early men lived by hunting at a time when the climate was very different from today. This was because of the Ice Ages which began about 600 000 BC and ended – perhaps for ever, perhaps only for a while – about 18 000 BC. During these Ice Ages, the temperature of the earth's atmosphere dropped. No one is quite sure why. The ice of the Arctic and the Antarctic spread outwards from the Poles. Britain as far south as the Thames was covered with ice, so was Canada and much of northern Europe. Mountains like the Alps, Pyrenees and Andes were covered with ice thousands of metres deep. The climate of those areas which the ice did not reach also changed greatly. Africa, for example, had much more rain. With so much water held in the ice, the level of the oceans fell. Britain was joined to Europe – the Thames flowing into the River Rhine rather than the sea – and North America was joined to Asia by a strip of land which now lies beneath the waters of the Bering Strait.

Those early men living near the edge of the ice became skilled at hunting particular animals. In what is now France and Germany they went after reindeer and bison; in what is now southern Russia, they hunted that ancestor of the modern elephant, the woolly mammoth.

The Lapp people who now live in the very north of Scandinavia, not far from the present edge of the Arctic ice, may well be the direct

Modern Lapp herdsmen round up the reindeer for the journey nearer the coast. Can you see anything on the photo which the early hunters would not have had?

How the Altamira paintings may have been created

descendants of the early hunters. There are about 30 000 of them who follow 300 000 reindeer as the herds move from one pasture of lichen to the next. From the reindeer they take all they need to survive: meat to eat, milk to drink, antlers for tools, skin and sinews for clothes and shelter. Only a century ago in North America, Red Indian tribes followed and lived off the buffalo in a similar way.

Near Altamira in Spain, an important discovery was made when a dog got lost down a foxhole. Several young boys searching for it stumbled on a series of caves. All over the caves were paintings of bison in red and black. The painters made their paints from colours extracted out of the local soil which they mixed with animal fat to make waterproof. The paint was put on with brushes of animal hair or pads of moss. Similar paintings have been found all over Europe, the best being in southern France. These were done between 20 000 BC and 10 000 BC.

Almost certainly the painted caves were places of religion or magic. The artists painted a successful hunt in the hope that by so doing the future hunts upon which their survival depended would be successful too. In these caves there have also been found little female statues which emphasise their child-bearing parts, the breasts and the stomach. If the women failed as child bearers the tribe would die out.

Around 13 000 BC the ice began to retreat. By 8000 BC Britain was once more an island and most of Europe clear of ice. The tundra landscape of moss, lichen, birch and willow which suited the reindeer disappeared. Instead there were forests of oak and ash, elm and lime. The reindeer herds moved north. Some men moved with them. Others stayed where they were and learned to adapt to new conditions. The Palaeolithic or Old Stone Age was drawing to an end and a new period in man's development, the Neolithic or New Stone Age was beginning.

Using the evidence: the case of the Kanam Jaw

On 29 March 1932, Louis Leakey was digging in some valleys near the eastern shores of Lake Victoria in Kenya at a place called Kanam West. With him were a number of African diggers led by Juma Gitau. Juma found first the fossil tooth of an extinct elephant, a deinotherium. Close by lay an apparently human tooth and jaw-bone.

Leakey was very excited by the discovery of this jaw. Since it was found among the remains of animals like the deinotherium which had long been extinct, Leakey decided that early man had lived at Kanam at the same time as the deinotherium; far earlier in fact than most experts then believed. He wrote at once to *Nature*, one of Britain's most famous scientific magazines, which published his discoveries in May 1932. The experts were very interested but not ready to go all the way with Leakey. They wanted to look closely at his evidence. Was this young man leaping to conclusions too quickly?

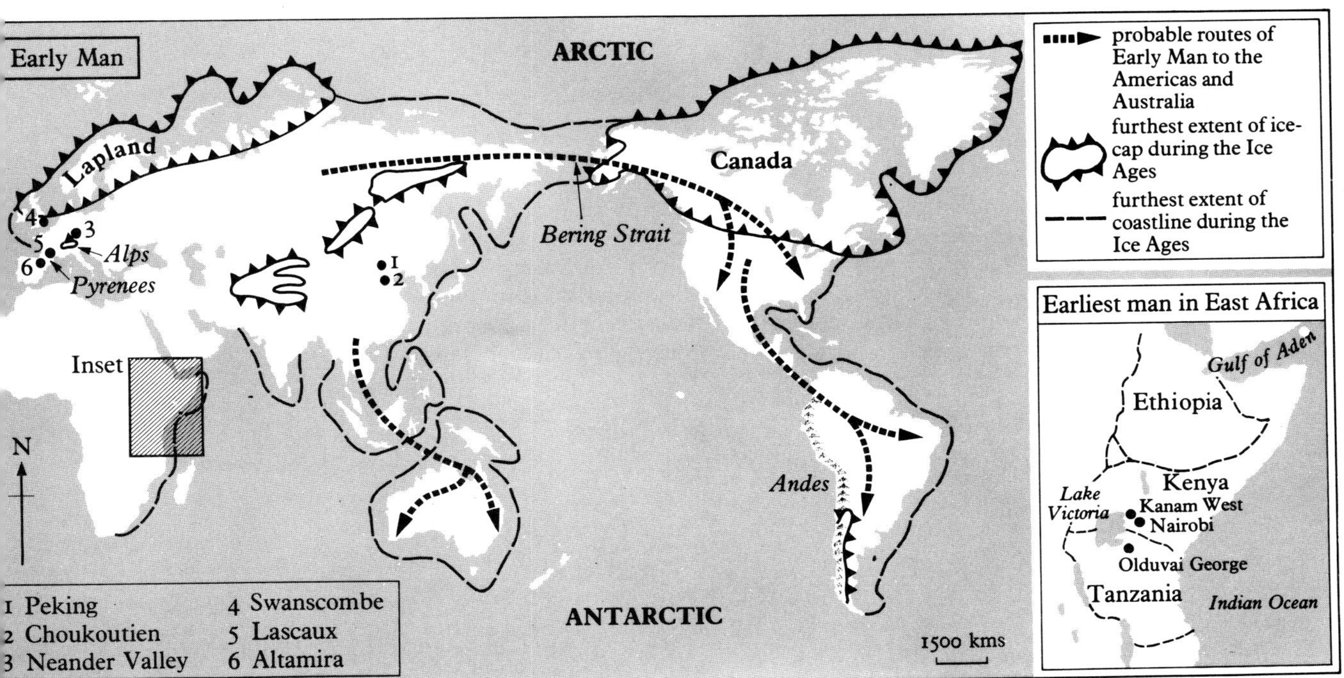

Everyone agreed that the bones had been found together. How had they got there though? Only *geological* evidence could prove Leakey was right. (A geologist studies the age and nature of the rocks which form the Earth's crust.) The different layers of rock, one on top of the other, can be dated fairly accurately. Bones, fossils and other objects found within each layer or stratum are of the same age as the rock itself. However, this is only true if the layers of rock have not been disturbed.

The jaw-bone at Kanam West might not always have been next to the deinotherium bones as Leakey thought. It might have been in a higher and later layer or stratum and brought down beside the earlier deinotherium bones by the effects of a cliff-fall or rain wash.

The only way to be sure that the jaw-bone had always been next to the deinotherium was for a geologist to test most carefully the soil in which the bones had been found. His tests would show if cliff-falls and rain washes had occurred in that particular area of Kanam West.

Before he left Kanam, Leakey marked the places where Juma had found the deinotherium tooth and the man-like jaw, with iron pegs. He also photographed their position. Then, bringing the fossils with him, he returned to England.

Unfortunately, when he came to show his fossils to the experts, a fault in his camera had completely spoilt his photos. Instead he used some taken by Miss Kendall, a friend of his wife, who had been visiting Kanam at the time and had taken some shots of the digging area. The experts were impressed but still needed the geological evidence, so Leakey arranged that Professor Boswell, a geologist, should visit Kanam and see for himself.

The visit took place in 1935 and was not a success. During the three years since Leakey's original discovery, local tribesmen had taken the iron pegs to make into harpoons and spear-heads. Also heavy rain had washed away parts of the hillside. Leakey found it hard to remember where exactly the 1932 finds had been made. Worse was to follow, as he noted in his diary for 18 January:

> Professor Boswell, Wayland and Kent spent the day at Kanam West and they say – and I suppose they are right – that they have located the exact position of Miss Kendall's photo and it was not Kanam West main gullies but is the Kanam West Fish Cliff gullies. This is serious . . . the Professor is in a bad humour over it. Apart from the absence of trees and of details in the gullies it is terribly like Kanam West and the mistake is not surprising though very regrettable.

As soon as he got back to London, Boswell wrote to *Nature*. 'I hold the opinion,' he said, 'that the geological age of the jaw is uncertain.' He considered that the exact position where the bones were found was not clear. Therefore, he said it was impossible to come to any firm conclusions about the rock layers from which they had come. It was therefore also impossible to date the fossil jaw with any accuracy.

This was a most serious attack. Not just on Leakey's ideas about the importance of the Kanam jaw but on his methods as an archaeologist,

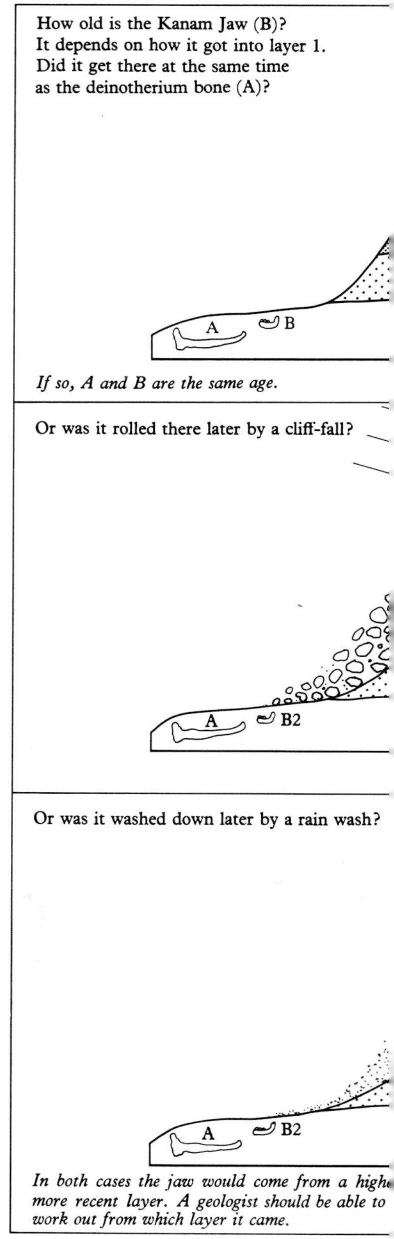

The rock layers in the Olduvai Gorge

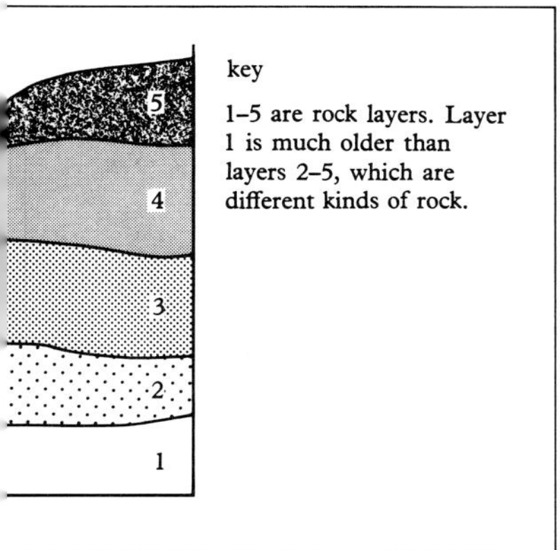

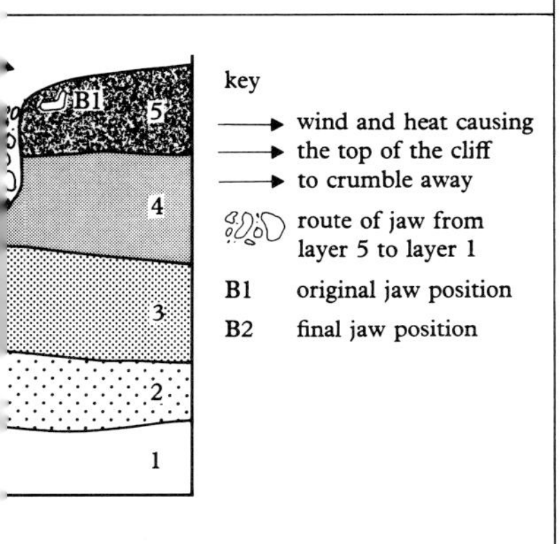

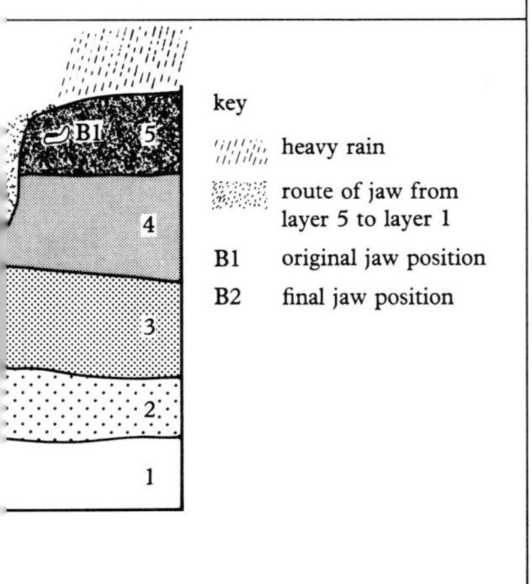

particularly on the ways he recorded and used evidence. Leakey, however, stuck to his guns. In a book published soon afterwards he wrote as follows:

The importance of the Kanam jaw lies in the fact that it can be dated geologically . . . and archaeologically, and that it represents the oldest known human fragment yet found in Africa. It is not only the oldest known fragment in Africa but the most ancient fragment of true *Homo* (real man) yet discovered in the world.

Questions and further work

1 (a) Where exactly was the jaw found?
(b) What made Leakey think that it was extremely old?

2 (a) What steps did Leakey take to mark the position of the discovery?
(b) What happened to the iron pegs?
(c) Why were Miss Kendall's photographs important and what eventually was found to be wrong with them?
(d) What other evidence did Leakey have to show the position of the jaw?

Study the diagrams opposite

3 (a) In what ways are rock and soil layers (strata) helpful to archaeologists? (See also pages 15 and 53.)
(b) Explain the meaning of a cliff-fall; *and* a rain wash.
(c) Show how they can make fossils appear much older than they really are.
(d) Why was it important to mark the exact position of the find and have a geologist check the soil?

4 (a) In what way did Boswell disagree with Leakey?
(b) What were his main reasons for disagreeing?
(c) Who do you think had the better case, Leakey or Boswell? Give reasons for your answer.

5 Imagine that you were Leakey in 1935. Make a note, as if in your diary, of the lessons you have learned from this unpleasant episode.

Dr Leakey at work in the Olduvai Gorge. Here he made some of the most important modern discoveries about Early Man.

2 Farmers and village-dwellers

Seeds, hardened into carbon after thousands of years

A stone pestle for grinding corn into flour

The walls of Jericho seen through the deep trench cut by Kenyon. How high are the ruined walls? How can you tell that they must be ancient?

Jericho and Jarmo

If you were an archaeologist and had dug up objects such as these, what could you say for certain about the people to whom they had once belonged?

At Jericho, beside the River Jordan in Palestine, an English archaeologist, Kathleen Kenyon, found objects such as these. The settlement in which they lay spread over four hectares. It had strong fortifications and probably contained about two thousand people. Using radio-carbon tests, she was able to calculate that it was about ten thousand years old.

Similar objects about nine thousand years old were also found by an American archaeologist, Robert Braidwood, at Jarmo, which lies in Iraq in the foothills of the Zagros mountains. The Jarmo sickles had beautifully polished cutting edges. The animal bones were from goat, sheep, cattle and dog, while among the seeds were remains of wheat, emmer, barley, peas and beans.

Excavations such as these tell us most of what we know about the Neolithic or New Stone Age. Braidwood was excited by the discovery of sickles, the remains of wheat and barley, pestles and mortars and animal bones. Although the people of Jarmo may well still have been hunters, clearly they were also farmers. They needed the sickles to cut the corn, the pestles and the mortars to grind the corn into flour. The animal bones came from their herds. If Man the Hunter was always on the move, Man the Farmer had to settle in one place. The great fortifications of Jericho which Kenyon found are good evidence that the people of Jericho meant to stay where they were. Their grindstones, pestles and mortars show that their main food was the corn which they grew on the land around them.

We know much more about these early farmers of 8000 BC to 3000 BC than about earlier men. Because they are closer to us in time, their remains are buried less deeply and are less decayed. Yet compared with later people, such as the Mesopotamians or the Egyptians, we still know very little about them. This is chiefly because they had not yet learned to write.

The first villages and towns

The 1470 Man lived nearly three million years ago. The first farmers begin to appear between eight to ten thousand years ago. Settling down to farming is quite a recent change in man's way of life. It is also one of the most important. Farming led to better food supplies; better food supplies to more people; more people to the growth of towns and cities. In towns and cities men lived and followed occupations which had little to do with farming. They might be kings or tax collectors, priests or teachers, traders or craftsmen, builders or designers. With towns and cities came the first civilisations.

A civilisation means a more organised and more secure society. People living in Jericho led settled lives; they had homes and possessions, and knew where their next meal was coming from. Law and order was maintained by a government. These people enjoyed a higher standard of living than they could have had in simple farming villages.

Farming first began in the area shaded on the map. Wild wheat and barley grew there naturally. For thousands of years men picked and ate

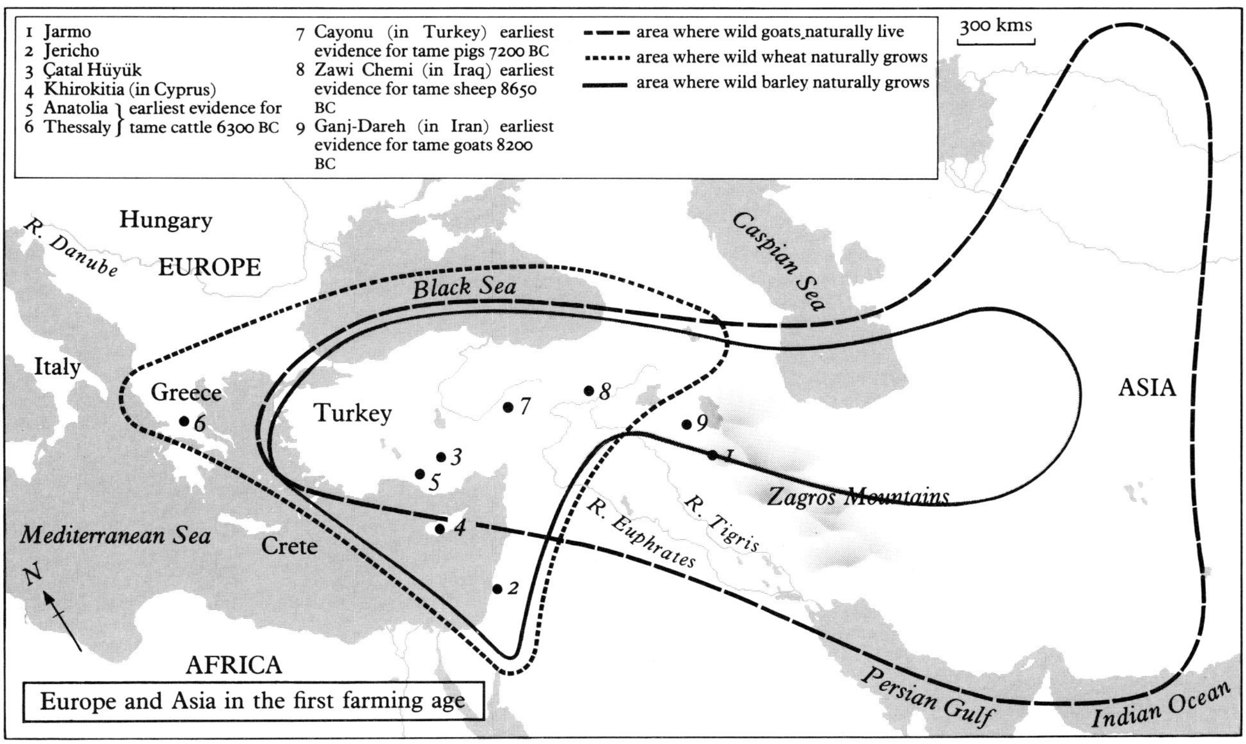

Europe and Asia in the first farming age

the ears of wild wheat and valued it for its nourishment. Then perhaps one spring a member of a hunting group, which came frequently to the same hunting camp, may have planted some seed and been able to harvest it the same autumn. So the first principle of farming was learned. Wild sheep, cattle, pigs and goats also lived in the same part of the world. As villages were built in the places where the corn grew best, the villagers began taming animals. Already the hunters had tamed the dog, probably from wolf cubs captured in the wild. These animals were trained and bred in captivity to help in the hunting. Since grazing animals do not move far from their grazing lands, their taming was not difficult. At first the farmers simply took care only to kill a proportion of males of the wild herds to supply their food needs. The size of the herds was kept up by new births each spring. Only slowly did they begin to fence the herds in and experiment with selective breeding in order to produce more milk-producing cows, fatter pigs and woollier sheep.

Houses at Khirokitia, Cyprus

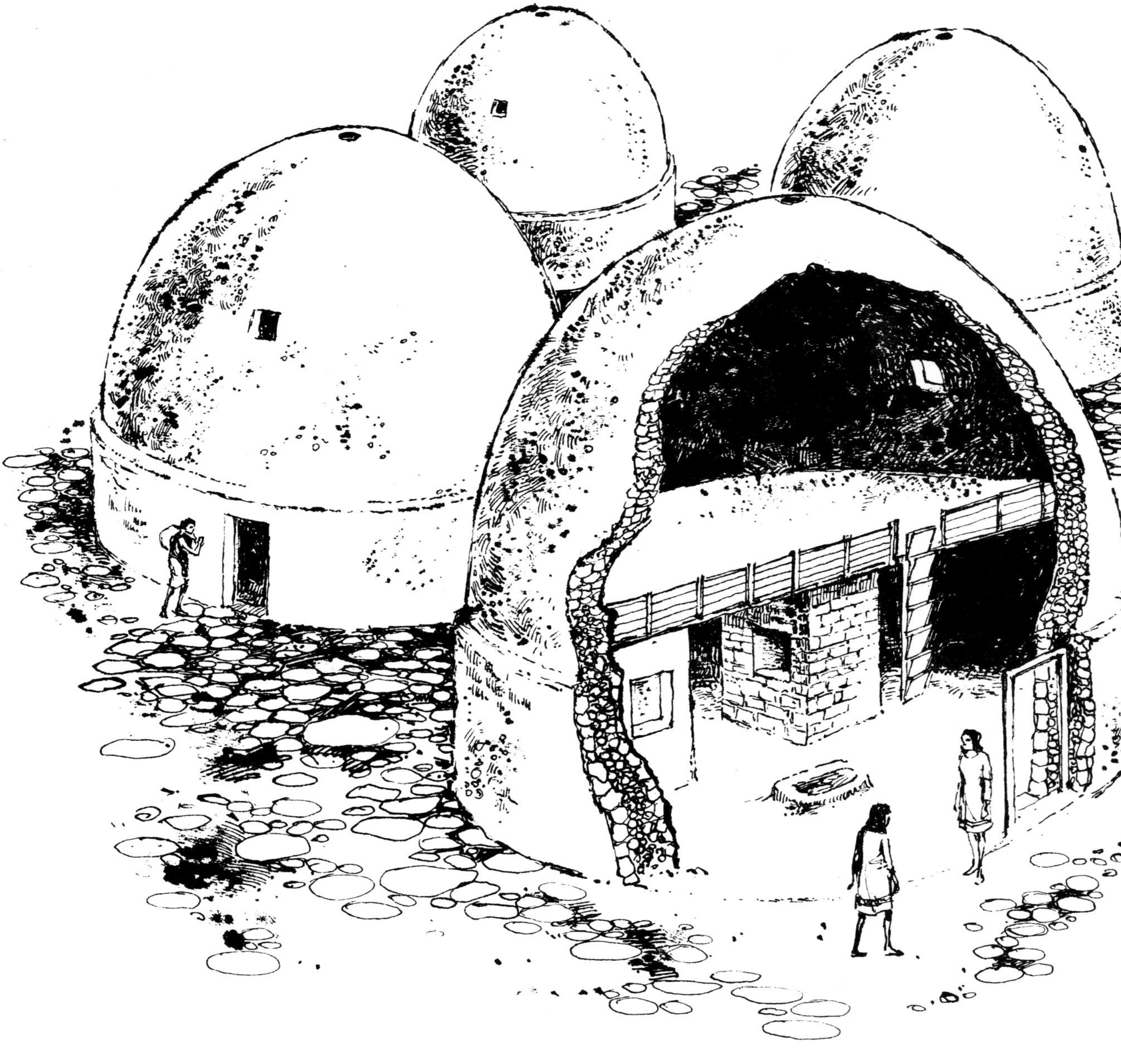

Farmers need different tools from hunters so new tools were invented. Stone was still the main tool-making material. It was to remain so until about 3000 BC in western Asia and for much longer in other parts of the world. Stronger and smoother axes were needed to clear good farmland of trees and bushes; hoes and ploughs were needed to prepare the soil, and sickles to reap the grain. In some places where the stone was specially good for making tools, mines were dug which supplied the valuable stone to farmers over a wide area. (See the Using the evidence section on page 31.)

Early weaving equipment

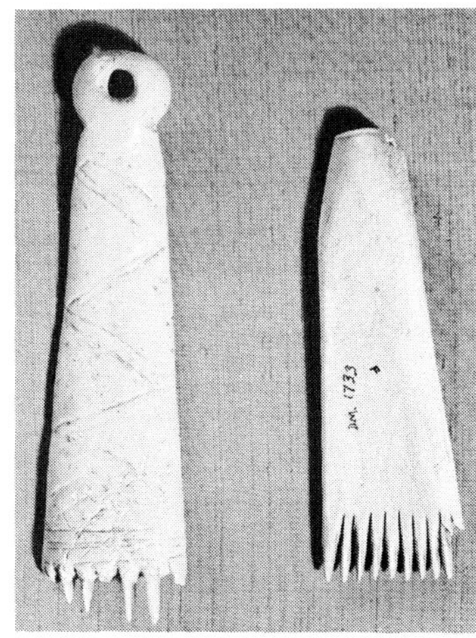

In the good years when the weather was kind, farming made it possible for the first time for men to have more food than they needed to survive. Some of the extra was kept to guard against the bad times. The rest they exchanged for things they needed (like tools) or simply enjoyed (like jewellery), which other men could make better than they. So trading began, first locally, then over larger distances. Some men could stop farming and earn their living as craftsmen. In a village near Jarmo in about 6500 BC there was a butcher, a beadmaker and a craftsman in bone.

The homes in the villages of settled farming families reached a far higher standard than the caves and flimsy tents of the hunters. The remains upon which this artist's reconstruction is based date from about 5200 BC. The outside walls are strong and weather-proof. Inside you can see the built-in oven, the central hearth and upstairs the sleeping compartment with its sleeping mats.

The skills of pottery and weaving were also learned early by these farming people.

Better farming meant more food; more food meant more people; and more people needed more land. By 6000 BC farming peoples can be traced moving from Turkey into what is now modern Greece and by boat to the island of Crete. By 5000 BC the movement was continuing westwards and northwards to Hungary and southern Italy. Using the two great rivers of central Europe, the Danube and the Rhine, as their main route they reach Holland by about 4000 BC. There, the farming villages were quite different to those, say, in Cyprus. The long, oak-framed houses, with twig and clay walls and steeply pitched thatch roofs, housed a number of related families and also their corn and their animals. They clustered around the village longhouse, the meeting place for the whole village which usually numbered about three hundred people.

About 3500 BC the first farmers to brave the sea crossing from northern France landed on the south coast of Britain. Others soon followed. Making their way along the chalk and limestone hills across southern and eastern England, they searched out the best farming lands. By 3000 BC farming villages could be found all over western Asia and Europe, in India and China too.

In the Americas the picture is different. North America was perfect hunting country with wide plains full of animals like the buffalo, elk and deer, and with broad rivers full of salmon and other fish. Most North Americans (the Red Indians) remained hunters until modern times. The first settled farming in Central America began about 5000 BC. Maize was the main crop and its cultivation eventually spread both south to Peru and north into what is now the southern part of the USA. In most aspects of life, the Americas were behind the rest of the world. The first known American pottery dates from 3200 BC, weaving 2500 BC and building in stone 1800 BC.

The word *megalith* comes from Greek and means *great stone*. It is a good word to describe the most impressive monuments left by the

The stone skeleton of a Neolithic chieftain's burial place, Lanyon Quoit, Cornwall. The smaller stones and earth round the sides have long since disappeared. How do you think the huge roof slab was raised into place?

Neolithic farmers: they were tombs for their chieftains. Usually they were an oval of upright boulders capped with a large roofing slab. The gaps between the uprights would be filled up with smaller stones. When the body was finally placed inside with some pottery, an axe or two, and perhaps some beads, the whole tomb was covered with earth. Often these megalithic tombs were huge. One at Bagneux in central France has a roofing slab which weighs eighty-seven tonnes. Another at Rodmarton in England contains more than 5000 tonnes of rock and stone which would have taken two hundred men at least a year to quarry and move into place using rollers and sledges. The great megalithic building period was from 3000 to 1500 BC in western Europe. That such monuments could be built proves that the Neolithic farming people could cooperate on difficult and complicated building projects.

Using the evidence: Grimes' Graves

In the strange countryside of the Norfolk Breckland, about six kilometres to the north-west of Thetford lies a curious pitted area. Today it is known as Grimes' Graves. All around stand the pines of Thetford forest. It is a gloomy and mysterious place. The local inhabitants were puzzled by these pits for thousands of years. Only in the last hundred years have archaeologists been able to unravel their secrets. This is what the pits look like today from the air. Have you any idea what they might be?

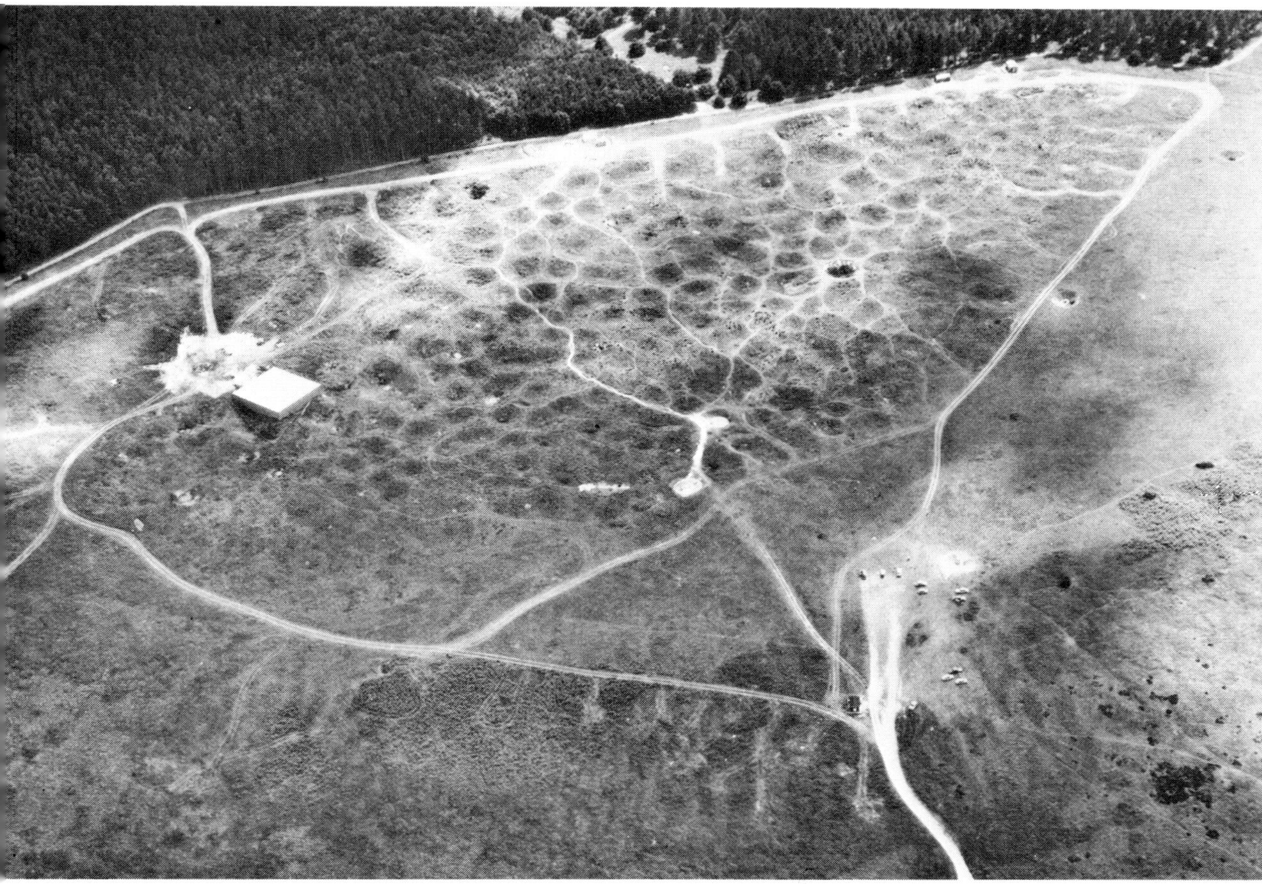

The Anglo-Saxons who gave the pits their name believed them to be the work of their chief god, Grim. In 1739, a *History of Norfolk* described them as a Danish military camp. A century later two local parsons, the Revd Manning and the Revd Pettigrew, dug a little into the pits. A military camp, they agreed, but a British one dating back to before Roman times.

1 How do you think they came to these conclusions?
2 What else might Grimes' Graves have been?

Serious excavations began in 1868 under the direction of Canon W. Greenwell. What he had uncovered three years later can be seen here.

A cross-section of Pit One

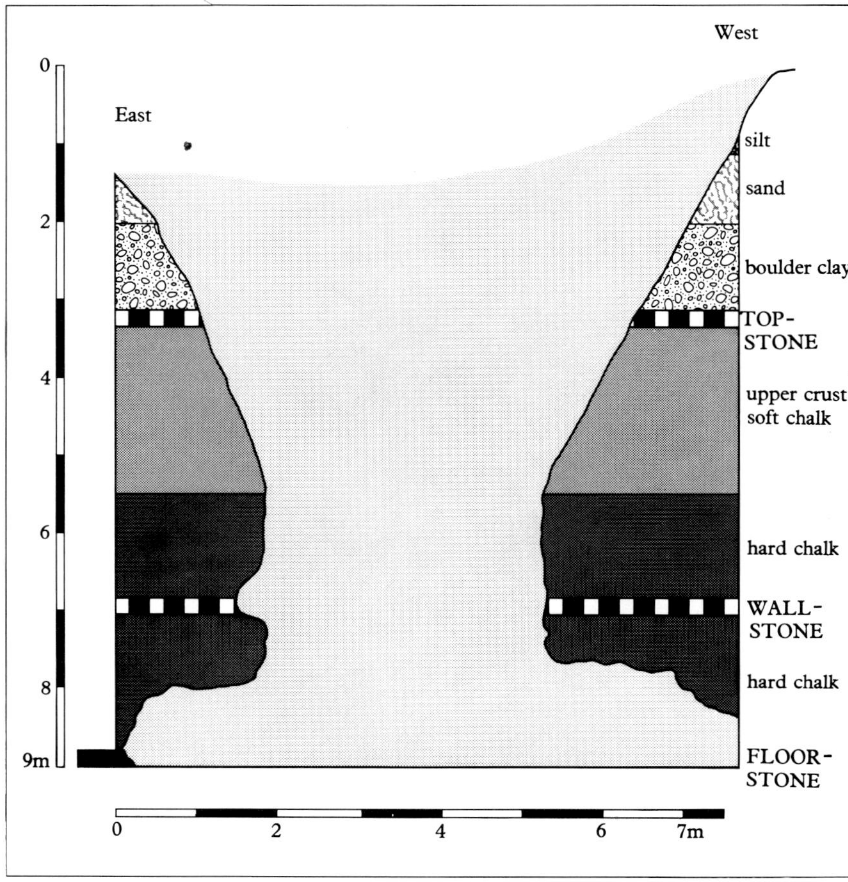

3 What do you think these cave-like openings are?

4 What do you now think Grimes' Graves originally were?
(*Clue:* topstone, wallstone and floorstone are different types of flint found in the chalk. Floorstone is the best for making flint tools.)

Excavations continued in various parts of the site until 1939. Among the many objects found during the digging were these.

Objects found at Grimes' Graves

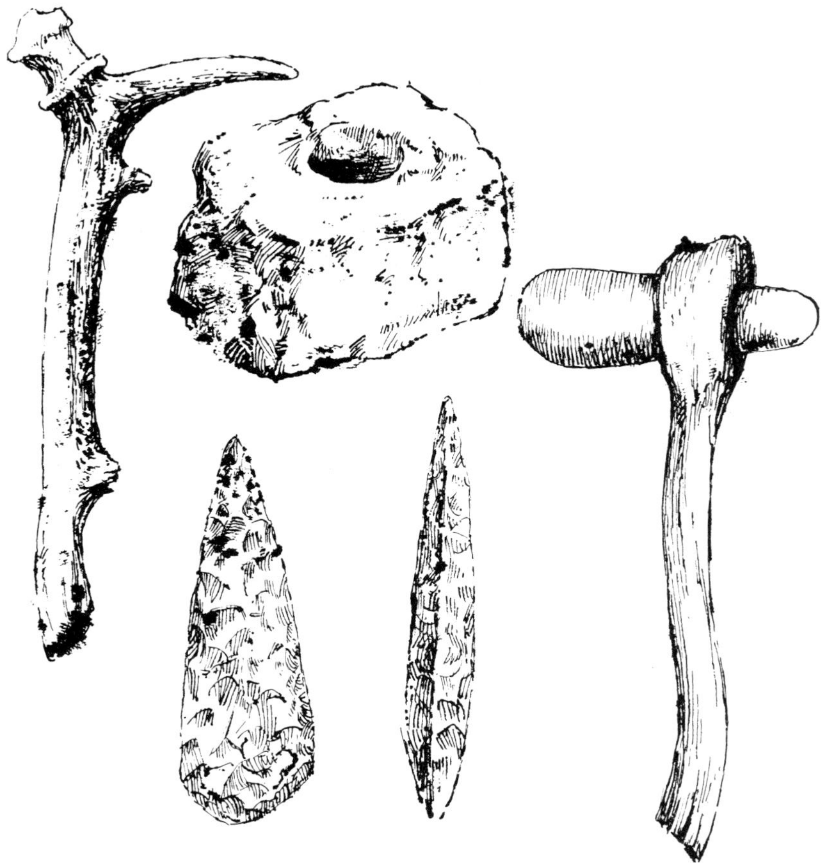

5 Note down how you think each of these objects might have been used.

In Pit Fifteen which only contained flint of poor quality, this small model only 108 mm high was found perched on a chalk outcrop. At its feet was piled a triangular heap of mined flint on top of which were seven red deer antlers, apparently arranged with care. Close by lay a chalk lamp.

The model found in Pit Fifteen

6 How do you explain this extraordinary arrangement of objects?

Now compare your answers with those of modern archaeologists.

The findings of modern archaeology

Archaeologists are sure that Grimes' Graves are flint mines. The surface of the area was found to be dotted with flints, some of which were already roughly chipped into tool shapes. The pits themselves reach down to the floorstone, from which the best tools were made, and no farther; where there are underground galleries they follow the floorstone seam through the chalk. A comparison with flints from other

An artist's reconstruction of work at Grimes' Graves

places and radio-carbon tests date the active life of the mines at about 2300–1700 BC. A strong local demand for flint tools, probably to clear the Breckland woods for farming, encouraged the search for floorstone. It was first found on the surface to the north-west of the site and the miners pursued the seam in a south-westerly direction digging down as much as twelve metres (as in Pit One) to reach it.

Almost all the objects discovered in the pits are to do with the miners' work. Their main tool was a pick made from the antler of the red deer. Two hundred and forty-four of these were found in Pits One and Two alone and it has been estimated that more than fifty thousand were used during the active life of the mines. The point of the pick would have been inserted into a crack or soft spot in the floorstone, hammered tight with a hammerstone and then levered free bringing a floorstone block with it. The toughest parts would have been attacked with bone picks and flint axes. Though the main pits were lit by daylight, the galleries needed artificial light, hence the chalk lampholders which probably contained a candlelike grease and wick.

How the miners reached the bottom of the deepest pits and raised the flints to the surface is not yet certain. Grooves in the chalk where the galleries meet the main pit wall suggest the rubbing of ropes and there is some evidence that a tree trunk may have lain across the top of Pit One.

The discovery which most excited archaeologists was that of the small chalk model which was found in 1939. She is believed to be a pregnant woman representing a goddess of fertility worshipped by the Neolithic people of the area. Pit Fifteen was not a good one, the floorstone being of poor quality. Before they moved on in search of a better, more fertile mine, the miners probably decided that they should make an offering to their fertility goddess in the hope that she would bring them luck. So they left the model in Pit Fifteen with the pile of flint at her feet and the carefully arranged antler picks and the lampholder.

7 Study carefully the artist's drawing. Much of it is based directly on evidence about which you now know; other parts are intelligent guesswork by the artist for which there is little or no direct evidence. Make a list first of those parts of the picture which you know from the evidence to be absolutely correct. Then make another list of those parts which are likely but not certain to be correct. Then note any way you think that the artist may be wrong.

8 Imagine that you are one of the team of miners who opened up and worked Pit Fifteen. You are taking part in the ritual ceremony shown opposite. Describe the thoughts running through your mind, your experiences in the mine in recent days, and your hopes and fears for the future.

3 Writing

The importance of writing

Imagine everyone suddenly forgot how to write and read. How difficult life would become: shopping without a shopping list; taking medicine or servicing the car without being able to read the instructions. Signposts and maps would be useless to us. We would have to rely instead on the directions of strangers. For advice, help and company we would have to depend on those people we could actually speak to, face to face. To know what happened yesterday, or a month or a year ago we would have to rely on memories and the memories of our family and friends.

Writing and the historian

Tomb A is the tomb of a chieftain who died on the island of Anglesey about 2000 BC. His name and the kind of man he was we can never

Tomb A

Tomb B

know. Tomb B is the tomb of Cyrus, one of the greatest of the kings of Ancient Persia, an outstanding soldier and statesman, merciful to his enemies, just to his subjects. He died in 530 BC and was buried in Pasargadae, the city which he himself founded. Men wrote about Cyrus in his lifetime and soon after; some of what they wrote can be read to this day. The unknown chieftain in tomb A could not write nor could any of his people, which is why we know so little about him.

Without written evidence, people in the past are faceless shadows. They lack personalities. With written evidence we can begin to get to know them as individuals. So written evidence is treasured by historians. Indeed, some would say that history only properly begins when Man learned to write and the earlier years are best called prehistory.

Cuneiform and hieroglyphics

The first known writing is about 5500 years old. It was simple picture writing carved in stone in the Sumerian city of Kish and was probably a tax record. By about 3000 BC the Sumerians were using soft clay tablets on which they wrote with reed pens. If they wished to keep what they

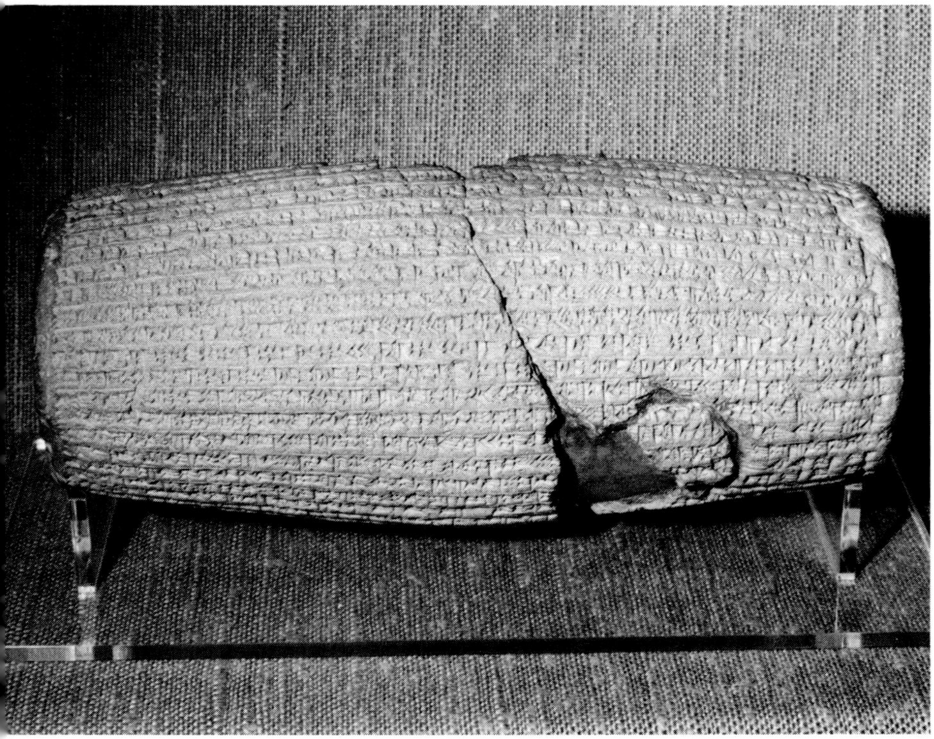

Beautifully-carved hieroglyphics from Thebes, about 2000 BC

The Cyrus cylinder, made of baked clay, is now in the British Museum. The cuneiform writing tells how Cyrus freed the people of Babylon from the wicked rule of King Nabonidus.

had written all they needed to do was bake the clay tablets. Since the mark the pens made was wedge-shaped, today their writing is known as cuneiform. (*Cuneus* is Latin for *wedge*.) As time passed their writing included fewer pictures and more symbols. The latter could be drawn quickly and clearly in wedges. Cuneiform was first used by traders and by tax collectors to keep accounts of what had been paid and what was owed to them. Then it came to be used by priests and kings. As more complicated ideas needed to be put into writing so different signs were used for ideas.

Later signs were used for syllables; that is, parts of words, which when combined together made another word. For example, a word like *betray* would be made by combining the sign for a *bee* with the sign for a *tray*. Eventually there were more than six hundred cuneiform signs which made it a most difficult writing to learn.

At the same time the Egyptians were developing their own kind of writing. Since it was first discovered in temples and tombs it has been named hieroglyphics, from the Greek words meaning sacred carvings. The first hieroglyphics date from about 3000 BC. They are carved in stone, painted on walls and coffins, or drawn in pen and ink on papyrus. Hieroglyphics still looked like picture signs and were impossible to write quickly. Two other forms, the hieratic and the demotic, were later used for speedier writing on papyrus.

Hieroglyphics continued to look like pictures of simple objects like lions, feathers and hands. They were used either to show ideas or, as in

*Demotic writing on papyrus.
This is more squiggly than the hieroglyphic picture-writing, more like modern writing and easier to write quickly.*

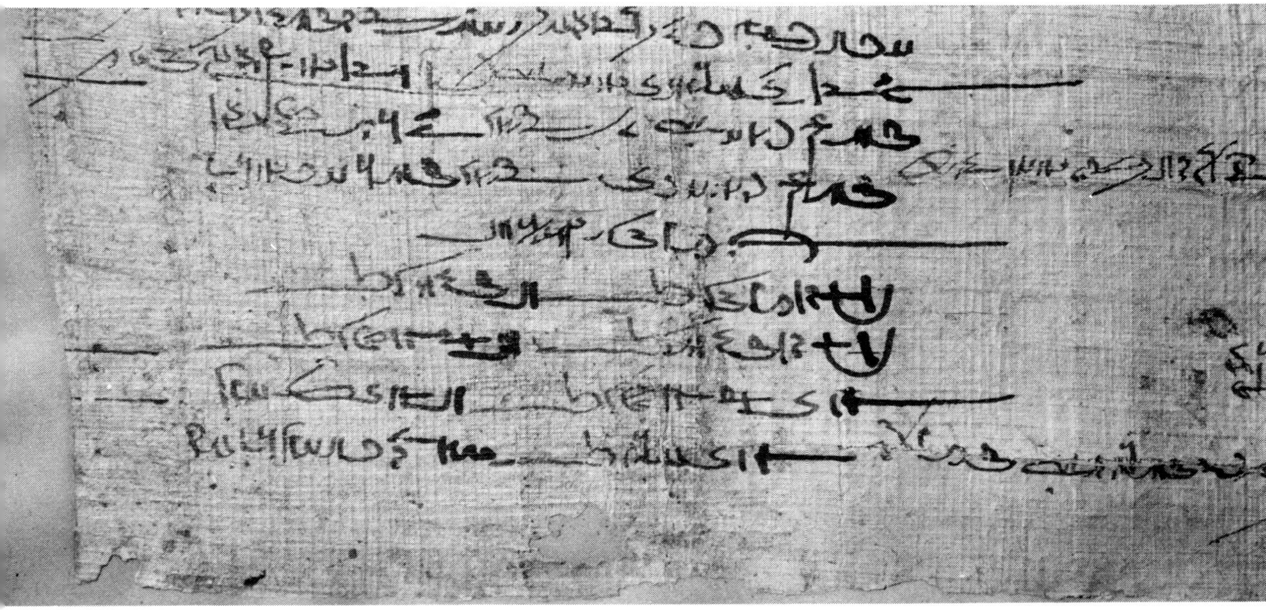

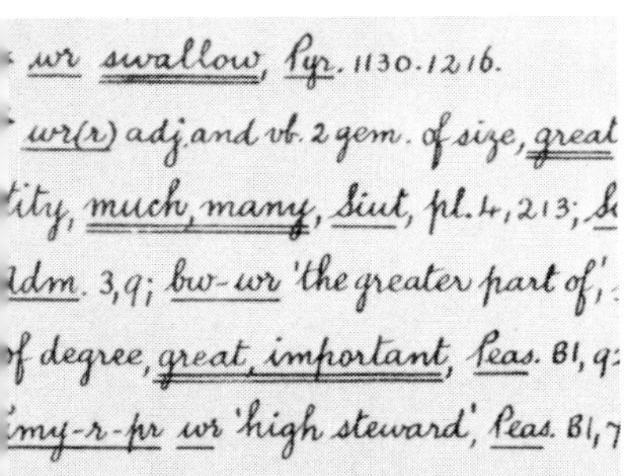
wr swallow, Pyr. 1130.1216.
wr(r) adj. and vb. 2 gem. of size, great
tity, much, many, Siut, pl. 4, 213;
Adm. 3, 9; bw-wr 'the greater part of',
of degree, great, important, Peas. B1, 9
imy-r-pr wr 'high steward', Peas. B1, 7
252; wr r 'too much, too great, for.
wr (1) n. greatness of size, Urk. IV, 16
60; excess of supplies, Sh. S. 54; Les. 7
uantity', Urk. IV, 1293, 13; n wr n 'inc
3) interrog. how much?, Gr. § 502.
wrt (1) n. greatness of rank: 'whose lo
l. 9, 350; what is important: dd. i wr

A page from a modern hieroglyphic dictionary. Note how the sign for a swallow can also mean 'great', 'how much', or 'what is important'.

cuneiform, part of a word or a single sound. There were more than seven hundred hieroglyphic signs so it, too, was a most difficult kind of writing to learn.

In the eighteenth and early nineteenth century many examples of cuneiform and hieroglyphic writing were found. Historians were most excited. The snag was that no one could read them. Until they were deciphered (i.e. the meaning of the signs was worked out) they were no more use in explaining what happened in the past than a pattern on a pottery jug. They were eventually deciphered by a number of scholars – using brains, pens and paper. This achievement is very important for our knowledge of the ancient world.

The deciphering of cuneiform

At the end of the eighteenth century a German by the name of Niebuhr wrote an account of his travels in Arabia. At the palace of the Persian kings at Persepolis he had carefully copied some cuneiform writing which many European scholars tried to decipher. Only in 1802 was any real progress made. In that year, a young German schoolteacher, Grotefend, made a bet with a friend that he would decipher the inscription. It seemed crazy since Grotefend had no special knowledge of ancient languages. None the less he won it.

This is how he did it. Other scholars had already worked out that there were three different kinds of writing at Persepolis. Grotefend concentrated on one of these, Old Persian. He guessed that these

On the Rock of Behistun, King Darius (third from left) boasts of his successes to his captives.

The writing in three languages, cut around the figures, was copied by Major Rawlinson at great risk to himself.

inscriptions were in praise of Persian kings. Like later Persian inscriptions (which could be read) they would all begin with the same kind of phrase namely, X (the name of a king), Great King, King of Kings, son of Y (name of a king), Great King, etc. If he had guessed correctly, then he should be able to find the cuneiform word for king since it would appear so often. This he was able to do. He then found a pattern of signs appearing which would make sense if they meant X, king, son of Y, king, son of Z (not a king). His next step was to make a list of all the Persian kings who might have had their praises written on the walls of the palace at Persepolis who were father and son and whose fathers had/had not also been king. He then checked his list against his cuneiform pattern. To his delight only one set of names could fit: Xerxes, King, son of Darius, King, son of Hystaspes. Hystaspes had only been a noble. These three royal names unlocked the secret of Old Persian cuneiform. They gave sound values to enough cuneiform signs for the values of many words to be found.

There were many types of cuneiform other than Old Persian. To decipher them remained a most difficult task. This rock helped greatly. Travellers passing along the road beneath it in AD 1837 would have seen a strange sight: Major Henry Rawlinson dangling from a rope half-way down the cliff-face. He was hard at work copying down the inscription. Although he was an excellent climber, he was risking his life. Two thousand three hundred years earlier, the stone carvers of King Darius had cut the inscription 500 metres above the valley floor. Moreover, they had carefully polished the area of rock around it. Twice Rawlinson nearly slipped to his death. The copy was finally completed by a local youngster who clawed his way across to those places beyond the reach of the English major.

The effort was worth it. Rawlinson discovered that Darius had used the Behistun Rock to boast of his victories in three separate languages: Old Persian, Elamite and Babylonian. Grotefend had deciphered Old Persian. Through Old Persian the mysteries of Elamite and Babylonian should be solved. But cuneiform was not going to give up its secrets easily. While Old Persian was phonetic, i.e. each sign was a single sound, in Babylonian a sign might stand for a whole word or part of a word or even more than one word. Fortunately at Nineveh archaeologists had dug up many clay tablets which turned out to be guides for student scribes. They gave the sound values and meanings of a large number of cuneiform signs.

In 1857, a sealed envelope was handed in to the Royal Asiatic Society in London. It contained a translation by Fox-Talbot of an Assyrian cuneiform inscription. He suggested that the Society send the same inscription to the three greatest cuneiform experts of the time: Rawlinson, Hincks and Oppert. Each worked on his own and came up with very similar results. Fox-Talbot's experiment showed that the main problems of cuneiform had been solved.

The Rosetta Stone, which is now in the British Museum

The deciphering of hieroglyphics

This slab of black rock was found by French soldiers building fortifications in Egypt in 1799 near the port of Rosetta. It has three different kinds of writing on it, Egyptian hieroglyphic at the top, Egyptian hieratic in the middle and Ancient Greek at the bottom. If the message was the same in each of the three languages then it might be possible to decipher the unknown Egyptian languages from the known Greek one. Many scholars tried but the first to succeed was the Frenchman Champollion.

He was born in south-west France in 1790. At school, he was brilliant at languages and fascinated by Ancient Egypt. By the time he was seventeen he knew a dozen languages and his own school took him on as a teacher. As soon as he saw a copy of the Rosetta Stone he was sure that he would be able to decipher its hieroglyphics. It took him fourteen years of intense work. He succeeded where others had failed for a number of reasons. He was immensely patient in comparing each section of the Stone with the others and with other inscriptions from the tombs and temples of Egypt. He had also taught himself Coptic, a language used by some Egyptians between AD 300 and AD 1500. But perhaps the most important reason was that his basic approach was quite different from that of other scholars. They believed hieroglyphics to be little pictures which either stood for a whole word or part of a word. Champollion became sure that sometimes they must be like letters in our modern alphabet and stand for a sound only.

This was the vital step in the right direction. In the Greek section of the Rosetta Stone he found the name of the king, Ptolemy. His knowledge of Coptic told him that the Egyptians would have been likely to pronounce his name Ptolmys. In the hieroglyphic section of the Rosetta Stone certain hieroglyphs were surrounded by an oval. These were already believed rightly to be names of kings and were called 'cartouches'. In 1822, Champollion was sent copies of the hieroglyphic inscriptions on the Obelisk of Philae. On this he was able to discover the hieroglyphic form of what were probably the names Ptolmys and Cleopatra. Comparing these two names he was reasonably sure that he had found the hieroglyphs for three of the sounds common to both names: *p*, *o* and *l*. He then guessed that just as in English *f* and *ph* have the same sound value, so two different hieroglyphs might have the same sound value for the fourth common sound in the two names, *t*. If this were so he could get twelve sounds from the two names. Moving on from these twelve, he was able to recognise the name Alexander in its Egyptian form of Alksentis in another cartouche.

Champollion now felt that complete success was close. Working furiously he collected together as many cartouches as possible from the years 300 BC to AD 100 when the names of the Egyptian kings were well-known and he was able to identify eighty of them in their hieroglyphic form. Then he went backwards in Egyptian history and was able to decipher cartouches of Thutmose and Ramses. 'I've got the answer,' he gasped to his brother, before taking to his bed for five days!

He published a book explaining his methods, wrote a dictionary of hieroglyphics and led an expedition to Egypt to study the tombs and temples in detail. When he died in 1832, still a young man, others continued his work. Today experts can read most hieroglyphic inscriptions except those of the earliest pharaohs.

The Obelisk of Philae, once sun-drenched beside a temple on an island in the Nile. It now stands darkened by the English weather in the gardens of a Dorset country-house.

Using the evidence: following the footsteps of Champollion

Here is the name Ptolemy as written on the Rosetta Stone.

Here is the name Cleopatra as carved on the Obelisk of Philae plus the sound values given to it by Champollion.

Here is the name Ptolemy as carved on the Obelisk of Philae plus the sound values given by Champollion.

Questions and further work

1 How is the Philae Ptolemy different from the Rosetta Ptolemy? (This does not matter since the Egyptians wrote both ways.)

2 Find and draw (a) the hieroglyphs which are common to both Ptolemy and Cleopatra and (b) the two hieroglyphs with the sound value *t*.

3 Draw the other 7 hieroglyphs and note beside them the sound value of each as they are used in the Cleopatra and Ptolemy cartouche.

4 Here is the Alexander cartouche. (a) How many of the hieroglyphs did Champollion have the sound values for? (b) What did Champollion discover to be the Egyptian form of Alexander? (c) Bearing that in mind, draw the other hieroglyphs in the Alexander cartouche and work out their sound values. (d) In what ways is the sign for *k* different from the others?

Important steps in deciphering

5 What was the key Old Persian phrase in cuneiform to which Grotefend was able to fit the correct names?

6 What names did he fit? Why was this such a big step forward?

7 What have the Rosetta Stone and the Behistun Rock in common? List the languages on each.

8 Describe the part played by (a) Rawlinson, (b) the Nineveh tablets and (c) Fox-Talbot in the deciphering of cuneiform.

9 If  = 10 and  = 1 and  = loaves and  = barley cakes,

(a) What does this cuneiform list from a baker's shop say?

(b) Write in cuneiform 33 loaves and 24 barley cakes.

Mesopotamia

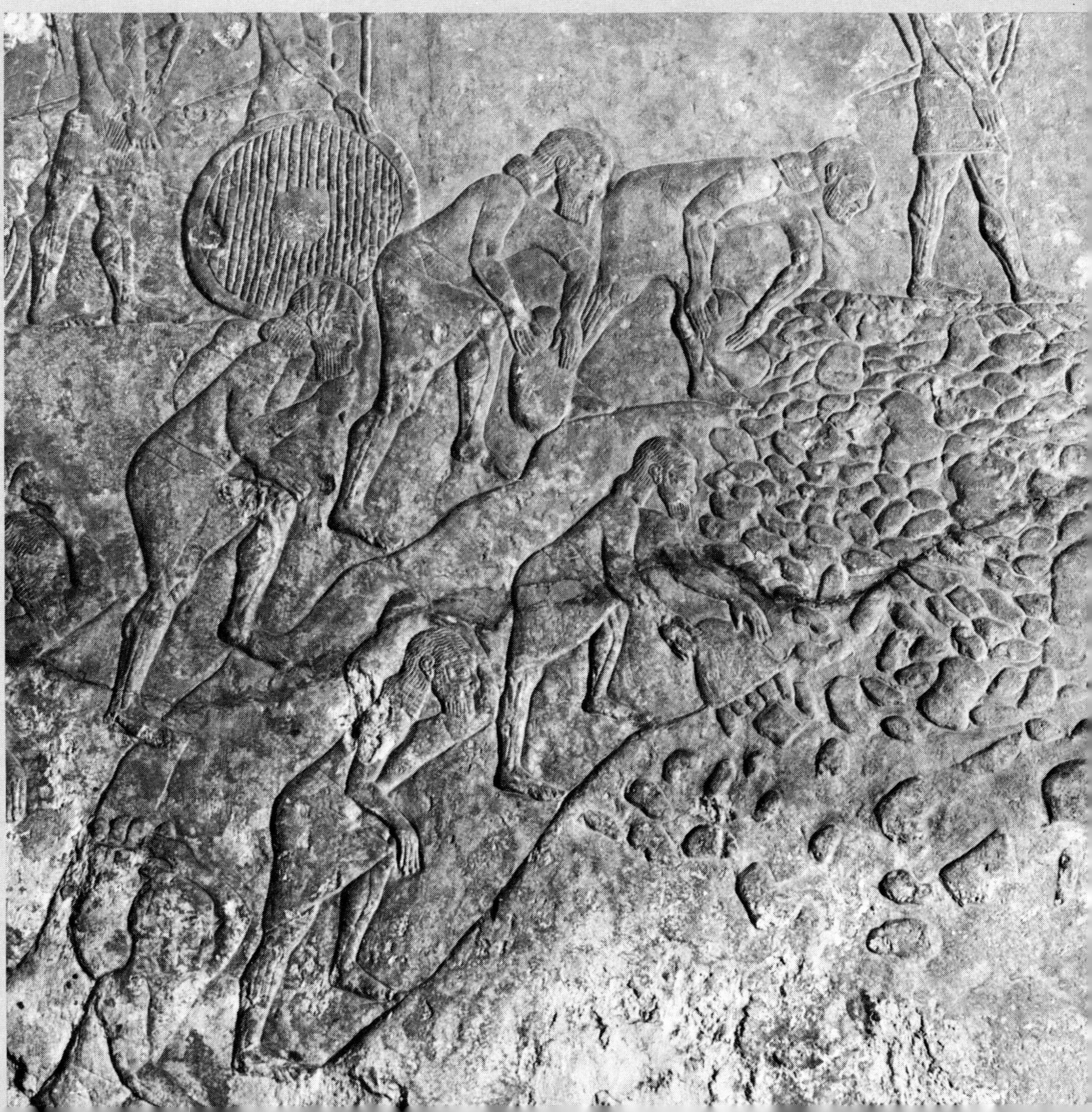

4 The land of the two rivers

South and east of the Jarmo hills the land fell away into a wide, hot wasteland which stretched southwards for thousands of kilometres. Through it, however, flowed two great rivers, the Euphrates and farther to the east, the Tigris. Both rivers flooded often and a band of fertile soil was laid across the otherwise desert wastes. This area the Greeks called Mesopotamia, the land of the two rivers.

The discovery of Mari

Among the low dusty hills on the west bank of the Euphrates just inside the modern Syrian border with Iraq some Syrians found an old statue while digging a grave. Soon a French archaeological team began excavations. What they found in these dull-looking hills was one of the most important and fascinating cities of Mesopotamia – Mari.

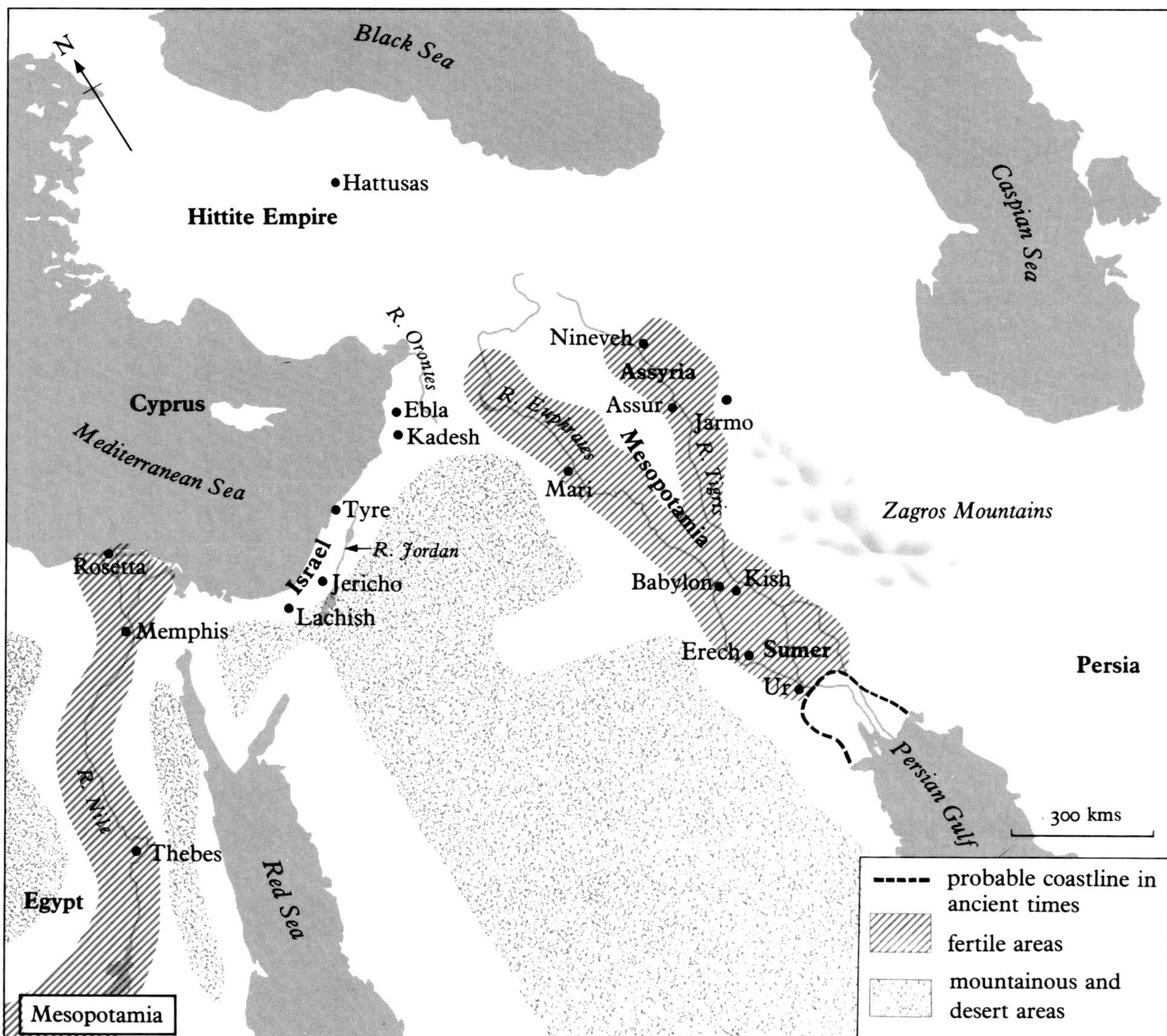

What have they found?
Two of the French team gently clear away the earth.

The find. The French team with the Goddess of the Flowing Vase safely excavated and thoroughly cleaned.

A cheerful wall-painting from the Palace of Mari

Here you can see some of the discoveries which were made early in the Mari dig. After six years' work the remains of a great palace with temples alongside it had been cleared. This palace of Mari was one of the marvels of the ancient world.

Though huge and like a fortress from the outside, inside it was comfortable with cool and airy rooms, tiled bathrooms, efficient toilets and drains. It was beautifully decorated with wall-paintings and statues.

The French archaeologists made another most important find: 25 000 clay tablets covered with cuneiform writing (see chapter 3). On these tablets the kings of Mari had ordered that important information should be kept: where their money came from, for example, and how it was spent; with whom the citizens of Mari traded, and which of the neighbouring kings were friends and which enemies.

From these tablets historians learnt much about Mari and about other parts of Mesopotamia. Before the Mari tablets were found it was thought that between 1800 BC and 1750 BC there was only one great king in the area, Hammurabi of Babylon. This view was based on scraps of evidence from other excavations. The Mari tablets tell a different story. 'There is no king who is mighty by himself,' reads one. 'Ten or fifteen follow Hammurabi, the man of Babylon, a like number Rim-Sin of Larsa, a like number Ibalpiel of Eshnunna.' Because of the evidence of the Mari dig, historians have had to change their views about Hammurabi and other parts of Mesopotamian history.

So we know about Mesopotamia through archaeology and through what the Mesopotamians wrote about themselves. Further evidence can be found in the writings of other peoples. Of these the Egyptians, the Jews (see pages 114–20) and the Greeks (see pages 121–68) tell us most. This chapter and the next two tell us of the major civilisations of Mesopotamia: Sumer, Assyria and Babylonia.

Sumer

The banks of the two great rivers were fertile. But they could not become good farmland until they were properly irrigated and their flood waters controlled by canals and dams. The first men in Mesopotamia settled only where the banks were high enough to be out of danger from flooding and which drained well of their own accord.

Low-lying land beside the River Euphrates

Here they were able to make a good life since their crops grew excellently. In the nearby marshes were fish, duck and the reeds for roofing their huts. Then they began to win the less well-drained areas for their crops and animals by cutting small canals and building simple reservoirs. Crops increased and villages grew in size.

Between 4000 BC and 3000 BC a people from the north, known as the Sumerians, took over the southern part of Mesopotamia. They were skilled farmers and craftsmen. In addition they had learnt how to work together in large numbers so that tasks beyond the powers of smaller groups could be achieved. The efforts of a whole family or even of a whole village were not enough to build the dams, reservoirs and canals to make fertile large areas of Mesopotamia which would also be safe from floods. Under the direction of their kings, the Sumerians were able to do all this work.

The first city-dwellers

Sumer was a collection of city-kingdoms. The city was the home of the king and his officials who supervised the vital irrigation works, decided who should farm which land and defended the people from their enemies. So rich were the farmlands that they were able to produce far more food than was needed by the farmers themselves. Many people were therefore able to live in the city and follow occupations which had little or nothing to do with the land. In the cities of Sumer were traders, shopkeepers, craftsmen and artists, royal officials and tax collectors, priests and teachers. With these first cities came the first civilisation (see chapter 2).

Sumerian craftsmen made two great advances. Firstly they began to use the wheel. Just how it was invented is not completely clear. Probably some clever man watching his friends straining away at a laden sledge hit on the idea of placing sections of tree trunk beneath it to help it along. By 3250 BC the Sumerians had wheeled carts and, soon after, pulleys for raising water from their wells.

The pictures on this so-called 'Standard of Ur', now in the British Museum, are made from mother of pearl and mussel shells. The top line shows Sumerian warriors; in the middle are enemy prisoners and at the bottom, horse-drawn chariots. How do you think the wheels were made?

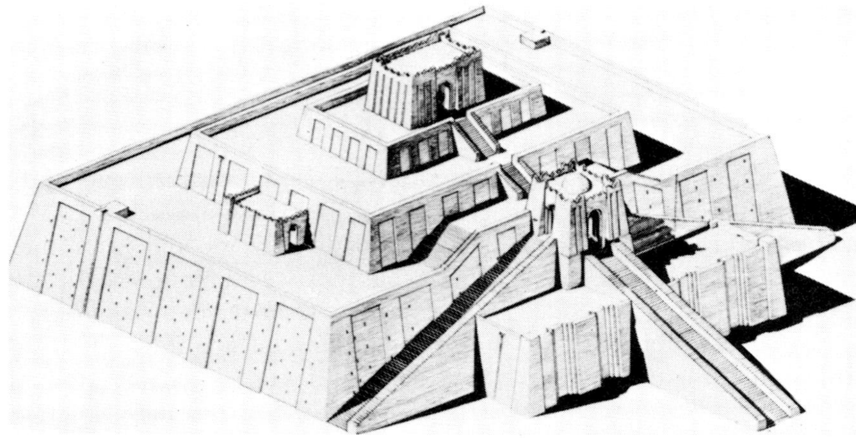

The ziggurat of Ur, as it may have been. At the top was the holiest place in the city.

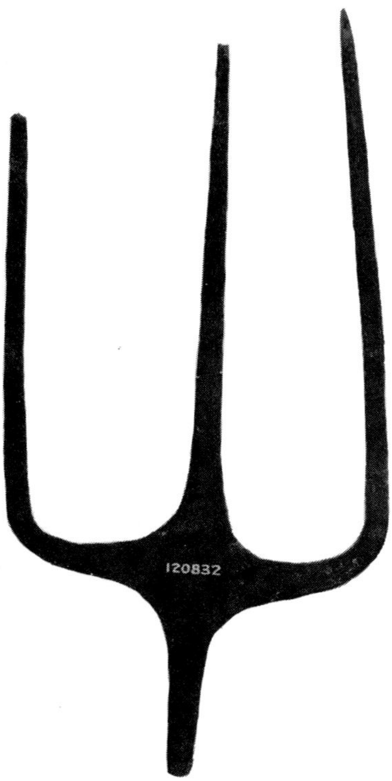

A Sumerian fishing-spear made of bronze

Secondly they discovered how to make bronze by combining copper with tin. Copper had been in use since about 8000 BC. Possibly it was first discovered by the chance lighting of a fire beside copper-bearing rock. Someone who saw the pure copper melted out from the rock perhaps realised what had happened and repeated the process. The pottery-firing ovens of Neolithic Man were hot enough to smelt copper and by 6000 BC copper jewellery was made in many places in western Asia. On its own, however, copper is too soft to make good tools. Bronze, by contrast, makes a sharper cutting edge and wears better. Since most of the copper of Mesopotamia was smelted from rock which also contained tin, it is likely that bronze was first made by chance. Soon, however, the Sumerians learnt how to make it properly. Slowly but surely bronze took over from stone as the chief material for tool-making. What historians call the Bronze Age had begun. It was to last for about two thousand years until iron replaced bronze as the major tool-making metal in western Asia and in Europe around 1000 BC.

Sumerian traders also made an advance as important to the progress of the human race as the wheel or bronze. Around 3000 BC they started to make picture signs on clay tablets so that they had some record of their sales and purchases. This was the beginning of writing, the story of which is told in chapter 3.

The Sumerians also became excellent mathematicians. Though they could count in tens and hundreds, they preferred to use 60 as their basic arithmetical unit. From them come our 360 degree circle, our 60 minute hour and our 60 second minute. They had schools and a special training course, which lasted years, for those who wished to master the skill of writing the terribly complicated Sumerian letters and so join the class of scribes or writers. They also had a set of laws which were carefully written down. They dealt harshly with wrongdoers. For example, should a house fall down because it had been badly built, and the owner was killed, then the builder was likely to be put to death. If a doctor through carelessness was responsible for his patient losing his eye, then he could expect to lose his hand.

The Sumerian city we know most about is Ur, the ziggurat of which you can see opposite. It was excavated by an English team, led by Leonard Woolley between 1924 and 1934 (see also the Using the evidence section). Between 3200 BC and 2500 BC, when the Persian Gulf came much closer and the Euphrates ran past its walls, it was a rich and powerful port. The remains of lengthy quaysides have been found and inside the fortified walls many of the houses are two storeys high with spacious rooms finished in plaster and whitewash facing on to a paved central courtyard. At the city's centre lay the Sacred Area where stood the palace, the public buildings and the temples. Towering over all else was the pyramid-shaped ziggurat. At the top was the shrine of Nanna, the Moon God. On New Year's Day a procession of priests mounted to the top of the ziggurat and there made sacrifices to Nanna so that he would protect the city and its lands throughout the coming year.

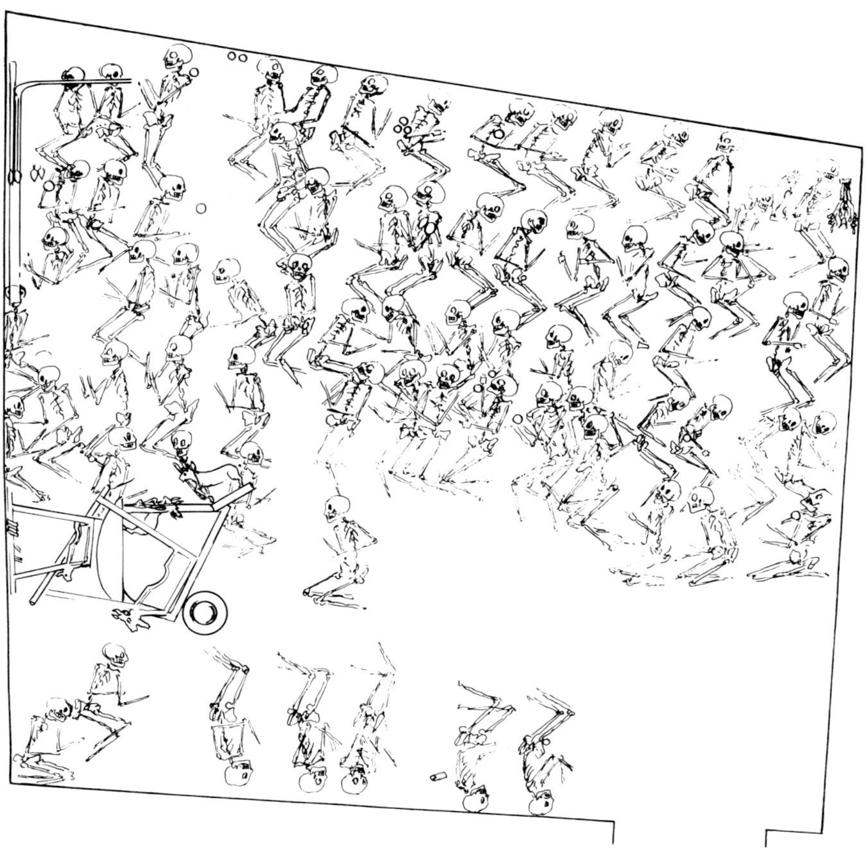

Woolley's sketch of the Death Pit of Ur as he found it

Beside the Sacred Area, Woolley found the royal cemetery. As well as many beautiful and precious objects, he found the remains of an astonishing and terrible event. Deep down in the brick-lined vault of the tomb of Queen Shub-Ad were more than sixty female skeletons. The fragments of their clothes and jewellery told Woolley that they were noblewomen from the royal court. Nearby were soldiers with their spears beside them, a harpist clutching his harp and oxen still harnessed to their wagons. The hands of most of the skeletons were raised as if to their mouths and little clay cups were scattered on the floor of the tomb. It seems that the servants of the dead king or queen followed the body to the tomb vault. There they took poison so that their master or mistress need not go on to the life to come alone.

The cities of Sumer fought each other constantly, mainly about water supplies and land. They also had to defend themselves from other peoples who enviously eyed their rich lands. For a time Kish was the strongest city; then Erech, whose mysterious King Gilgamesh became the hero of many later stories (see the Using the evidence section); then it was the turn of Ur; then of Lagash. The first king to unite the land of Sumer was an outsider, Sargon the Great. During a long life he conquered Sumer and much of the rest of Mesopotamia. After his death, most of the Sumerian cities fell to barbarian tribes who were eventually driven off about 2100 BC by Ur-Nammu, king of Ur. He rebuilt the great ziggurat and made possible Sumer's last period of prosperity. It only lasted a short time. Other invaders came. Ur was captured, its king taken away a prisoner. The new cities of wealth and power were farther north, first at Mari, then at Nineveh and then at Babylon.

A lady's head-dress from the Death Pit

Using the evidence: a mystery at Ur

In the summer of 1929, Woolley's diggers were driving a great shaft down through the mound of the ancient city of Ur. They were searching for the earliest human settlement upon which the city had later grown. They would know that they had reached it when they reached soil which no longer contained the fragments of pottery, bones and building materials which proved that people had once lived there. The remains immediately above this untouched ground would be the earliest human settlement.

At last after many days came the cry from the bottom of the shaft, 'We are now at ground level.' Woolley clambered down to investigate. He prodded the soil and ran it through his fingers. He stood there puzzled. Here was certainly a new layer of soil which contained no sign of human settlement, but it was clay, not at all the type of soil which he was expecting. He ordered the shaft to be deepened still farther. Three metres down, the band of clay ended and to the amazement of the diggers new signs of human settlement appeared.

The photograph shows the shaft and the diagram, which is based on Woolley's sketch, the clay band with the remains of human settlement both above and below it.

How could such a thick layer of clay, quite different from the surrounding soil, have got above one town and below the next? Woolley, using both archaeological and written evidence, was able to solve the mystery. Can you, using the same clues as Woolley?

(A) The clay must once have been silt carried by water.

The 'Flood' shaft and the men who dug it. The clay layer cannot be seen in the shadows but runs horizontally across the shaft beneath the steps.

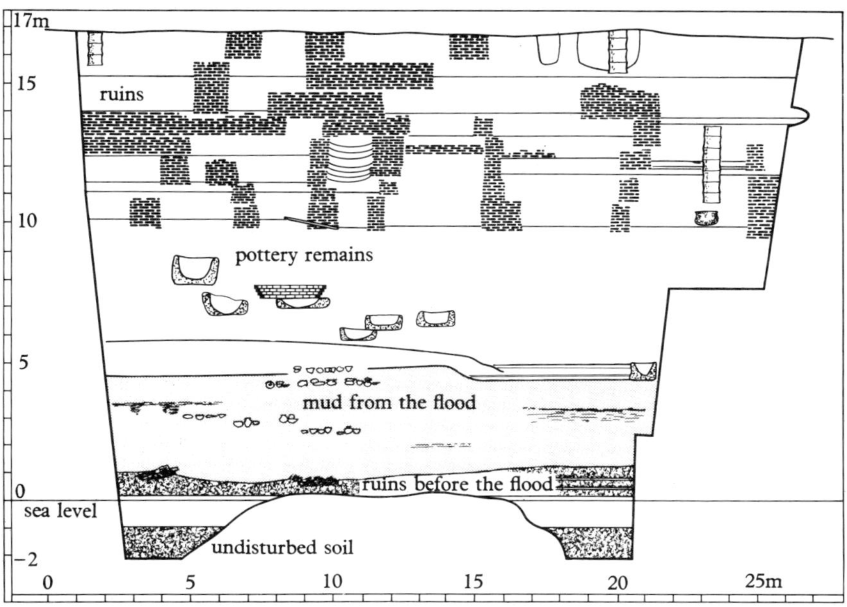

Woolley's sketch of the 'Flood' shaft

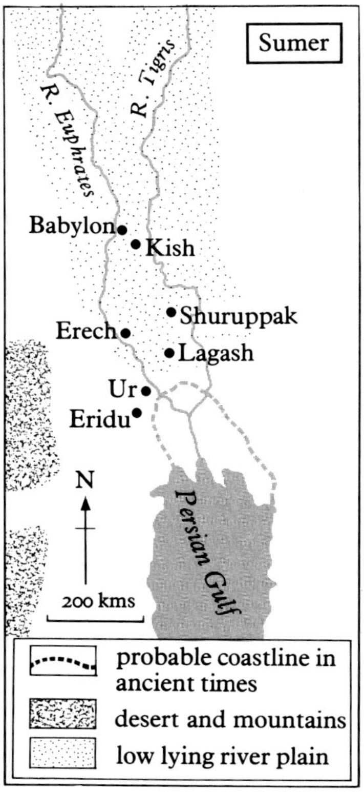

(B) Look at the map showing the old coastline, the main rivers and the position of Ur.

(C) Scientific tests showed that the clay was different from that normally laid down in the valleys of the Tigris and Euphrates. It contained the remains of tiny organisms which live not in fresh water but in the sea.

(D) The story of the great king, Gilgamesh, can be read on cuneiform tablets. It was first written down about 1700 BC and was based on stories older still which had been handed down from one generation to the next. All sorts of adventures happen to Gilgamesh while he searches for his ancestor Utnapishtim. When at last he finds him, Utnapishtim tells him of this catastrophe which befell the world and which only he survived.

For one day the South Wind blew, gathering speed, submerging the mountains, overtaking the people like a battle. Adad's rage reached the heaven, turning all light to darkness. Six days and six nights raged the wind and the flood and the cyclone devastated the land. When the seventh day came, the cyclone, the flood, the battle was over. All mankind was turned to clay. The ground was flat like a roof.

Note particularly the direction from which the wind blew and how the countryside looked when the water had gone down.

(E) Further geological tests have shown that the clay band dates from about 4000 BC.

(F) River engineers have calculated that to lay three metres of clay would need a depth of 7.5 metres of silt-laden water.

(G) Further digging elsewhere in Mesopotamia has uncovered similar clay bands. There is one at Kish, 46 centimetres wide. Kish is about 220 kilometres up the Euphrates from Ur.

(H) 7.5 metres of water at Ur would mean a flood over southern Mesopotamia 440 kilometres long and 160 kilometres wide.

(I) About 2000 BC the Sumerians made this list of their earliest kings. The first eight are divided from the next by these words:

The Flood came
After the Flood kingship was sent down again from Heaven.

Questions and further work

1 Clues (A), (F) and (H) are geological and scientific. How do they suggest that early Ur disappeared beneath three metres of clay?

2 (a) In which two clues are the Sumerians writing about their past?
(b) What terrible event a long time ago do they both mention?

3 Using (a) Sumerian written evidence and (b) geological and scientific evidence, what dates can you give to this terrible event?

4 In Woolley's opinion the band of clay was laid down by a flood so enormous that it was remembered by later generations in the *Epic of*

King Gilgamesh

Gilgamesh and in the Bible story of Noah's Ark as the Flood which destroyed almost all mankind. Using all the clues, but especially (B), (C), and (H), explain as clearly as you can how such a huge flood could have happened.

5 Imagine that you were an inhabitant of the first city of Ur who saw and survived the great flood of 4000 BC. Either write or make sketches for a wall-painting about what happened to you.

6 Read the story of Noah's Ark in the Bible in Genesis 6–9. Where was Noah living at the time of the Flood? In what ways are the stories of Noah and of Gilgamesh similar?

5 Assyria

Nineveh

The Assyrian people lived beside the Tigris river in northern Mesopotamia. Nineveh was their greatest city. All the peoples of the land between the two rivers were warlike. They had to be, to defend themselves from the frequent attacks of desert and mountain tribes. The Assyrians, however, were the fiercest of all. For five hundred years between 1100 BC and 600 BC their violent kings, leading ferocious and excellent armies equipped with iron weapons and horse-drawn chariots, spread terror through western Asia.

An early warrior-king of Assyria was Tiglath-Pileser I. In the eleventh century BC he fought his way westwards to the Mediterranean and made the rich cities of Phoenicia pay him tribute. He also defeated Babylon, Nineveh's greatest rival. He boasted that:

> Against twenty thousand warriors and their five kings I fought and won. . . . Their blood I let flow in the valleys and on the mountains. . . . I cut off their heads and outside their cities like heaps of grain I piled them up. . . . I burned their cities with fire, I demolished them, I cleared them away.

The Winged Bull of Sargon, eighth century BC. This magnificent beast stood beside the entrance to Sargon's Palace at Khorsabad.

The ruins of Nineveh. A nineteenth-century English archaeologist sketches some early finds.

Yet another foe bites the dust of defeat before the Assyrians. Jehu, King of Israel, surrenders to Shalmaneser.

Assurnasirpal with a courtier

Not surprisingly the lands which he had conquered rose in revolt as soon as they heard that he was dead.

The Assyrian Empire was rebuilt by Assurnasirpal II. He improved the army and added to it new siege weapons including battering rams with iron heads. He plundered his way through Syria and Phoenicia. He won so much loot from his expedition that he was able to build himself a completely new capital at Nimrud. When it was finished he celebrated by inviting 70 000 guests to banquets which lasted ten days. For this celebration, 2200 oxen, 16 000 sheep, thousands of game birds, gazelles and fish were slaughtered.

Assurnasirpal's grandson, Tiglath-Pileser III, fought less for plunder than for power. He wished to make an Assyrian empire which would last. Where his armies conquered, there he placed Assyrian officials to rule in his name. The Assyrian armies were unstoppable. Led by Tiglath-Pileser, they spread the empire westwards towards Egypt and eastwards towards Persia. Led by his grandson, Sennacherib, they made Judah pay tribute (see the Using the evidence section). They besieged and captured Babylon which had risen in revolt. Sennacherib's treatment of the city was merciless. First he burnt the buildings, then he diverted the Euphrates so that mud-brick ruins were washed away. 'I dissolved it in water,' he wrote in triumph, 'I annihilated it making it like a meadow.' Sennacherib, however, was a builder as well as a destroyer. He made Nineveh his capital and there erected a mighty palace with more than eighty rooms. He also improved the city's water supply by an impressive system of canals and aqueducts.

Sennacherib came to a violent end, being murdered by two of his sons. After a family struggle, a third son, Esarhaddon, became king. Now the Assyrian armies turned on Egypt. The Egyptian pharaoh might rule the oldest and richest empire in the world but his armies

Assurbanipal hunts lions

Assurbanipal feasting in a garden with his queen

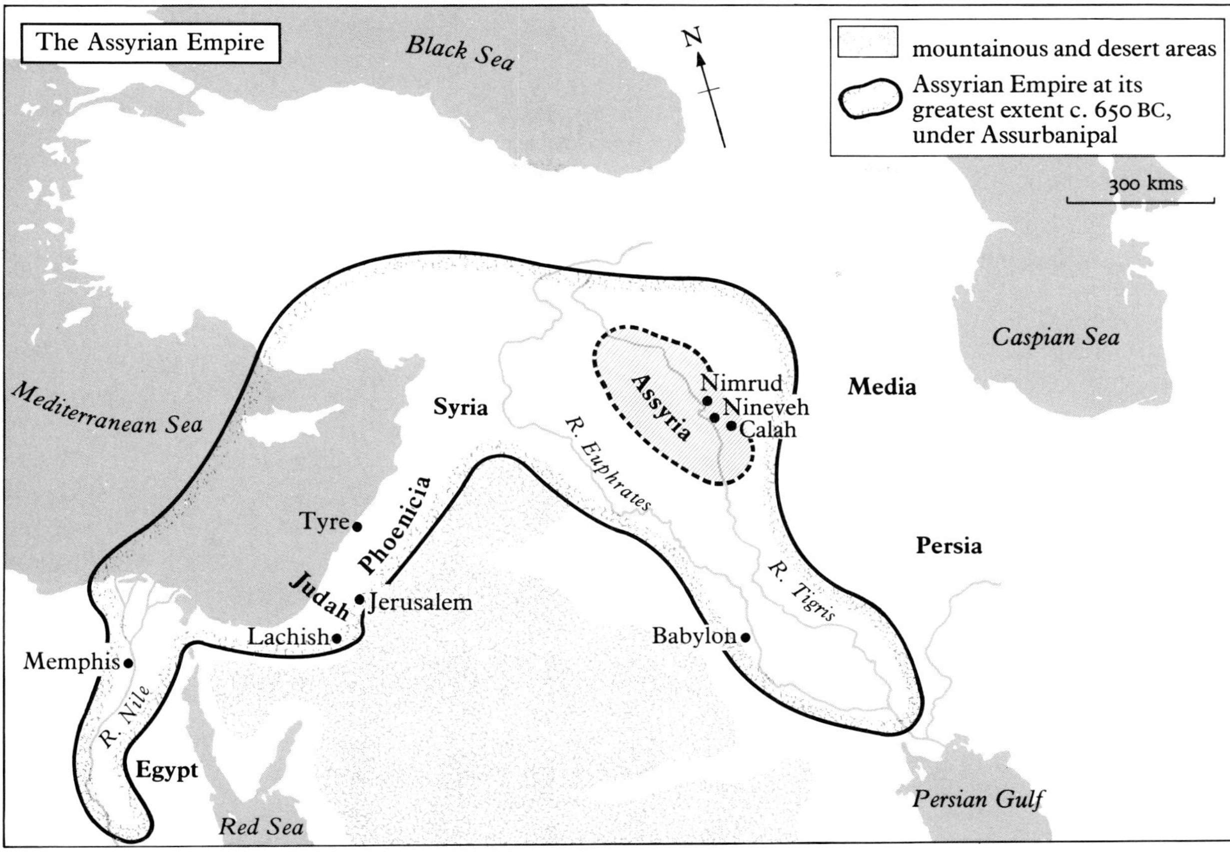

were no match for Esarhaddon's. Memphis, the Egyptian capital, fell after only a month's fighting. By the end of 671 BC Egypt had become just another province of the Assyrian Empire.

During the reign of Assurbanipal, the Assyrians ruled more of the world than any people before them. They treated their conquered lands cruelly and continued to plunder them. The cities of the Tigris grew rich from this plunder. Assurbanipal's palace in Nineveh was decorated with Egyptian gold and ivory, Syrian silver, Persian lapis lazuli (a deep blue stone) and Phoenician cedarwood. It had a garden and a zoo stocked with plants and animals from every part of the empire. Fierce warrior though he was, Assurbanipal also prided himself on his intelligence. 'Marduk, the greatest of gods,' he wrote, 'has given me an inquiring mind and considerable powers of thought.' His palace included a library of 22 000 clay tablets and he seems to have had a special interest in mathematics and science.

Assurbanipal was able to hold this large empire together. His successors could not. The cruelties of Assyrian rule provoked revolt after revolt. In 616 BC the Babylonians joined forces with the Medes and together they attacked their hated masters. Nineveh was captured and destroyed by fire in 612 BC. Three years later, all Assyria had been conquered, never again to appear as an independent power.

Using the evidence: Sennacherib attacks Israel, 701 BC

The Assyrian evidence

In 701 BC Sennacherib, King of Assyria, invaded Judah. His army besieged Lachish, one of the strongest fortresses of the Jews. This relief was carved in Sennacherib's palace in Nineveh, after the siege. It is now in the British Museum.

From his throne, Sennacherib watches the siege

Lachish as the Assyrians found it in 701 BC

A tower on the Lachish wall is attacked by the Assyrians

1 Of the soldiers which you can see on the relief, which are the Assyrians and which are the Jews? How can you tell which are which?
2 List the various ways in which the defenders are trying to drive off the attackers.
3 Sketch as clearly as you can the siege-engine which the Assyrians are pushing towards the tower from the left.
4 Explain what the following might be for:
   (a) the pole at the front of the siege-engine
   (b) the soldier in the engine with his back to the tower
   (c) the archers on and beside the engine.
5 What evidence can you find on this relief that the Assyrians were cruel as well as skilful fighters?

The Sennacherib cylinder, a six-sided baked clay tablet

We know from other evidence that Sennacherib captured Lachish. What happened next is not so clear. On this six-sided tablet is Sennacherib's version.

As for Hezekiah of Judah, him I shut up like a caged bird in his royal city of Jerusalem. I built earthworks against the city walls and whoever came out of the city was made to pay for his crimes. Those of his cities which I had captured, I took away from his kingdom. I increased the tribute which he paid me and a yearly tax. As for Hezekiah, he was frightened by the splendour of my power and his best troops deserted him.

6 What does Sennacherib say were the main results of his war with Hezekiah?
7 What was his opinion of Hezekiah?
8 Does anything seem to have gone wrong for the Assyrians?
9 Did he actually capture Jerusalem?

The Jews' version

There is an exciting account of Sennacherib's attack on Judah told from the Jewish point of view in the Bible (2 Kings 18 and 19). The following are the main points:

Now in the fourteenth year of the reign of King Hezekiah, Sennacherib, king of Assyria attacked all Judah's fortified cities and took them. Hezekiah then sent to the king of Assyria at Lachish this message – 'I have done wrong. Whatever you ask of me that I will do.' So the king of Assyria made Hezekiah, king of Judah, pay three hundred talents of silver and thirty talents of gold. Hezekiah gave all the silver that there was in the temple and in the royal treasury; he also cut the gold from the temple doors and from the pillars of the royal palace.

Then the king of Assyria sent three of his generals with a great army against Jerusalem. Heartened by the prophet Isaiah, Hezekiah and the people of Jerusalem refused to give in. Then it happened one night that the angel of the Lord struck down 5180 of the Assyrian army. When they woke in the morning, all around were dead bodies. So Sennacherib, king of Assyria, departed and returned to Nineveh.

10 According to the Bible, Sennacherib's attack was a great disaster for Hezekiah yet it could have been worse. Explain:
   (a) in what ways it was a great disaster;
   (b) how it could have been worse.

11 (a) Who is the 'Lord' this Bible account refers to?
   (b) What do you think the phrase 'the angel of the Lord struck down' might mean?

12 In what ways do the Assyrian and Jewish versions:
   (a) agree
   (b) disagree?

13 Though the disagreement is a big one, neither side may actually be lying. Explain how this may be so.

14 Imagine that you are a Phoenician engineer employed by the Assyrians to repair and service their siege-engines during the Judah campaign of 701 BC. Describe your experiences that year.

Lachish has fallen. Its people are led off into captivity.

6 Babylonia

The earliest written laws known are those of Hammurabi, King of Babylon (1792–1750 BC) which are written on this black stone pillar. The king is on the left, offering his laws to a seated god.

Babylon

After defeating the Assyrians, the Babylonians and Medes split the Assyrian Empire between them. The Medes took the north and east, Babylon the south and west. For nearly two thousand years Babylon had been an important city. The next seventy years, however, especially the reign of King Nebuchadnezzar, were the most glorious in her history.

Babylon stood on the Euphrates where the main trade routes of the ancient world met. Babylonian ships, usually manned by Phoenician sailors, traded down the river and along the coast of Arabia and India. Merchant caravans reached deep into Persia and Asia Minor. Consequently the city was a busy centre of trade and commerce. Shops and offices lined the many riverside quays, and keeping accounts and writing trading agreements on cuneiform tablets kept the scribes busy. Babylon was also a great centre of learning and of religion. The priests seem to have been very interested in astronomy. Using their temple towers as observatories, they carefully noted the movements of the moon and of the planets. They calculated the phases of the moon to within seconds of the time now measured by modern scientific instruments, and the movement of the planet Mercury more accurately than was done by any other ancient civilisation, including the Greeks and the Romans. They also designed a satisfactory calendar based upon the phases of the moon.

King Nebuchadnezzar is famous because in the Bible he was the king who invaded and conquered Judah, captured and destroyed Jerusalem and took many Jews back to Babylon as prisoners. In fact he fought fewer battles than the Assyrian kings.

He had a fairer claim to fame as a builder. During his long reign Babylon turned into one of the most beautiful cities in the world. The best description which we have of the city was written by the Greek, Herodotus (see the Using the evidence section). We can also read the descriptions of other Greek travellers. For them the most wonderful part of the city were the famous Hanging Gardens. An artificial hill of terrace upon terrace was planted with every sort of flower and tree. Water for them was raised by machinery from the river below. The story goes that Nebuchadnezzar had them made because his new young queen was homesick for the green hills among which she had grown up.

The period of Babylon's glory lasted only a few years more after Nebuchadnezzar's death. His successors were no match for the tough Persian king, Cyrus the Great, who moved against Babylon after he had conquered the Medes in 549 BC. Though defeated in battle, the Babylonians were not discouraged. They retreated, Herodotus tells us, inside their massive fortifications with enough food to last for years. They neglected their defences and continued to feast and celebrate. Cyrus, however, diverted the waters of the Euphrates so that his soldiers were able to wade along it where it ran through Babylon. They attacked under the cover of night and seized the strongholds of the city before the Babylonian king knew that the attack had started! After the Persians, the Greeks ruled Babylon. By 300 BC the main trade routes no longer passed through the city and it began to decay. The buildings turned to ruins and were used as brick quarries by nearby villages and towns. The irrigation system was neglected, the Euphrates changed course and the sands blew in from the desert. Today, for all the rich remains uncovered by archaeologists, it is difficult to imagine this was once the world's biggest and busiest city.

All that is left of Babylon, the biggest and busiest city of Mesopotamia. The River Euphrates, which has changed its course since ancient times, can be seen beyond the ruins.

Using the evidence: what was ancient Babylon really like?

Herodotus, who probably visited Babylon about 450 BC, describes the city in the first book of his *Histories*. He was the first writer whose work survives to write about the past because he thought it both interesting and important. For this reason he is known as the Father of History (see page 153). Later Greek and Roman historians were very rude about him. In their opinion he was too ready to believe fantastic tales which he had heard on his travels. They even nicknamed him Herodotus the Liar. Modern historians are usually less rude but some still think that he exaggerates greatly. Here we have, however, a way of checking how accurate Herodotus is. From AD 1899 to 1914 a team of German archaeologists, headed by Robert Koldewey, uncovered the remains of Nebuchadnezzar's Babylon. In the pages that follow Herodotus' description is set alongside the archaeological discoveries of Koldewey. Compare the two and decide for yourself how good a guide to Babylon Herodotus really is.

Babylon: this artist's sketch shows the decorated walls beginning to appear, thanks to the efforts of German archaeologists

Babylon as the archaeologists found it

The size of ancient Babylon is difficult to work out because the Euphrates follows a different course, and marsh now covers part of the city. So far about 18 kilometres of wall have been found and 250 towers.

The archaeologists soon found remains of huge fortifications. The outer wall was 7 metres wide, 13 metres inside it was a second, 8 metres wide, and inside that defending the inner fortress a third, 4 metres wide. The space between the two outer walls was filled with earth almost to the height of the ramparts so there was space enough for a chariot to pass either along the walls or in the space between them.

The ziggurat temple of Bel or Marduk, as the god was also known, was

Babylon as Herodotus described it

Babylon lies in a wide plain, a vast city in the form of a square with sides nearly 23 kilometres long and a circuit of some 90 kilometres, and in addition to its enormous size it surpasses in splendour any city of the known world.

It is surrounded by a broad deep moat full of water, and within the moat there is a wall 25 metres wide and 100 metres high. . . . On top of the wall they constructed, along each edge, a row of one-roomed buildings facing outwards with enough space between for a four-horse chariot to pass. There are a hundred gates in the circuit of the wall, all of bronze. . . . The great wall is the chief armour of the city; but there is a second one within it, hardly less strong though smaller.

The temple is a square building, 400 metres each way, with bronze gates,

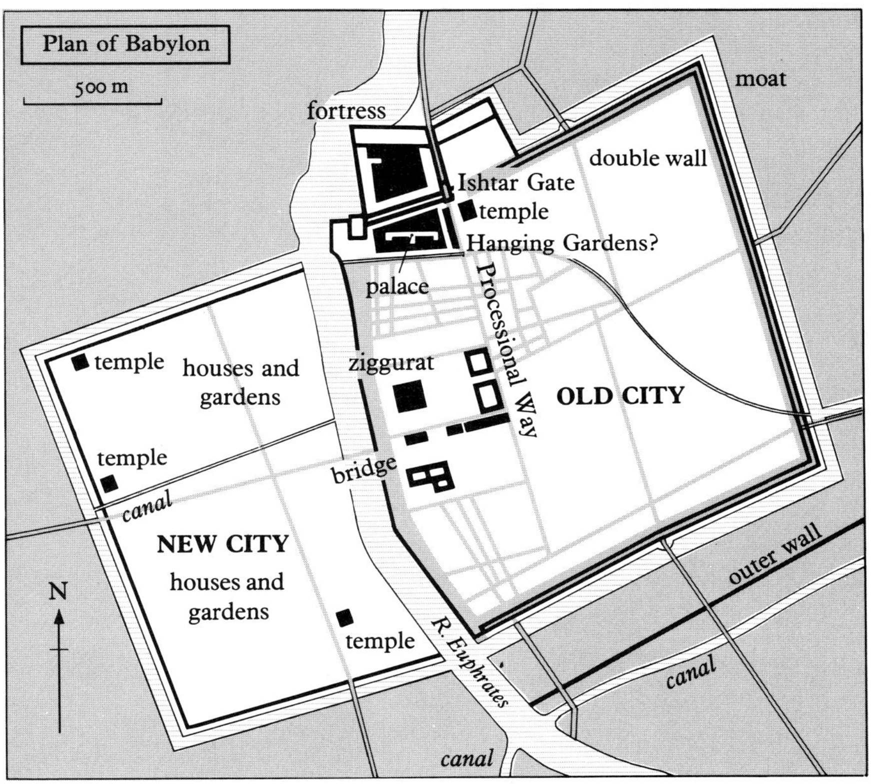

The discovery of the Sacred Way. A photo from Koldewey's excavations.

Babylon – a modern reconstruction

found to be the biggest in Mesopotamia. It stood in a sacred area about 400 metres square and was itself 100 metres square at the base rising to a height of 100 metres. Koldewey calculated that 58 000 000 bricks had been used to build it.

The most exciting discovery which Koldewey made was a street and a gateway into the Sacred Area. The street which Koldewey called 'the Processional Way' was 25 metres wide and ran quite straight for a kilometre until it reached the Ishtar gate of the Sacred Area. The street was paved with marble and limestone slabs on each of which was written, 'Nebuchadnezzar, King of Babylon am I. The Bel street I paved with Shadu slabs for the procession of the great god Marduk. Marduk, Lord, grant eternal life.' The high sides of the street and the Ishtar gate were covered with bright blue enamel tiles, the street being decorated with yellow lions, the gate with bulls and dragons. Marduk (Bel) was the chief god of Mesopotamia and the Babylonians believed that their city was particularly favoured by him. This street was built specially for the procession of the priests of Marduk.

and was still in existence in my time; it has a solid central tower 200 metres square with a second erected on top of it, and then a third and so on up to eight. All eight towers can be climbed by a spiral way running round the outside and about half-way up there are seats for those who make the ascent to rest on. On the summit of the topmost tower stands a great temple with a fine large couch in it, richly covered and a golden table beside it.

There are a great many houses of three and four storeys. The main streets and the side streets which lead to the river are all dead straight.

Cuneiform writing on a brick from Babylon

Questions and further work

1 Draw a diagram of the fortifications of Babylon, based on Herodotus' description. How different are the fortifications uncovered by Koldewey?

2 List the main points of Herodotus' description of the Temple of Bel.

3 (a) Did Koldewey find anything like this temple?
(b) In what ways was the temple ziggurat which he found different from the one described by Herotodus?

4 (a) What important part of Nebuchadnezzar's Babylon did Koldewey find which Herodotus does not mention?
(b) Had it been built at the time Herodotus visited Babylon? Explain your answer.

The Ishtar Gate – rebuilt in a Berlin Museum

(c) How surprising do you think it is that Herodotus does not mention it?

5 How reliable a guide to Babylon do you now believe Herodotus to be? Explain your answer.

6 Imagine that, like Herodotus, you have climbed to the top of the ziggurat of Bel. Using all the information which you now have about Babylon, sketch the view of the city stretching away beneath you.

Egypt

7 The Egypt of the pharaohs

The Valley of the Kings

This is the Valley of the Kings, a desolate valley which winds its way into the hills not far from the great city of Thebes. Four things in particular are worth noting. First, the soil is very dry and sandy since rain seldom falls. As a result when the ruins of Ancient Egypt disappeared beneath the surface, the dry, soft sand which covered them preserved them remarkably well.

Secondly the entrances which you can see running into the hillside are entrances to the tombs of the pharaohs or kings of Egypt. For all Egyptians, life on this earth was a preparation for the life to come. They

The Valley of the Kings near Thebes

took tremendous care of their tombs and with the way in which they buried dead bodies. Inside the tombs they placed a dead person's belongings so that he could live again at least as well as he had lived on earth. As a result, much was buried and survived beneath the sand.

Thirdly almost every square centimetre which you can see has been dug over by archaeologists at least once, sometimes two or three times. In the last hundred and fifty years such rich and exciting discoveries have been made that expeditions have come from all over the world in the hope of finding more. Not surprisingly this valley, where the most powerful and rich of the Egyptian rulers were buried, attracted them like bees to a honey pot.

Fourthly, note the low stone wall in the left foreground of the photo. Behind it is the entrance to the tomb of the pharaoh Tutankhamen. This entrance had been hidden beneath the remains of huts of workmen who were building a later tomb and had been missed by many archaeologists. More important, it was missed by the tomb robbers who had managed to find and steal the valuable possessions buried in the other tombs in the Valley of the Kings. It was discovered in 1922 by an English team led by Howard Carter and paid for by Lord Carnarvon.

Left Tutankhamen's tomb: the antechamber

Below The golden coffin of the young pharaoh, made by craftsmen of marvellous skill

The tomb had four separate rooms. In the antechamber you can see on the left part of the royal chariot, on the right some bedroom furniture. There were statues, jewellery and pottery of exceptional beauty. The second photograph shows the golden coffin which lay inside two wooden ones. These coffins lay inside a massive stone container which, in turn, was surrounded by four further wooden barriers. Inside the gold coffin was the body mummified according to the usual Egyptian custom.

By mummification, the Egyptians aimed to preserve as much of the

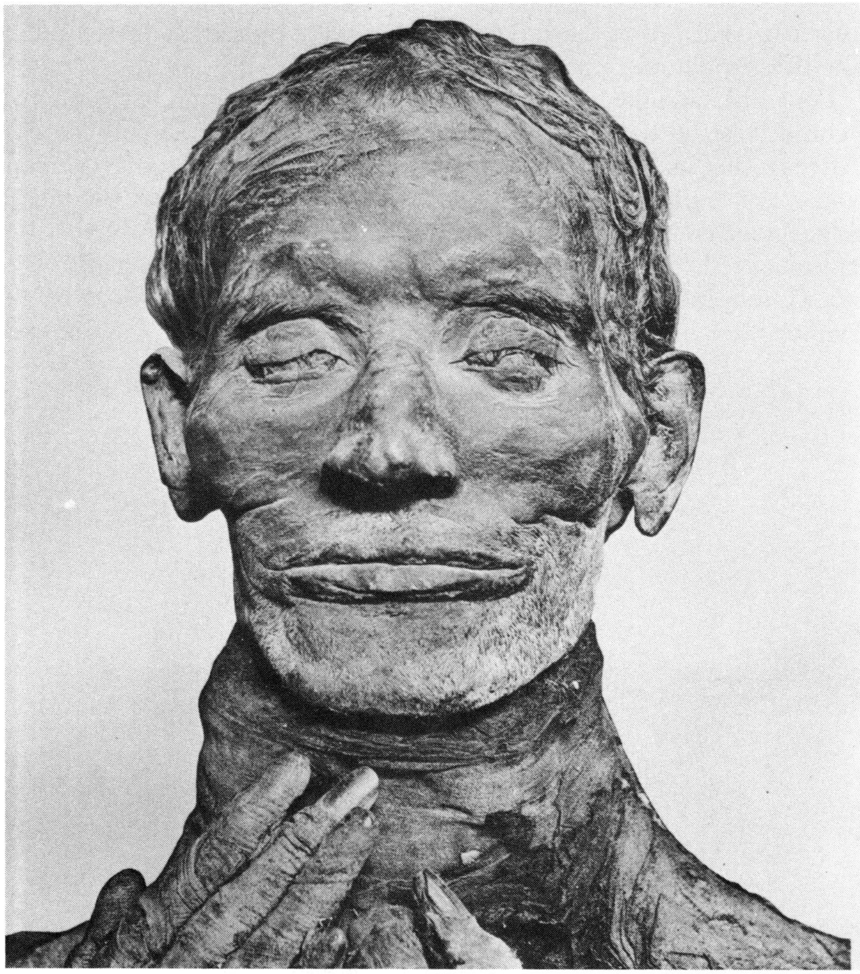

His friends would still recognise him, though he is now nearly 4000 years old. The mummified head of Yuaa, father-in-law of Pharaoh Amenophis III. You can still make out the hair of his beard and eyelashes.

body as possible for the life to come. They removed the innards except the heart and kidneys, then coated the body inside and out with special salts, spices and oils. Finally they wrapped it in many layers of linen cloth before placing it in the tomb. If done in the most careful and expensive way, which only the families of pharaohs and nobles could afford, mummification successfully preserved a person's appearance for thousands of years. We have a better idea of what Egyptians looked like than we have of any other ancient people.

The Theban tombs also tell us about many Egyptians other than the pharaohs. Within a stone's throw of the Valley of the Kings is the hillside where the noblemen of Thebes were buried. The tomb of Meket-Re, who died about 2000 BC, contains a number of models of his estates. They give us a vivid idea of how he and his family lived (see chapter 8).

Menna was a government official about 1370 BC whose job it was to make sure that the taxes due from local landowners were properly paid in grain. The walls of his tomb are covered with paintings of him at

work. You can see him in the top row. He stands in the kiosk on the left with a staff in his hand. He is supervising a man being beaten. Below, the harvested corn is winnowed and threshed. The Egyptians wrote on stone, wall-paintings and papyrus (an early kind of paper, made from papyrus reeds): much of their writing has survived (see chapter 3).

A wall-painting from the tomb of Menna, Thebes

We also have the writings of some early historians. An Egyptian called Manetho, who lived between 200 BC and 300 BC, wrote quite an accurate description of the pharaohs of Egypt from 3100 BC listing them in the order in which they reigned. Many foreigners also came to Egypt, marvelled at and wrote about what they saw. The most entertaining description which we can read now is by Herodotus. He gives a particularly good account of mummification.

The rule of the pharaohs

The Nile flows from the lakes and mountains of central Africa northwards to the Mediterranean. As it flows through Egypt there is a short stretch of fertile land on each bank, then desert. This land is made fertile by the Nile's floods. The snows of the mountains of Ethiopia and central Africa melt in the spring, and the floodwaters of the melted snow reach Egypt in late summer and overflow the river banks, spreading fertile silt wherever they reach. Once the floodwaters go down, the Egyptian farmers sow their grain which ripens easily in the hot sun. The Nile is the life-blood of Egypt. Without it there would only be desert.

Wandering hunters first entered the valley about 5000 BC. They soon changed to farming, sowing grain, herding sheep and cattle and living in reed or mud huts. The Nile, however, brought disaster as well as life. Sometimes the floods were so great that the villages were swept away, sometimes so small that fields which desperately needed moisture and silt were left dry. As in Mesopotamia, the inhabitants got together. They built dams, cut canals and stored grain from the good harvests as an insurance against bad ones. Again as in Mesopotamia, they were ruled by kings. The word used was *pharaoh* which means *he who lives in the great palace*.

By 3400 BC there were only two pharaohs in Egypt, one ruling Lower Egypt (the Nile Delta mainly) the other Upper Egypt which was the rest of the country ruled from the city of Nekhen. The first pharaoh to unite the whole country, so Manetho tells us, was Menes, about 3100 BC, who made Memphis his most important city.

These early pharaohs were very powerful. Their people believed them to be Horus, the Sky God, in human shape and that when they died they sailed in a heavenly boat to join the Sun God, Re. Through their officials they supervised the irrigation of the fields and the storing of the grain. Through their tax collectors they made themselves rich by taking a good share of the ample crops of the Nile valley. They left behind them dramatic proof of their power in the pyramids which held their tombs. So far about eighty pyramids have been discovered (see the Using the evidence section). The labourers who hauled the slabs into position were not slaves but ordinary Egyptian peasants, who came to work on the pyramids during the flood season when they could not tend their fields. Building a temple-tomb for their god-king was reason enough for performing their back-breaking labour. No other memorials in the world are anywhere near the size of the pyramids. No other building made such demands on the muscle-power of so many people as did the Great Pyramid of Khufu (Cheops).

The first pyramid-building pharaoh was Zoser. His step-pyramid at Saqqara was designed by the world's first known architect, Imhotep, about 2800 BC. It was the first large stone building in the world. The famous pyramids of Giza followed two to three hundred years later and pyramids continued to be built until about 2200 BC.

Then came the close of what is called the Old Kingdom and with it the end of pyramid-building. The pharaoh could no longer control the local princes. Irrigation schemes were neglected. There were poor crops, starvation and fighting between cities. In this fighting Thebes did well and at last a Theban prince, Mentuhotep, was strong enough to unite the whole country and make himself pharaoh about 2050 BC. Then followed some three hundred years of peace and improvement known as the Middle Kingdom. The irrigation schemes were repaired and enlarged. Copper from Sinai was mined in large quantities. Thebes was the capital of Egypt and as the country grew richer, became an impressive city of temples, palaces and tombs (see page 86).

A mysterious episode followed about which we know little. The Theban pharaohs became weaker in the two hundred years from 1770 BC to 1570 BC. Foreign princes called the Hyksos, who had already been settled in the Delta area for many years, grew stronger.

Thebes again led a revival of Egyptian power. In 1567 BC a Theban prince, Amosis, made himself pharaoh and drove the Hyksos from the country. So began what is called the New Kingdom. It was to last five hundred years and would see Egyptian power at its greatest as warrior-pharaohs pushed southwards into Arabia and eastwards across Palestine. They too built on a colossal scale, like Ramses II (1304–1237 BC) at Abu Simbel.

The man standing at the entrance gives you a good idea how large these statues are. This temple at Abu Simnel was built by Ramses II.

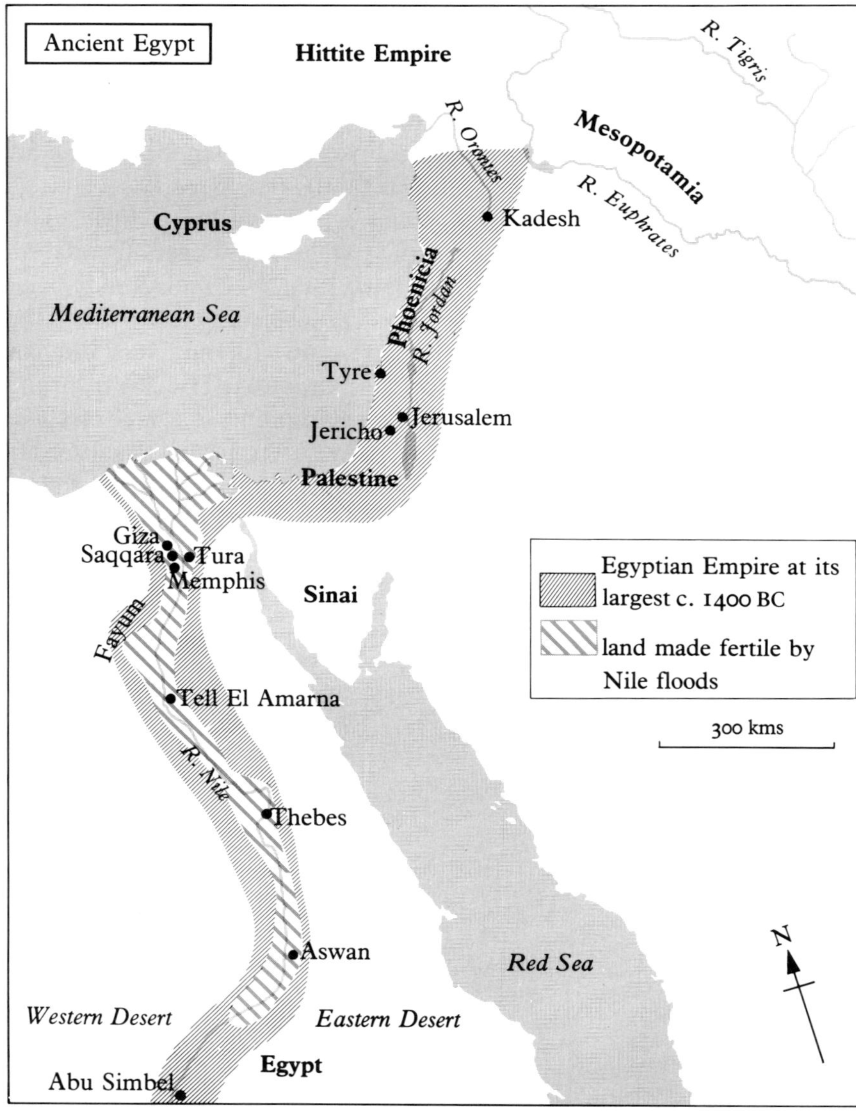

Two crises upset the New Kingdom. On the death of her husband, Queen Hatshepsut refused to give way to the rightful pharaoh, her stepson, Thutmose III. Instead she ruled alone for another twenty years. Thutmose was not at all happy with this situation. When at last she died, he had her name removed from all official records and monuments.

In the fourteenth century BC the pharaoh Amenhotep IV tried to change Egyptian religion completely. He believed that there was only one god, Aton. He took the name Ikhn*aton* and founded a new capital which he called Akhet*aton*. We know he was an odd-looking man with a long head, thick lips, spindly legs and a pot belly. By contrast his wife, Nefertiti, seems to have been unusually beautiful. Wall-paintings show them living apparently in great happiness with their six children.

However, later there seems to have been a revolt led by the priests of the old religion, during which Amenhotep may have been murdered. The old religion returned and every mention of Amenhotep and his god Aton was chiselled off the temples and palaces.

From about 1000 BC Egypt grew weaker. Sea raiders attacked the northern coast, and foreign armies invaded from the north-east. First came the Assyrians, then the Persians, the Greeks and finally the Romans. In the temples, however, Ancient Egypt lived on. Men continued to worship the old gods and hieroglyphic writing was still used. These last remains of Ancient Egypt did not finally die out until the Christian religion spread through the Roman Empire in the fourth century AD.

The nobleman Nebamun hunts wildfowl in the Nile marshes. A cheerful painting from the walls of his tomb.

Ancient Egypt is usually remembered for its pharaohs, its priests, its temples, tombs and palaces. There was much more, however, to Egyptian civilisation. It produced brilliant craftsmen in every kind of stone and metal; clever mathematicians who could understand fractions and square roots, and who worked out a 365-day calendar; doctors with a useful knowledge of the human body, healing medicines and pain-killing drugs. Their writers told fairy stories and composed love poems, which were sung accompanied by the harp and flute. They also made collections of wise sayings to guide good behaviour. Their civilisation changed little in three thousand years. The Egyptians believed in doing things in the correct, established ways. At the same time they enjoyed life. Their wall-paintings and stories show their love of bright colours, flowers and feasting.

The Great Pyramid. In the foreground are the huge brick claws of the Sphinx.

A copper chisel – one of the main tools of the pyramid-builders

Using the evidence: building the pyramids

At the time the pyramids of Giza were built the Egyptians had only simple building tools. We know these included sledges, ropes, levers, copper chisels, the 90° set square and the merket. There is no evidence to suggest that they had wheeled transport or pulleys for raising heavy weights.

Yet the Great Pyramid of Khufu (Cheops) is to this day the largest stone building ever put up anywhere in the world! It is almost 147 metres high and 230 metres square at its base. The Houses of Parliament and St Paul's Cathedral together would both comfortably fit inside it. It is built of approximately 2 300 000 stone blocks each weighing on average two and a half tonnes. Some, however, are much heavier. The granite slabs which cover the pharaoh's burial chamber deep inside are each about fifty tonnes. French engineers inspected the three pyramids in 1799 when they visited Egypt with Napoleon's army. They calculated that with the stone from the pyramids they could build a wall right round France three metres high and half a metre wide!

Even more remarkable is the precision with which these huge buildings were made. The Great Pyramid's sides run north–south and

The Aswan quarries. Wood was wedged into these slots. Soaked with water the wood swelled and split the stone.

Granite for an enormous monument left half-quarried when it cracked in the quarries at Aswan.

east–west. In both directions they are only a fraction of a degree out of line. The base is so flat that the south-east corner is less than a centimetre higher than the north-west. To achieve similar results, modern builders need complicated machinery and scientific instruments.

How did the Ancient Egyptians do it? Archaeologists and historians have puzzled over this question for more than a hundred years now and are still not sure that they know the right answer. Here are some of the most important pieces of evidence which they have to make use of. Study the evidence. Then have a go at solving the puzzle yourself.

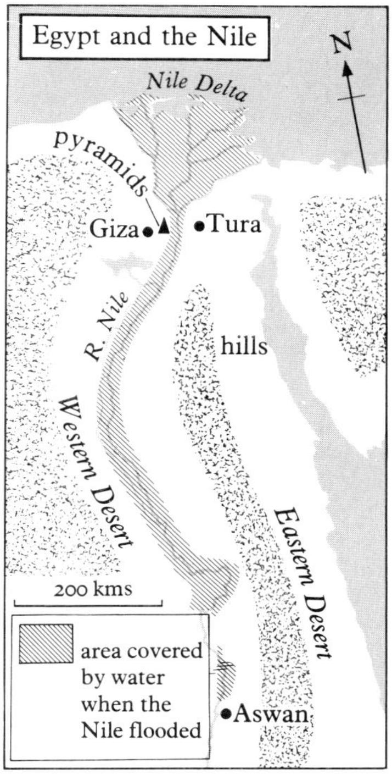

The puzzle of the pyramids

Getting the stone to the Giza site

The Great Pyramid contains three types of stone. Poor-quality limestone which was quarried nearby, good limestone from Tura and granite from Aswan (see the map).

1 How did they quarry (a) the limestone (b) the granite?
2 How did they transport the stone for most of the journey?

Prince Diehuti-hotep – all sixty tonnes of him – on the move

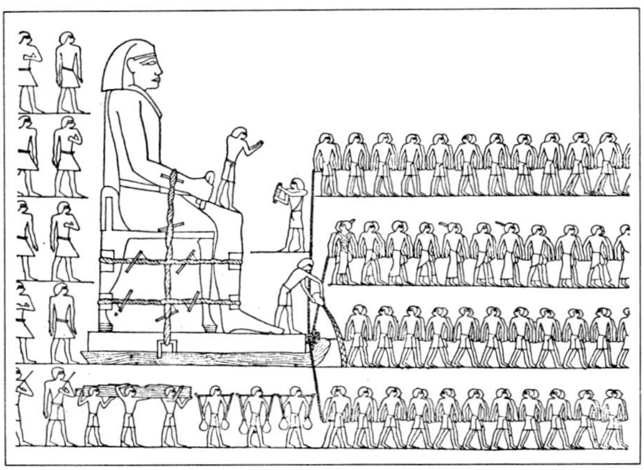

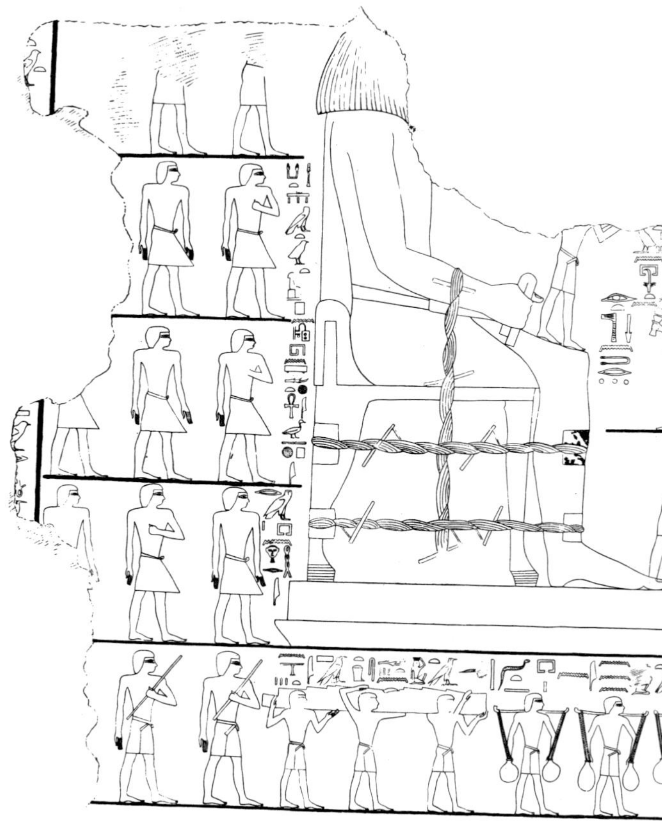

Getting the stone from the Nile to its place in the pyramid

There is no picture of the pyramids being built. There are pictures, however, of other building works of a later date. This one shows a seven-metre-high statue of Prince Diehuti-hotep being moved, about 1800 BC. It probably weighed about sixty-one tonnes.

3 (a) Find the man in charge. What is he doing? What is the man in front of him doing? (c) What is the statue mounted on? (d) How is it made secure? (e) How is it moved? (f) How many men are pulling? (g) How is its movement being made easier? (h) If the statue reaches rough ground how will it be prevented from tipping?

When another unfinished pyramid was uncovered recently, the remains of a wide earth ramp were found along one side.

4 Using the information in the picture, sketch in as much detail as you can of a forty-tonne granite block being moved: (a) from the Nile to the building site; (b) up the pyramid to its position, which would be near the centre about half-way up.

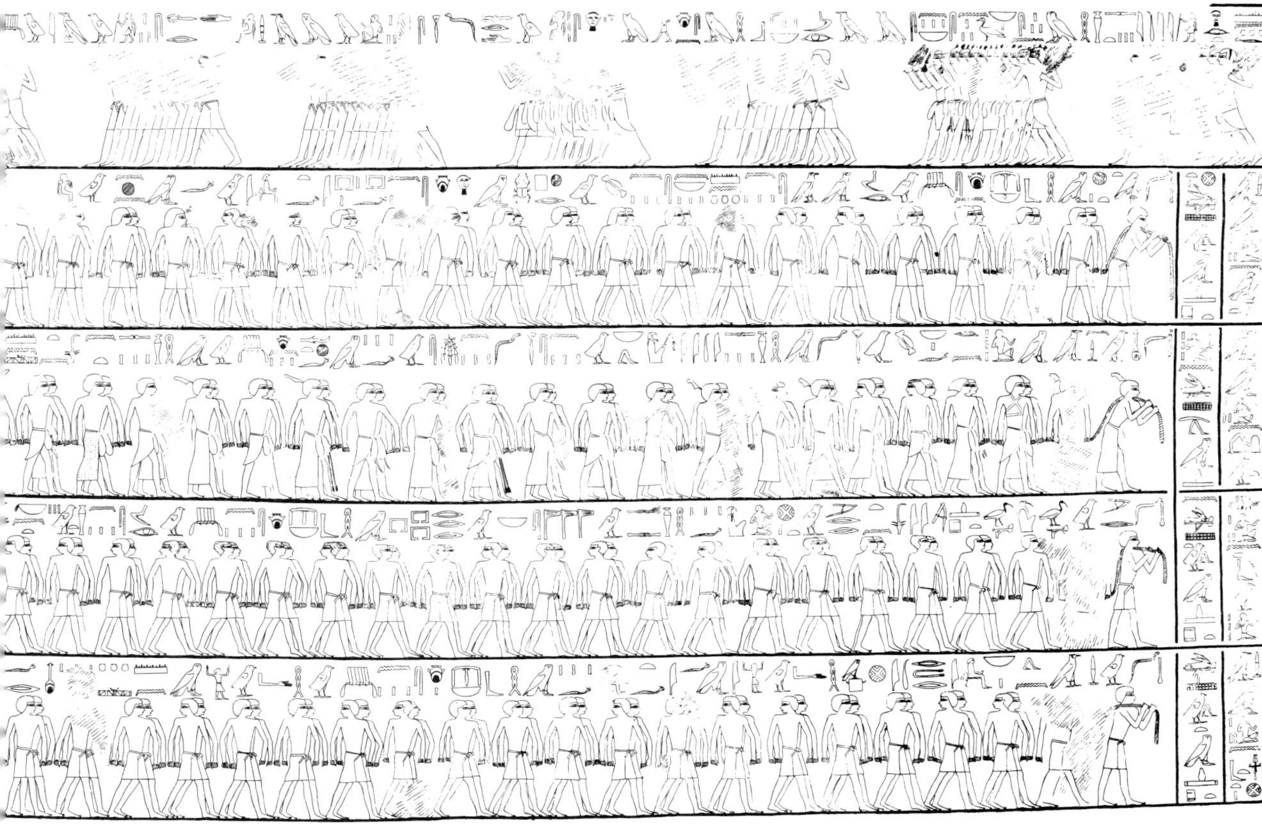

The Pyramids of Giza

Preparing the site for a pyramid

Levelling the site and getting the sides correctly lined

(A) The most level surface available to early civilisations was the surface of water in a still canal.
(B) In a later temple picture, the pharaoh is shown marking out the lines of a new temple after studying the stars of the Great Bear constellation.
(C) Quite an easy way of fixing due north is to mark the position of a star as soon as it rises at night, its setting point, and then divide in half the angle so made. Such a calculation was well within the power of the Ancient Egyptians.

5 Sketch the pyramid builders:
   (a) getting the line of the sides right;
   (b) getting the base level.
6 Compare your answer to the 'puzzle of the pyramids' with the experts' answer which now follows. List the ways in which your answer is different from theirs.

The answer of the experts

Good limestone was quarried at Tura on the eastern side of the Nile, ordinary limestone near the building site. It was cut out with copper chisels and wedges. The granite from Aswan was probably cracked by two methods – either by lighting fires beside it then throwing water over it, or by battering it with hammers of obsidian (a very hard black volcanic glass) to make wedge slots and then pushing in the wooden wedges which would then be soaked. The stone would be shifted from the quarries to the banks of the Nile on sledges hauled by teams of men. Most of the journey would be made by boat down the Nile. At flood time boats could get to within 400 metres of the pyramid's building site.

From the boats to their place on the pyramid the boulders were again shifted on sledges pulled by teams of men. The movement of the sledges was made easier by placing wooden rollers beneath them and by soaking their path with water. The area of the pyramids was levelled by using narrow mud channels criss-crossing the base which gave the diggers a level to work to. North–south was found by a careful study of stars and some simple mathematics.

The experts cannot agree how exactly the stone was taken up the pyramid. Most think some kind of earth ramp must have been used.

The remains of the workmen's village have been found close by and experts agree that there were about 4000 professional stone cutters at work on the pyramid at any one time. Patiently working with copper tools these men were skilled enough to reach the remarkable standards of precision shown in the cutting and placing of the stone blocks. We need further discoveries, a wall-painting, a written description, the remains of another unfinished pyramid for example, before we can be quite certain how these vast monuments were built.

8 Life in Ancient Egypt

The greatest city of Ancient Egypt was Thebes, 980 kilometres as the crow flies from the mouth of the Nile. It was one of the marvels of the Ancient World, spreading over sixteen square kilometres with the Nile flowing through its heart. Its temples and palaces were so numerous that the Ancient Greeks spoke in wonder of 'Thebes of the Hundred Gates'. Although more than three thousand years have passed since most of its monuments were built, it is still an incredible sight today.

However, how did the ordinary Thebans live? Their houses and workshops of mud-brick have vanished beneath the Nile as well as their farms and waterways. But in 1920 American archaeologists made a discovery which gave flesh and blood to ordinary Thebans in a way that a pharaoh's treasure never could (see the Using the evidence section). What they found were twenty-three models showing daily life on the estates of a Theban nobleman called Meket-Re. He died about 2000 BC and had the models placed in his tomb so that he could enjoy in his life after death the same kind of life that he had lived in this world. Just by our looking at them, the world of Meket-Re and his estate workers, though gone now for almost four thousand years, comes vividly and accurately to life.

The site of Thebes. In the top left of the photo you can just see the Nile, on the banks of which were temples and palaces. The city proper stood on the plain (centre left) and more palaces and temples ran along a line where the hills and plain meet. The temple-tomb of Queen Hatshepsut can be seen below the mountain cliff. Just off the picture (to the right) is the Valley of the Kings.

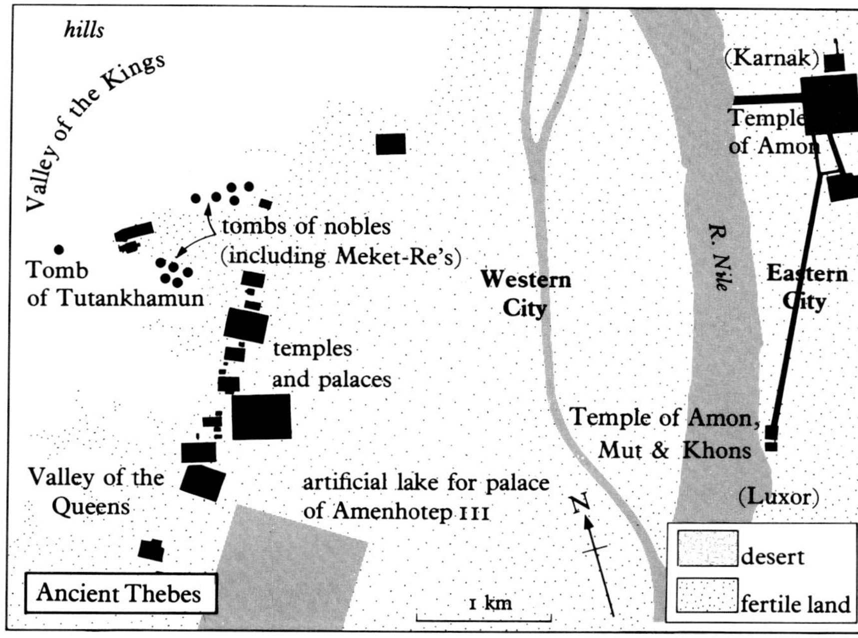

A tour of Meket-Re's estates

(This imaginary tour is based directly on the tomb-models. Try to find people and objects mentioned in the text in the photographs.) Imagine yourself as a noble from the city of Memphis passing through Thebes on your way to Nubia. You have been able to arrange an introduction to the great noble, Meket-Re, and have been promised a tour of his famous estates.

You arrive soon after sunrise on a late summer's morning. The gate-keeper shows you into the garden-court where the fruit of the sycamore figs, standing beside the ornamental pond, is ripening to a reddish-brown. The landowner awaits you beneath the porch which shades the main entrance of the house. He apologises for not offering you refreshments but he has urgent business to attend to. Government officials have come to inspect his cattle and to calculate the amount of taxes which he has to pay this coming year. If you could go with him straight away, you could view this important event and then visit the rest of the estate.

There is already much going on around the cattle sheds. The cattlemen, who can easily be recognised by their thick black hair and by their wooden sticks, are shouting at the tops of their voices as they line up the cattle. On the shaded dais four scribes are getting their writing equipment ready. From their shaven heads you can tell that they come from a superior class to the cattlemen. They have set out their writing palettes and ink cakes but have yet to unroll their papyrus and unpack their pens from the large chests which they have brought with them. The government inspector, shaven-headed like the scribes, is already there,

chatting with the head cattleman whom, clearly, he knows well. On Meket-Re's arrival, a respectful hush falls. He takes the one seat on the dais and his son, In-Yotef, sits on the floor beside him. To begin the inspection, the head cattleman salutes him, raising his right hand to his left shoulder. Then, as the cattlemen drive the herd at a slow but steady pace past the dais, the scribes make an immediate record on their papyrus. At the same time the government inspector, standing down in the yard, does his own count using his fingers. Two cattlemen help him. The cattle come in all shapes, sizes and colours: black, red, piebald and spotted. When the last animal has been driven past, the inspector and chief scribe compare their numbers. The inspector takes his leave taking two of the papyrus rolls with him for his records.

The tour proper can now begin. First stop is the cattle stalls which are divided into two parts. In the first the animals munch away at their own speed; in the second they are being fattened for slaughtering by forced feeding. The cattlemen have fixed ropes to their lower jaws and hand-feed them with grain and straw.

The slaughterhouse or butcher's shop is on the opposite side of the yard. Just before you arrived, two bulls had had their throats cut. They

Scribes at work in the granary

Left The cattle-inspection as it was found in the tomb. You should be able to find Meket-Re, In-Yotef, the scribes and the cattlemen.

The cattle-shed

lie on their sides with their legs bound and their blood running off into bowls. In one corner bowls of blood are being heated, while in another a pintail duck is being plucked. All the work is strictly supervised by an overseer, who carries a list on papyrus of all the animals to be slaughtered that day.

Unlike the other estate buildings, Meket-Re's granary is open to the sky and can quickly be identified by its walls which rise to points at each corner. Inside the entrance, four scribes make a careful record of all the measures of grain which enter and leave the granary. No errors can be allowed, as grain is not just the main food of everyone on the estate: it is the landowner's main source of wealth, which he will offer in exchange for those things he wants from other Theban landowners or craftsmen. The three main storage bins lie beyond and can be approached by a flight of steps. Five labourers are standing on the low partition walls busily dumping grain into the bins. To protect their skin from the rough sacks, they have thrown a corner of their kilts over their shoulders.

You follow one of the labourers carrying a sack on his shoulder to the building next door from which come some interesting smells. This one building contains both the brewery and the bakery; the former on the right of the entrance door, the latter straight ahead. In both areas, however, the beginning of the process is the same. The labourers take the grain from the granary and crush it in limestone mortars with heavy pestles. They then pass it to the first female workers you have seen on this estate. Clad in white shifts, they bend over their gritstone mills and grind it into flour. The flour is then mixed into dough.

In the brewery the next stage is to add yeast to the dough and then make little cake shapes which will be left for a day or so to rise. They are then mixed with water and, in barrels open to air, left to ferment. After a short time, the fermenting mixture is poured into clay jars which are then stoppered and sealed.

The brewery is busy enough but the bakery is even busier. Besides the workers preparing the dough, mixing it by hand in vats, two cake-makers squat on their haunches as they shape the dough into buns and loaves. An attendant watches the four ovens; two square ones in one half of the bakery, two round in the other. In the centre, beside the partition wall, stands a basket full to the brim of long thin loaves, freshly baked to a rich brown.

Next door in the weaving shed there is not a man to be seen. Thirteen women, again all wearing simple white shifts, are making cloth. Three, who sit against the wall, are preparing the flax fibres for the spinners. They twist the fibres loosely into short lengths. Standing nearby the spinners spin the lengths into thread on long spindles which they hold in their left hands. By the opposite wall, two women finish preparing the yarn for the weavers, using three pegs spaced out on the wall. Five more women weave it into cloth on the looms on the floor.

The brewery and the bakery. How do you know which is which?

The weaving shed

Meket-Re's travelling boat is on the right with a kitchen tender beside it. What are the men on the prows getting ready to do?

Your time is fast running out and one thing which you must do before leaving Thebes is to worship at the Temple of Amon which lies some way down river and on the opposite bank. Meket-Re will not hear of your going there on your own. He leads the way to the jetty on the river bank where his small fleet of boats is moored. His captain has made one of his travelling boats ready to sail. The oarsmen are on board and servants are loading the kitchen tender with baskets of bread, jars of beer and wine and cuts of meat. On the jetty, the young In-Yotef says goodbye. He is anxious to take out the sporting boat and see if he can harpoon some fish before the sun sets.

The travelling boat leaves the bank and turns downstream towards the city with the kitchen tender following at a respectful distance. Coming upstream are two fishing canoes, the trawl between them containing fish.

Papyrus fishing-boats

Meket-Re and his musicians (models from the travelling boat)

Out in mid-stream the rowers find their rhythm and Meket-Re's musicians, one a blind harpist, the other a singer, begin a gentle duet. The music continues until the temple is reached and while Meket-Re prays with you in the Temple of Amon, his cooks get to work aboard the kitchen tender. Before you finally continue on your journey you eat an excellent meal aboard the travelling boat enjoying the cool of the river breezes and a magnificent view of the famous city.

Using the evidence: the models of Meket-Re

Read the account of the discovery, then answer the questions about it.

A team of American archaeologists, led by H. E. Winlock, had been excavating the tomb of Meket-Re during the winter of 1919–20. They had found little of interest and, with the end of the normal digging season nearing, were depressed. One evening, in the middle of March 1920, Winlock who was back at the team's headquarters got a note from Burton, one of his team who was still up at the tomb. 'Come *at once*,' it read, 'and bring your electric torch. Good luck *at last*.' Winlock hurried back to the tomb. At the entrance was a little knot of excited Arabs and in the gloom of the tomb corridor stood Burton and the headman. Winlock's own account continues:

Burton pointed to a yawning black crack between the wall of the corridor and the rock floor. He said that he had tried to look in with matches but they didn't give enough light and told us to try the torches. At least a hole here was unexpected but we had looked into so many empty holes. Anyway I got down flat on my stomach, pressed the torch into the hole, pressed the button and looked in. . . .

Was this the discovery they had been hoping for?

Burton and I sat down dazedly to talk it over. He told me how . . . one of the men . . . had noticed that the chips had an unaccountable way of trickling into a crack as fast as he dug. At first the man hadn't paid much attention. It was just one of those crazy whims of the Americans that made them want to dig out such a place anyway. Still he had called the headman of his gang and together they were scraping the stones away from the crack when Burton arrived. . . .

In the morning our work began in earnest and three terrific days followed. Burton rigged up mirrors to throw sunlight down the corridor and took a photograph of the crack in the rocks. Then we dug in front of it and found in the floor of the corridor a little pit about a yard square, and waist-deep. It had been carefully filled with chips of the very rock it was cut in and both ancient thieves and modern archaeologists had taken this filling for the living rock of the mountain and passed over it. The side of the pit under the wall of the corridor was built of mudbricks and when we had photographed them and taken them away we were looking into a little low chamber about three yards square and scarcely four feet high in which no man had entered for four thousand years. Rock had fallen from the roof – in doing so it had opened up the crack we had looked into the night before – and had upended one of the boats and broken others but except for this nothing had been disturbed. Our only fear was that as fresh air got into the chamber more would come tumbling down and we were torn between our desire to get everything out safely before we had a catastrophe and to get a complete set of photographs and plans of everything just as we had found it. It was just luck that made both possible, for after we had finished tons of rock began to fall. Still we escaped the misfortunes of our French colleagues digging half a mile away. They had a man killed by rock falling in a tomb chamber while we were working on this one. . . .

As we worked along through those three days and nights we began to realize what it was we had so unexpectedly discovered. The tomb was that of a great noble of four thousand years ago. He himself had been buried in a gilded coffin and a sarcophagus of stone in a mortuary chamber deep down under the back of the corridor where thieves had destroyed everything ages before our day. Only this little chamber had escaped and it was turning out to be a sort of secret closet where the provision was stored for the future life of the great man. . . . In short we had found a picture of the life of a great noble such as he hoped to live in eternity which was nothing more or less than the one he had led on earth forty centuries before.

Winlock's workmen bring the models down from the tomb. Half of the models are now in New York, half in Cairo.

Questions and further work

1 What was the first clue that there might be a hidden chamber?

2 Here is an outline plan of the tomb of Meket-Re as Winlock drew it. Copy the outline, and on it label the burial shaft leading to the chamber where Meket-Re's body had been placed, the burial chamber, the model-chamber and the entrance.

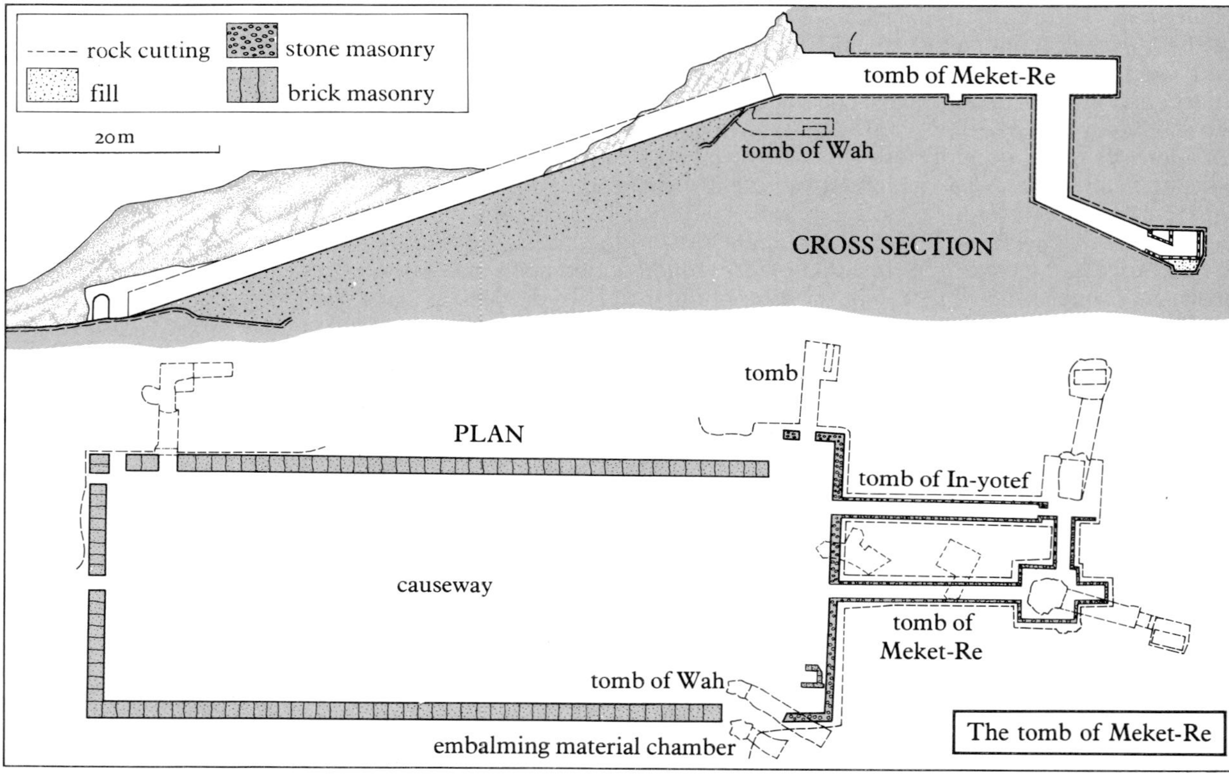

The tomb of Meket-Re

3 Why had the tomb robbers missed the model-chamber even though they had got right into the tomb?

4 What catastrophe did Winlock fear as they began moving the models from the chamber?

5 Describe the ways in which Winlock's team made a record of their discovery.

6 (a) Why did Meket-Re have these models made?
(b) The models are made of wood and have little value as works of art. Why did Winlock and historians of Ancient Egypt get so excited about them?

7 Imagine you are In-Yotef, or a scribe, or one of the men in the brewery, or one of the women in the weaving shed. Describe a typical day in your life on Meket-Re's estates 4000 years ago.

The Spread of Civilisation

9 The wider world

Before 2500 BC cities and towns existed only in western Asia and in Egypt. Then other civilisations grew up in many other parts of the world. This chapter looks at just three areas: India, Central America and China.

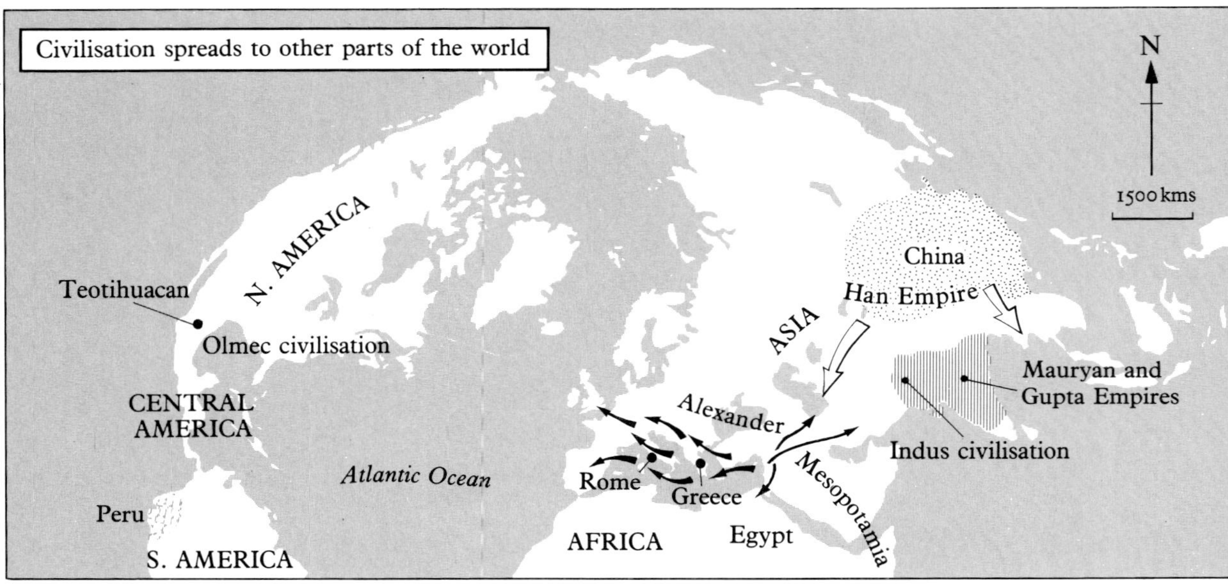

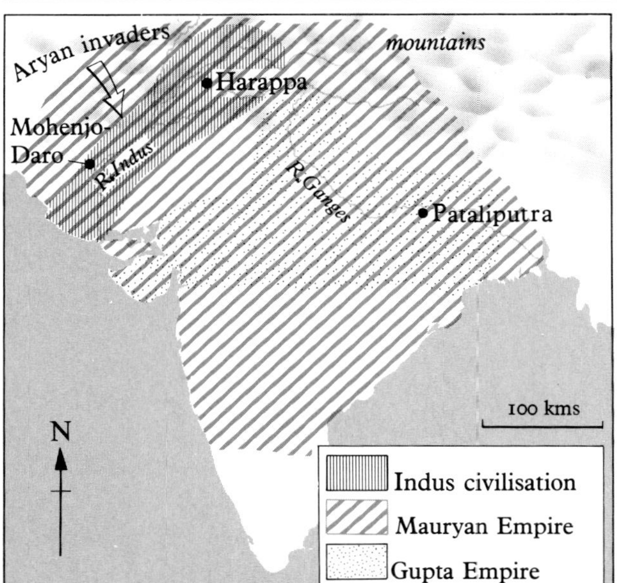

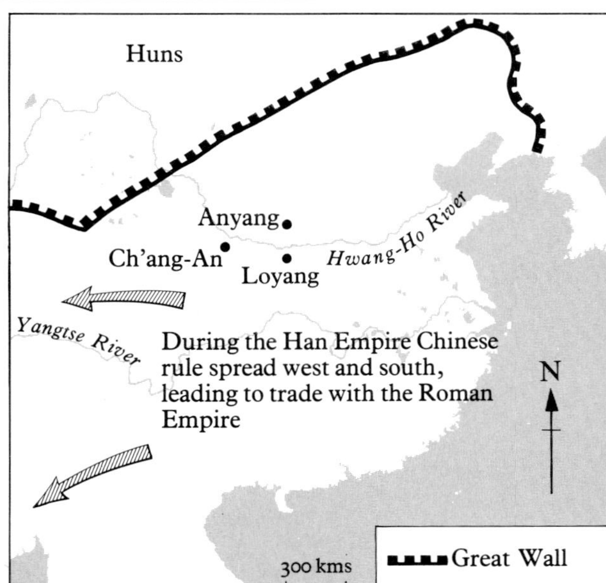

Ancient India

About 2300 BC when the pyramid-building pharaohs were still ruling in Egypt and Sargon the Great was master of Sumer, another great civilisation was reaching its height in the wide plain of the River Indus. This Indus civilisation began in the same way as in Mesopotamia (see chapter 4). Farming villages along the fertile river banks were able to produce enough food to support town life. The towns were centres of trade. They traded especially with Mesopotamia through the island centre of Dilmun (modern Bahrain).

Mohenjo-Daro – a street drain of sensible design

Two great cities have been discovered so far, Harappa and Mohenjo-Daro. Both had about thirty-five thousand inhabitants who lived in houses of baked mud-brick. The streets were long, straight and well-drained. Crossing each other at right angles, they divided up the cities into neat squares. There were a number of different types of houses, which suggests two main classes of citizen. Some houses, large and well-designed with sanitation as good as anywhere else in the Ancient World, probably belonged to rich merchants. Others, cramped in size and huddled together among the shops and workplaces, must have belonged to peasants and to craftsmen. The chief public buildings were a central fort, an office block, a granary and circular working platforms for pounding grain. A huge bath may well have been a religious centre since no temples have been found. We know these people could write because inscribed trading seals have been dug up, but this writing still needs to be deciphered.

The Indus civilisation lasted about seven hundred years. Its end around 1750 BC may well have been violent (see the Using the evidence section). At roughly the same time Aryan tribesmen, warlike and

Carved stone seals, from Mohenjo-Daro, and used perhaps for trade. The writing on these seals has not yet been deciphered.

nomadic, moved in from the north-west. Eventually they conquered both the Indus and Ganges plains and made the dark-skinned inhabitants their slaves. Two great religions of the Far East were then formed, Hinduism and Buddhism.

The *Vedas*, or Holy Books, were written by Hindu priests between approximately 1500 BC and 1000 BC. They taught that every human being had to be reborn many times before reaching the state of perfection and that the gods divided men into five separate groups or *castes*. A man's caste when he was reborn depended on how he had lived in his previous life. The top caste contained the Brahmins (the priests who would not be reborn), the next Kshatriya (the nobles and warriors), then Vaisya (farmers and merchants), Sudra (servants) and lastly at the bottom Candala (the untouchables for whom the most unpleasant jobs were kept). Hindus believed that the untouchables had been criminals in a former life. The work you did, the person you married, even the people you ate with were limited to the caste into which you were born. The upper castes had a rich and pleasant life at the expense of the lower.

Quite different were the ideas of Gautama Buddha (around 563–483 BC). He left his noble home at the age of twenty-nine, unhappy with its comfort and anxious to find the true way of living. After six years' searching, the truth finally came to him. For forty-nine days he sat beneath a tree, deep in thought. He spent the rest of his life explaining to all who were ready to listen the real meaning of life. He described Four Noble Truths and an Eightfold Path to good behaviour. All men, whatever their caste, could benefit from Buddhist teaching. It appealed, therefore, to members of the lower castes and to rich merchants who felt particularly hard done-by in the caste system. Buddhism and Hinduism were to become bitter rivals.

Lions from the top of a pillar in Asoka's palace

Immediately after the sudden arrival and departure of Alexander the Great in 326 BC (see pages 165–6) Chandragupta Maurya created an empire in northern India. Asoka, the third Mauryan emperor, attacked and conquered Orissa on the east coast. '100 000 people were moved from their homes,' he himself wrote, '100 000 were killed and many times that number also died.' But he was so appalled by his own cruelty that he changed his life. He became a Buddhist and encouraged Buddhism throughout his empire. 'All men,' he declared, 'are my children.' He ruled his subjects as a kind but firm father might treat his children. He set new standards of justice and provided better roads and medical services. Asoka refused to lead his armies into war again except in defence of his people. He also became a vegetarian and forbade the sacrifice of animals. Buddhism lost much of its support in India and in later centuries, its main strength has been in south-east Asia, China, Korea and Japan.

Another great empire was set up in northern India in the fourth century AD. This was the Hindu Gupta Empire. It grew rich, trading with the Roman Empire, and a golden age in Indian painting, sculpture, dance and drama followed. Its astronomers and mathematicians were also advanced. One of them, Aryabhata, believed that the earth rotated on its axis and that it moved round the sun. He also calculated the length of the year using the Indian number system of nine digits and zero. This was much easier to use than the Greek and Roman system and eventually reached Europe by way of the Arabs. In the fifth century the Gupta Empire declined, trade with the Roman Empire lessened and during the following century the cities were destroyed by barbarian tribes, who broke through the northern mountain frontiers.

Using the evidence: the end of the Indus cities

'About 1750 BC the cities of Mohenjo-Daro and Harappa were abandoned, apparently after floods caused by a change in the course of the Indus' (*Reader's Digest History of Man*). Floods seem to have been an important reason for the decline of the Indus cities but was this the only one? Sir Mortimer Wheeler, who directed the main excavations at Mohenjo-Daro, preferred another explanation.

He discovered great fortifications. In one part of the city, there were skeletons lying not only inside the houses but in the doorways and streets. Close examination showed that many of them had broken skulls. He was reminded of a famous Indian legend in the *Rigveda* which was first written down by Hindu priests between 1500 BC and 1000 BC.

The hero is the god-king Indra who leads the Aryan invaders. He is always fighting and always victorious. Wheeler remembered the lines:

With your swift chariots O Indra,
You have overthrown twice ten kings with sixty thousand nine and ninety followers.
You go most bravely from battle to battle, destroying
Fort after fort with your great strength.
In blazing fire you burn up all their weapons.
You tear away their carefully built defences.
And your standard-bearer finds golden treasure.

Might not Mohenjo-Daro and the legend, he thought, fit together like Troy and Homer (see pages 134–5)?

What do you think?

Questions and further work

1 (a) What is the *Rigveda*?
(b) Who according to the legend is Indra?
(c) Who in history are the Aryans? When and where did they enter India (see pages 97–8)?

2 What conclusions can you come to from the skeletons found by Wheeler?

3 (a) What phrases from the *Rigveda* extract seem to you to suggest that the 'forts' destroyed by Indra were in fact the Indus cities? Explain your answer.
(b) Which phrases, if any, seem to you to make it unlikely? Explain your answer.

4 Imagine that you have been asked to rewrite the section in the *Reader's Digest History of Man* on the end of the Indus civilisation for the next edition. Rewrite it including Wheeler's alternative explanation in not more than a hundred words.

Central America

Huge, dark and terrifying, this Olmec 'big-head' broods over a religious area in Central America

The civilisations which eventually appeared in America, cut off as they were by the Pacific and Atlantic Oceans from all contact with the rest of mankind, were unlike any others. On their farms they kept turkeys, ducks, dogs and bees. The usual domestic animals of Europe and Asia (horses, cattle and sheep) did not exist. They had, however, many more crops, of which maize was the most widely grown, but they never invented a plough and used tilling sticks instead. Neither did they discover how to make iron and steel, nor did they use bronze except in small quantities. Their tools and weapons were made of stone or wood with razor-sharp edges of obsidian (a black volcanic glass). Their traders always bartered, never having coins, and their architects designed magnificent temples without arches or domes. They used wheels on children's toys but not for anything else!

The first civilisations of Central America were in what is now modern Peru and also on the Gulf coast of Mexico. In Peru the inhabitants became excellent weavers and, between 2000 BC and 1000 BC, began to build large religious centres in the mountains. On the Mexican Gulf coast, the Olmec people began a civilisation about 1300 BC which was to last more than a thousand years. Its statues and buildings were among the most remarkable of the Ancient World.

The Ancient Americans built pyramids too. This one at Teotihuacan is seventy metres high. It stood beside a temple, in the middle of a city with well-paved streets and underground drainage. A second, smaller pyramid lies in the background (right).

Mexico continued to be the centre of civilisation in the Americas. As the Olmecs faded away, farther north in the highlands the city of Teotihuacan grew to more than 100 000 inhabitants between AD 300 and AD 600 while at the same time, farther to the south in Yucatan, the foundations of the great Maya civilisation were being laid.

Ancient China

Settled farming seems to have begun in the northern river valleys of China about 3000 BC. The first farmers lived in simple wood and mud huts but from an early date they were able to make painted pottery. Gradually they learnt to make silk and to carve jade. Their religion was the worship of their ancestors. Their priests also foretold the future by using 'oracle' bones. They pressed a hot point against an animal bone. The shapes of the cracks so made on the bone surface revealed to them, they said, the secrets of the future.

Shang craftsmen were excellent bronze-workers. They also sacrificed humans, so the faces on this container may represent their victims.

The earliest Chinese dynasty (ruling family) known to us is the Shang which ruled the north China plain from about 1400 BC. The capital city of the Shang emperors was Anyang. There were also other cities of craftsmen and traders, whose inhabitants included skilled workers in bronze and some at least who knew how to write.

In the foundations of Anyang have been found the remains of 852 human skeletons. Men and women were apparently sacrificed as building began, to persuade the gods to protect future inhabitants of the city. In one place five chariots with their drivers and horses were buried among a larger group of soldiers.

But then Chou invaders attacked from the west. They destroyed the Shang dynasty and ruled China for nearly eight hundred years, the period of The Hundred Schools. Thinkers travelled from noble court to noble court explaining their ideas. The greatest of these was K'ung Fu-tzu (or Confucius as he is known in Europe). His lifetime (550–480 BC) coincided almost exactly with that of Buddha. Confucius believed that every man had great power to do good; the ruling class had been given their power to rule from Heaven so that they might bring out the best from their subjects. They should think of themselves as the mothers and fathers of their people. It was their duty to uphold law and order and to encourage loyalty, truthfulness and respect for parents, especially the father. They should also place in positions of responsibility men of talent, however humble their families might be. It was for this reason that Chinese officials had to sit difficult examinations before being appointed.

From 400 BC the Chou rulers were unable to control the overpowerful nobles. Two centuries of disorder followed, the period of The Warring States. It was ended by the Emperor Shih Huang-Ti who founded the Ch'in dynasty (the origin of the name China). He was a man of enormous energy and ambition. He forced the princes to accept him as ruler. He also made safe his northern frontier, by adding to existing sections of the defensive wall. Thus was created the Great Wall of China.

Shih had no time for the past: the future was much more interesting. He planned that his successors should rule the Empire which he had made 'for ten thousand ages'. The old days must be forgotten.

> Those who praise the old days in criticism of the present government shall be exterminated with all their family.... Thirty days after this decree is pub-

lished all who have not burned their [history and philosophy] books will be branded and sent to forced labour on the Great Wall.

But Shih Huang Ti's Empire lasted only four years after his death. He died while travelling across China and his scheming chief minister Li Ssu (who had master-minded the burning of the books) kept his death a secret. He placed a cart of rancid fish beside the imperial coach so that no one would smell the decomposing body and hurried back to the capital. There he had the second son made emperor before the Crown Prince knew that his father was dead.

Shih Huang-Ti's Great Wall snakes its way across the mountains of northern China. It is 3200 kilometres long. (Hadrian's Wall is only 110 kilometres.)

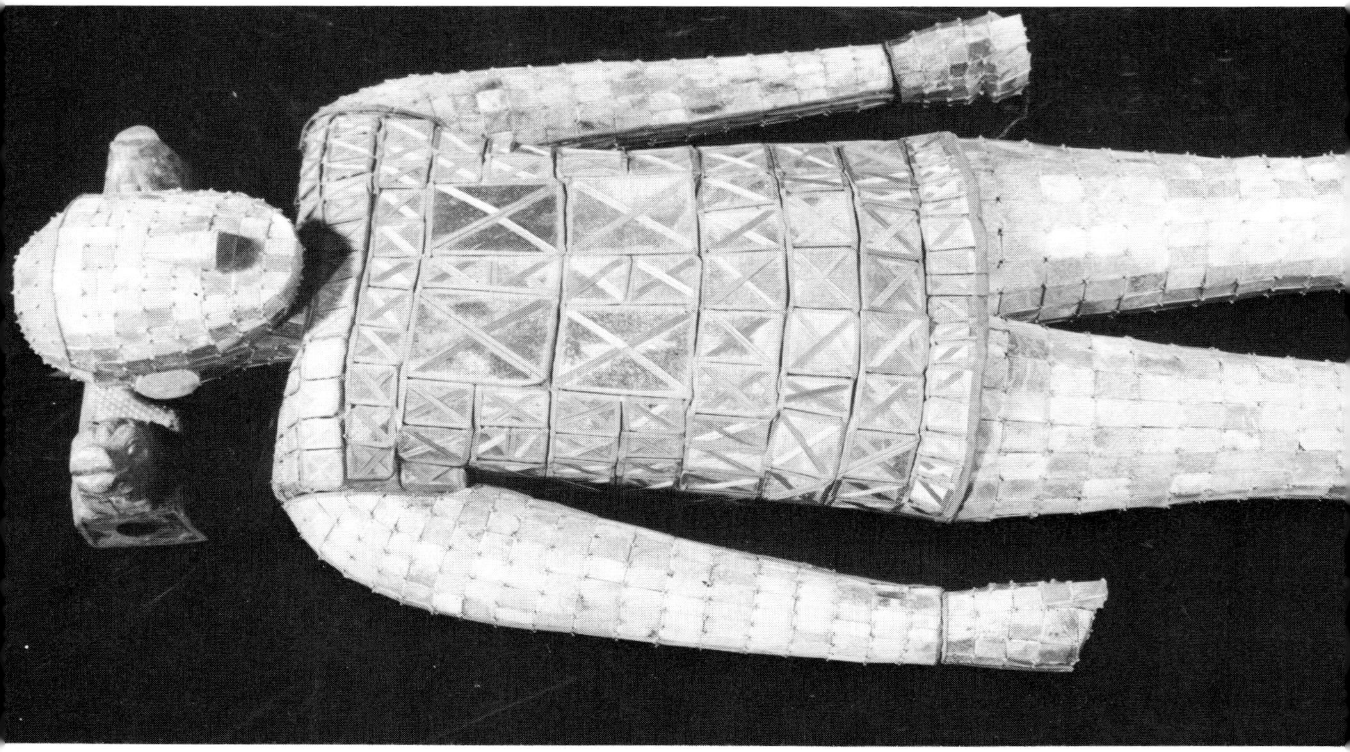

Han wealth – the jade funeral-suit of the Princess Tou Wan. Jade was supposed to keep away evil spirits.

The new emperor was a disaster. A writer of the time described him as:

> A base and greedy character who trusted his own judgement and did not listen to ministers of ability and experience . . . the officials governed very severely . . . the taxes were unbearable . . . the empire crushed under forced labour . . . crime increased.

A widespread revolt ended the Chin dynasty. After five years' hard fighting between rival generals Liu Pang emerged the winner and set up the Han dynasty (see the Using the evidence section).

The Han Empire (206 BC–AD 220) reached the height of its power at the same time as the Roman Empire. The two empires had much in common. The Han Empire was vast, the work of a number of warlike emperors, of whom the Emperor Wu (141–87 BC) was the most successful. It was well governed since its officials were clever and carefully trained according to Confucian ideas. It was prosperous too. Encouraged by the emperors merchants traded widely even to the edge of the Roman Empire. Education was good and the people inventive. As well as improving well-established Chinese crafts like silk-making and jade-carving, they invented paper, cast iron, the magnetic compass and the wheelbarrow.

The Han court with its formal and complicated ceremonies emphasised the god-like nature of the emperor. As time passed the emperor lost touch with his people. He rarely left his palaces and gardens. When he

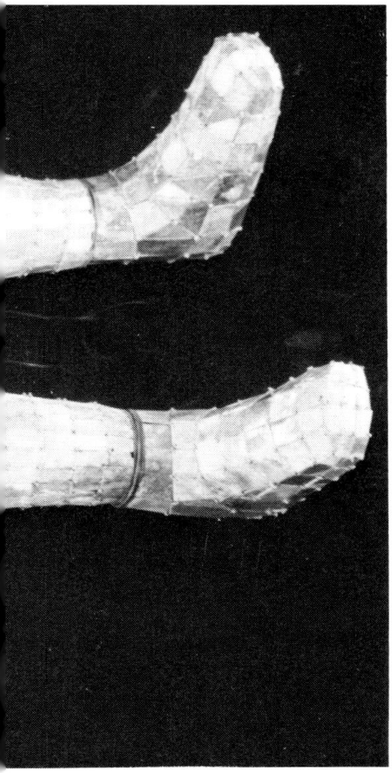

travelled, the roads were cleared and heavily guarded. Courtiers plotted among themselves and Han rule grew worse. One widespread rebellion, that of the Yellow Turbans, was only put down with difficulty. Thereafter the emperors were little more than puppets in the hands of their generals. The last was forced to give up his throne in AD 220.

Han artistry – one of the famous bronze 'flying' horses. The sense of galloping is given by balancing the whole weight of the animal on a single hoof.

Like the Roman Empire, the Han Empire was raided by barbarian tribes, though on a smaller scale. The famous library at Lo-Yang was completely destroyed and the former capital Chang-An ransacked. 'Not more than a hundred families were left,' wrote a survivor. 'Only four carts are to be found in the whole city and the officials have neither robes nor seals of office. . . . Weeds and thorns grew thickly as in a forest.'

Using the evidence: the victory of Han

The Chin Emperor was dead. Hsiang Yu led the Ch'in armies against the Han led by Liu Pang. Ssu-Ma Chien, the best historian of early China, describes the last part of their struggle:

For a long time Ch'in and Han battled together yet neither could win a decisive victory. The able-bodied men were weary of fighting while the old and young were exhausted by carrying food supplies. Hsiang Yu made a proposal to the king of Han.

'Because of us the Empire has been in tumult for many years. Let us settle the issue by hand to hand combat instead of involving all these men.'

The king refused with a smile. 'I prefer to fight with my wits not with brute force,' he said.

In the fighting which followed a skilful Han archer, Lou Fan, killed many Ch'in warriors.

Hsiang Yu in a fury buckled on his armour and rode out with his halberd to do battle. As Lou Fan raised his bow, Hsiang Yu glared and bellowed at him so fiercely that the bowman dared not meet his eyes or shoot but fled back to the ramparts.

Han warriors

The Han, well supplied with food themselves, cut off the Ch'in food supplies. Hsiang Yu finds that his soldiers are deserting him and that overwhelming numbers of the enemy are closing in on him. He spends the night drinking in his tent and writing a poem of farewell, which he sings with his beautiful wife, Yu. Then leaving Yu and most of his army, he and a few of his best warriors cut their way through the surrounding Han forces.

King Liu sent after him with five thousand men. By the time Hsiang Yu crossed the River Huai he had fewer than a hundred men with him. He lost his way and asked an old man in the fields to direct him. 'Go left,' said the old man, deliberately deceiving him. Leftwards led him into the marshes where he got bogged down and the Han cavalry caught up with him.

So he turned east to Tungcheng. By now only twenty-eight horsemen remained with him and his pursuers numbered several thousand. He knew that he could not escape so he spoke to his men:

'Eight years have passed since I rose in arms. In that time I have fought more than seventy battles . . . and was never defeated. That is how I won my empire. But now I am suddenly hemmed in here. This is because Heaven is against me and not because my generalship is at fault. Today I shall perish here but for your sake I shall fight gallantly and overcome the enemy three times. I shall break through their lines, kill their commander and cut down their flag so that you may know that it was Heaven that destroyed me and not my generalship which was at fault.'

Hsiang Yu broke through and killed a commander. But on reaching the bank of a river across which safety lay he refused to cross. Once more he turned to make a final hopeless attack against the Han horsemen. Wounded in a dozen places he turned to see Lu Ma-Tung the Han commander.

'Isn't that my old friend Lu!' he exclaimed. 'I hear the king of Han has offered a reward of a thousand gold pieces and the land of ten thousand families for my head. Let me do you a good turn.' With that he cut his own throat.

Ssu-Ma Chien goes on to say:

When he [Hsiang Yu] got rid of the Righteous Emperor and set himself up in his place, he could hardly complain when the kings and nobles turned against him. He boasted of his conquests, trusted only his personal judgements and did not follow the old ways. . . . Yet he never realised his mistakes nor blamed himself for his misfortunes. What a fool he was to say that Heaven was against him and that his generalship was not at fault.

Questions and further work

1 What is meant by 'Ch'in' and by 'Han' (see pages 102–104)?
2 On whose side was Hsiang Yu (see page 105)?
3 When did this fighting take place?
4 What evidence is there here that Hsiang Yu was a brave soldier?
5 (a) What evidence is there that he was a good general?
(b) What evidence is there that he was a poor general?
6 Liu Pang lost many battles but won the war. Why?
7 For what reasons does Ssu-Ma Chien think Hsiang Yu a fool?
8 Make a note of those parts of the extracts which give you the feeling that Ssu-Ma Chien may be exaggerating. Explain in what way you think he is exaggerating.
9 Explain how each of these facts affect your view of Ssu-Ma Chien's reliability.
(a) He was employed by the Han Emperor.
(b) He describes Liu Pang, the Han leader, as bad-mannered and not particularly brave.
(c) He wrote his history about a hundred years after the death of Hsiang Yu.
(d) The Chinese were the most careful keepers of historical records in the ancient world.

10 Phoenicia

The main road from Egypt to Mesopotamia ran northwards along the Mediterranean coast until it reached the River Orontes. Then it turned inland and ran eastwards until it reached the Euphrates valley. The coastlands through which it passed were mountainous, but there were also fertile valleys and good ports. Many armies marched this way, and great battles were fought. As often as not the inhabitants found themselves ruled by foreigners. They were conquered by the Egyptians, the Assyrians and the Babylonians, then the Persians, Greeks and Romans. For about five hundred years, however, from 1200 BC to 700 BC two remarkable peoples flourished in this coastal area. In the north were the Phoenicians and in the south the Hebrews. Though they lived beside each other they were very different.

Motya

The Greek historian Diodorus tells us that in 397 BC the Phoenician port of Motya in Sicily was attacked by Dionysius of Syracuse. The struggle for the city was long and bitter.

Although the enemy had managed to break through the walls and seemed to be masters of the city, the Phoenicians, high up in their houses, hurled missiles down upon them. King Dionysius therefore ordered wooden towers to be brought and fitted them with footbridges which they could push out on to the houses.

At last Motya fell to the Syracusans and most of her inhabitants were slain.

Motya is now a small, empty and privately owned island just off the coast of Sicily. Archaeologists have found there some important

Phoenician figures modelled in bronze. Notice their strange tall hats.

remains of the old Phoenician city. These include a surrounding wall with twenty square towers and four gateways, a temple and a stone staircase. Near the harbour was discovered a typical *cothon* or dry dock, used to repair ships. Statues from the temple, pottery and glass and some jewellery have also been found.

The cemetery of the city was on the mainland and connected to the island by a stone causeway. The sea is higher now than it was then and the causeway lies just below the waves, but local farmers still use it to get their carts across to the island.

So we know about Motya from a Greek historian and from excavations. This is typical of Phoenicia as a whole. The Phoenicians knew how to write but they usually wrote on papyrus, which has rotted away. (The climate of Phoenicia is damper than that of Egypt.) What writing there is on stone or baked clay does not tell us very much. The Greeks rarely had a good word for the Phoenicians. 'Bitter and bad-tempered', is one Greek description of them. 'Very obedient to those who rule them but cruel to those they rule themselves', is another. Was this a fair description? Or was it because the Greeks and Phoenicians were usually enemies? Without having the Phoenician point of view, we have no way of telling.

We know more about Phoenician trading ports such as Motya than about the great cities of the mainland. Phoenician Tyre and Sidon lie buried beneath later buildings and bustling modern cities. The remains of the ancient Phoenician cities are sometimes brought to light when the foundations of new buildings are being dug, but a small part and for a short time only.

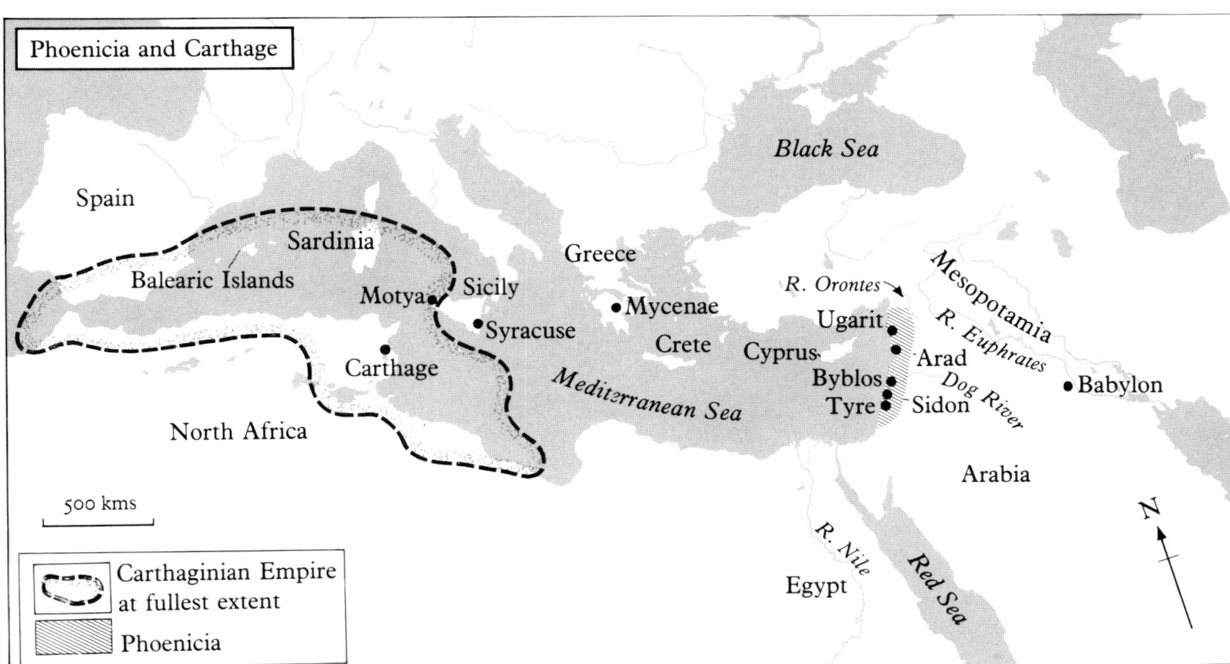

Other useful evidence comes from Egyptian wall-paintings and Assyrian reliefs (see the Using the evidence section).

The mainland cities and their colonies

The Phoenicians seem to have moved westwards from northern Mesopotamia and to have arrived on the Mediterranean coast about 3000 BC. Although they came as hunters, they quickly took up farming and trading. In 2600 BC Byblos was an important trading centre, being joined later by Ugarit, Tyre, Sidon and Arad.

The Phoenicians had to trade to live. Not enough food could be

The harbour, Byblos. Though the buildings are later, this photo gives a good idea of the Phoenician coastline with the mountains never far away.

The cedars of Lebanon. Only a small area remains of what was once a vast forest.

grown in Phoenicia itself so some was imported and paid for by the export of goods. The geographical position of the Phoenician cities encouraged trade. As well as being on the main road from Egypt to Mesopotamia, by sea they were in easy reach of Crete, Mycenae and all the cities of the eastern Mediterranean. The Phoenicians bought grain, cattle and sheep, and sold timber (especially cedarwood) and the products of skilled craftsmen, like jewellery, glass, pottery, ivory, carvings, perfume and clothing. Their most famous industry was linked with clothes. The men of Tyre made a most beautiful purple dye from the murex shellfish found along their coast. So valued was this 'Tyrian purple' that it came to be thought of especially as the colour worn by kings and emperors.

The Phoenicians exported works of art. This ivory carving of a lion attacking a man was found in an Assyrian palace.

With good timber to hand, they became the best boat-builders and seamen of their time. They learned how to steer by the stars at night. Even the Greeks were forced to agree that 'the men of Sidon steered the straightest course'. In their broad merchant ships they explored the Mediterranean and the coasts of Africa, Arabia and Spain (see the Using the evidence section). They also built powerful warships. These were driven by about fifty oarsmen, sitting in two rows, one above the other. A sharp ram running out from the bow, below the waterline, could rip holes in the enemy's ships.

Between 1000 BC and 600 BC trading ports and colonies (new lands settled by people moving from the existing cities) were founded all over the Mediterranean. The most famous of these was Carthage in North Africa. It was probably founded in 814 BC and grew larger and more powerful than any city on the Phoenician mainland. By the third century Carthage ruled much of North Africa, Spain and Sicily. Only after three great Punic Wars (see pages 173–5) did the Romans gain control of the western Mediterranean.

In 574 BC Tyre was captured by Nebuchadnezzar of Babylon. This began the decline of Phoenicia, which then became part of the Persian Empire. The Phoenicians, however, provided the Persian emperors with the best section of their navy. However, in 332 BC Alexander the Great completely destroyed Tyre (see pages 160–62) and effectively brought Phoenician history to an end.

A Phoenician merchant ship (carved on a Tyrian tomb)

The Phoenician alphabet

One invention of the Phoenicians is now part of everyday life, the alphabet. We have seen in chapter 3 how signs came to be used for sounds not words in cuneiform and hieroglyphics. However these were still clumsy and difficult forms of writing. About 1400 BC the Phoenicians began to use simple signs or letters for the main sounds of human speech, so making an alphabet of twenty-two letters.

To the Phoenician alphabet the Greeks added *a*, *e*, *i*, *o* and *y* which made an alphabet very like ours. Thanks to the alphabet, writing became faster and easier to learn. It also became a skill which could be mastered by many more people than a special class of scribes.

Using the evidence: the Phoenicians

The Phoenicians as explorers

Read this extract from Herodotus' *Histories*. See if you can work out in which direction the Phoenicians sailed.

As for Libya [Africa] we know that it is washed by the sea on all sides except where it joins Asia, as was first shown . . . by the Egyptian king Necho who sent out a fleet manned by a Phoenician crew to sail round and return to Egypt and the Mediterranean by way of the Pillars of Heracles. The Phoenicians sailed from the Red Sea into the Southern Ocean and every autumn put in where they were on the Libyan coast, sowed a patch of ground and waited for the next year's harvest. Then harvesting their grain they put to sea again. After two full years, they rounded the Pillars of Heracles in the course of the third, and returned to Egypt.

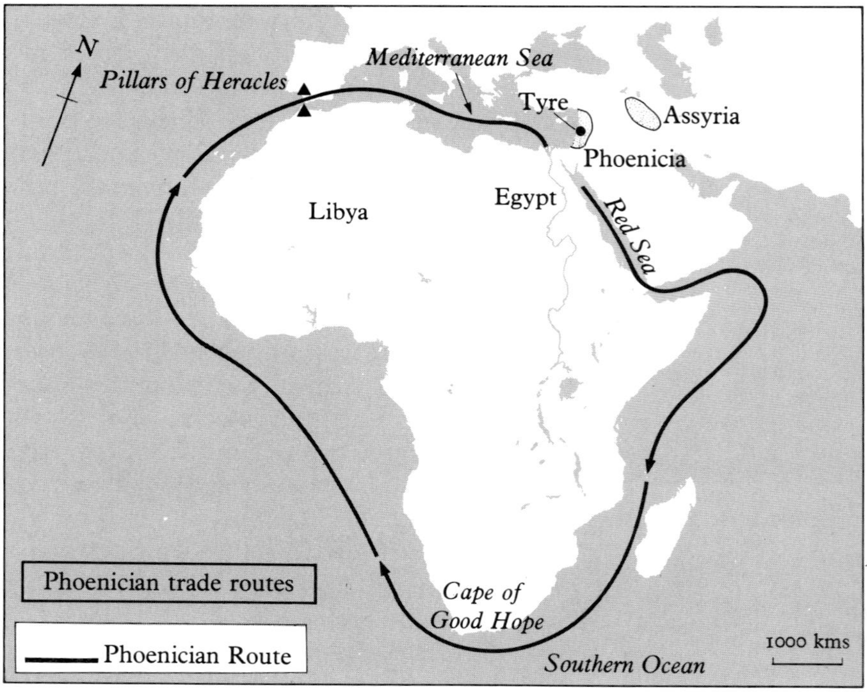

These men made a statement which I do not myself believe, though others may, to the effect that as they sailed on a westerly course round the southern end of Libya, they had the sun on their right, to the northward of them.

1 Using a modern atlas, find a map showing Africa and the Mediterranean. Compare it with the map of the Phoenician voyage and list the modern names for: The Red Sea, the Southern Ocean, Libya, Phoenicia, Tyre, Assyria, the Pillars of Heracles.

2 (a) Roughly how far did the Phoenicians sail? (You may find it helpful to place a piece of string or cotton along their route, then straighten it out and measure off with a ruler.)
(b) How long did the voyage take?
(c) How did they supply themselves with food for so long a voyage?

3 (a) If you were on a ship sailing westwards past the Cape of Good Hope at midday, where would you expect the sun to be?
(b) Read Herodotus' last sentence. Do you believe the sailors? Explain your answer. Why do you think that Herodotus did not?
4 Imagine that you were one of the crew of this successful expedition. Describe your experiences.

A Phoenician king in trouble about 700 BC

These two pictures are copies of a wall-relief, now destroyed, which stood in the Palace of Nineveh, the Assyrian capital. They show Sennacherib, the Assyrian king, attacking Tyre and Luli, the king of Tyre, putting his son on board a waiting ship which will carry him and his family to Cyprus and safety.

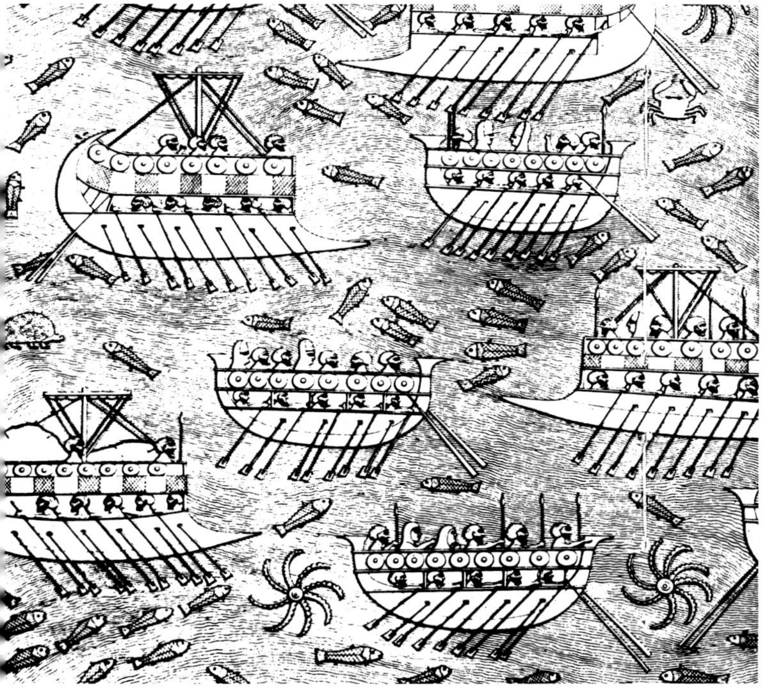

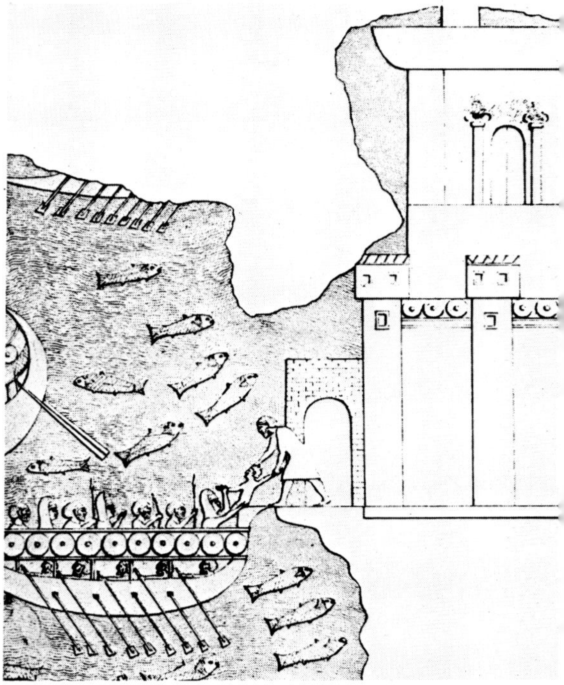

5 (a) How many types of ship can you see?
(b) Make a sketch of each.
6 (a) In what ways are they the same?
(b) In what ways are they different?
(c) For what do you think each type was designed? Explain your answer.
7 Look at the buildings, their size, shape and position. What do you notice about the city of Tyre about 700 BC?
8 Using *only* the evidence in the Herodotus extract and in the copies of the wall relief, write a paragraph about Phoenicia. You should be able to include something about ships, sailors, towns, ports, links with Egypt and with Assyria.

11 The Hebrews

Hebrew was the name given to the people who settled the lands to the south of Phoenicia between 1500 BC and 1000 BC and to their language. Later they became known as Jews. The lands in which they settled became known eventually as Palestine. In recent years Jews have returned to part of Palestine after a gap of almost two thousand years. They have made a new nation there which is called Israel.

We know a great deal about the Hebrews from what they wrote about themselves. The Bible tells not only the story of how the Hebrews first came to Palestine and what happened to them once they were there, but also of Jesus Christ who lived in Palestine from about 4 BC to AD 30. The problem with the Bible as historical evidence is that it was written not so much to describe clearly what actually happened but to spread a religious message.

The other important evidence for the history of the Hebrews is archaeological. The Bible's account of the Hebrews' conquest of Palestine and the archaeological evidence of the same time is compared in the Using the evidence section.

There is some evidence from Egyptian writings (see page 120) and from Assyrian reliefs and cuneiform tablets (see pages 60–62). There is one important Jewish historian, Josephus. He took part in and wrote about the Jewish War against the Romans from AD 66 to 70 and also wrote about earlier periods of Hebrew history.

From Abraham to the dispersion

Like the Phoenicians, the Hebrews moved towards Palestine from the east.

According to the Bible, they lived first in southern Mesopotamia. Then they followed their leader, Abraham, north to Haran and later

The Jew's most sacred place. The central chamber of the Temple of Jerusalem in which stood the Ark of the Covenant. The Covenant was the solemn agreement made with God which showed the Jews to be His chosen people. (A photograph of a model in the garden of a hotel in modern Jerusalem.)

westwards to the edge of Palestine. Some generations later, however, famine drove them into Egypt and eventual slavery. Boldly led by Moses and actively helped by their God, they managed to escape from Egypt and, after forty years wandering in the wilderness of Sinai, came near to Palestine once again. There, on the slopes of Mount Nebo from where the Promised Land could be seen across the River Jordan, Moses died and Joshua took his place.

The Bible says that the Hebrews then swiftly conquered Palestine with the aid of the Lord God of Israel. Using all the evidence, many historians now believe that Palestine was taken over slowly by the Hebrews between 1400 BC and 1000 BC. They suspect that there were already many Hebrews there before Joshua arrived. Whoever first wrote down the Joshua stories as they are told in the Bible exaggerated the speed and the size of his conquests.

Like the Phoenicians, the Hebrews enjoyed a golden age between 1000 BC and 700 BC. King David defeated the Philistines, dangerous enemies living in the coastal cities in the south. His power spread north and eastwards. David also won the city of Jerusalem which he made his capital. Solomon, his son, grew rich from the profits of trade and, with the aid of Phoenician architects and craftsmen, built a fine temple and other buildings in Jerusalem. Towards the end of his reign Solomon became more and more unpopular because of the taxes he imposed. The Hebrews quarrelled amongst themselves. Two separate kingdoms were formed: Israel in the north, and Judah in the south. Neither was any match for the reviving Mesopotamian empires. Israel fell to the Assyrians in 722 BC and Judah to the Babylonians in 586 BC. Both conquests led to many Hebrews being exiled to Mesopotamia.

When the Persians conquered Babylon, the Hebrews were allowed to

The road along which David may have marched when he conquered Jerusalem

return to Palestine. Reunited as one people they rebuilt the temple in Jerusalem, which had been destroyed by the Babylonians. Under the leadership first of Nehemiah, then of Ezra, their fortunes improved. They were, however, under foreign rule which they hated, especially if it interfered with their religion. Between 168 BC and 142 BC the five brave sons of the priest, Mattathias, led a revolt. All five lost their lives in the struggle but the Jews kept the right to worship as they wished. Further trouble arose after the Roman conquest of 63 BC. The Romans demanded that the Roman emperor be worshipped as a god. This the Jews refused to do. There was but one God, they argued, their God. They were also sure that a Messiah soon would come, a descendant of King David, to drive out the Romans and make the Jews a great people once more.

There were many who claimed to be this Messiah. Then about 4 BC Jesus Christ was born. His religious teachings upset the Jewish priest leaders more than the Romans. It was at their request that Pontius Pilate, the Roman governor, ordered his death by crucifixion. Christ's followers were convinced that he had risen from the dead. They formed the Christian church which, after nearly three hundred years, became the official religion of the whole Roman Empire.

Many Jews, however, did not believe Jesus was the real Messiah. Resistance to the Romans continued. Two major revolts centred on Jerusalem were crushed by the Roman army, the first in AD 70 the second in AD 135. The only way to deal with these stubborn Jews, the Romans decided, was to remove them from their homeland and scatter them throughout the Empire. This they did. Not for another eighteen hundred years, until the state of Israel was created in 1947, did Jews return to rule that land which they believed was promised to them by their God.

Right The coastal plain of Canaan as the invading Hebrews would have seen it from the inland hills. The Mediterranean is in the background.

Below The posts of the city gates of Roman Jerusalem made the holes in these worn stones. Christ must have walked across these stones to his death.

Bottom The end of the Jewish revolt, AD 70. The victorious Roman soldiers remove the famous seven-armed candle-holder from the Temple of Jerusalem.

Using the evidence: the conquest of the Promised Land

The Bible as history

The Hebrews stand on the slopes of Mount Nebo. Canaan (Palestine) can be seen in the distance. Moses has led them there from their terrible lives as slaves in Egypt through forty years of suffering in the Wilderness of Sinai. But now he is dead. The Bible continues: 'The Lord God spoke to Joshua. Moses, my servant is dead. Rise up and cross Jordan with all your people, to the land which I am giving them.' Joshua crossed the Jordan and straight away found his way blocked by the city of Jericho. This he besieged. 'And the Lord said to Joshua; see I have given Jericho and its King to you.' The Hebrews did not attack Jericho, instead they followed their God's instructions. 'The priests blew with their trumpets and it came to pass when the people heard the sound of the trumpets, they shouted with a great shout, that the walls fell down flat so that the Hebrews were able to go into the city and completely destroy it.'

After Jericho, the Hebrew army moved on to the city of Ai. 'And Joshua burnt Ai and made a heap of it forever, the King of Ai was hung on a tall tree.' Five Amorite kings then formed an alliance against the Hebrews but Joshua defeated them. After the battle, they hid in the cave of Makkedah but they were tracked down. Then Joshua 'smote them, slew them and hanging them on five trees and threw their bodies into the cave in which they had been hid. He covered the cave's mouth with great stones.'

The Hebrews then turned south, their target the city of Lachish. This fell on the second day of the attack and Joshua 'smote it with the edge of the sword and all the people that were in there.' One of the last and strongest cities to resist Joshua was Hazor, whose king organised another anti-Hebrew alliance which included a powerful regiment of horse-drawn chariots. 'Joshua did as the Lord God told him; he cut the hamstrings of their horses and burnt their chariots with fire. And he smote all the inhabitants of Hazor, completely destroying them; and he burnt Hazor with fire.'

'So Joshua took the whole land according to all that the Lord said unto Moses . . . and they rested from war.' Most Bible scholars would date the conquest about 1230 BC.

The ruins of the once-mighty city of Hazor

1 (a) From where did the Hebrew army enter Canaan?
   (b) How much of the Promised Land had Moses conquered?
   (c) How much of the Promised Land did Joshua conquer?
2 Explain in your own words with the help of pictures or diagrams how the Hebrews captured Jericho. It would be worth reading the full Bible account in Joshua, 6.

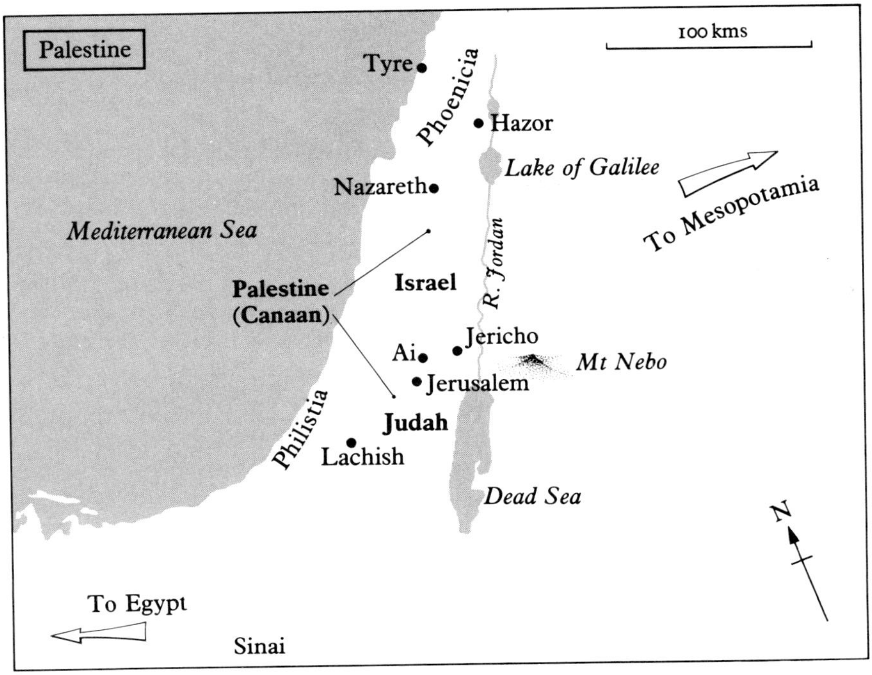

The archaeological evidence

Many of the sites of the cities mentioned in the Bible have been excavated. Here are some of the findings.

Jericho

A very old city, parts go back as far as 7000 BC. For the years 1500–1200 BC only a little has been found. The city seems to have been deserted by its inhabitants about 1325 BC and not to have been lived in again for hundreds of years. This could have been caused by a Hebrew attack. Parts of the fortifications did collapse, perhaps as the result of an earthquake but a long time before the time of Joshua's supposed attack.

Ai

No one lived on the site of Ai between 2200 BC and 1000 BC.

Lachish

This was attacked and destroyed about 1230 BC. The destroyer could have been the Egyptian, Merenptah, whose army was in the area in 1229 BC (see the second piece of Egyptian evidence, page 120).

3 (a) In what ways do the *biblical* and *archaeological* evidence agree and disagree about the fall of Jericho?
(b) In what ways do the *biblical* and *archaeological* evidence agree and disagree about the fall of Ai?
(c) In what ways do the *biblical* and *archaeological* evidence agree and disagree about the fall of Lachish?

The Egyptian evidence

The two most important pieces of evidence from Ancient Egypt are both in writing.

The first is a letter dating from between 1390 BC and 1365 BC. It was written in Canaanite by a Palestinian prince, Suwardata, to the pharaoh explaining what was happening in Palestine and asking for help.

The King, my Lord should know that the Habiru [Hebrews] have risen in the land which the King, my Lord, has given to me and that I have beaten them. The King, my Lord, should know that my brothers have left me: and that I and Abdu-Kheba alone are left to fight the Habiru. . . . May it please the King to send me aid. . . .

The second is a hymn in praise of the victorious pharaoh, Merenptah, carved in stone on a temple wall. It dates from 1229 BC and near the end come these lines.

Canaan [Palestine] is defeated and all its evil with it, Gezer is conquered. Yanoam is blotted out. The People of Israel [the Hebrews] is desolate, it has no children. Palestine has become the widow of Egypt.

4 (a) When did Suwardata write his letter? Was it before or after the date of Joshua's conquest?
(b) What sort of people does he make the Habiru out to be?
(c) Where, roughly, are the Habiru living?

5 (a) What is the date of the Merenptah hymn?
(b) Roughly where does it show the Hebrews to be living?

6 Make a time-chart of the years 1400 BC to 1200 BC (1400 at the top, 1200 at the bottom, each line to mark twenty years. You will need eleven lines in all.) On it place all the evidence we have of the Hebrews in or near Palestine beginning with Suwardata's letter 1390 BC and ending with Merenptah's hymn of praise 1229 BC. Include the Forty Years in the Wilderness of Sinai and the Flight from Egypt.

7 Clearly the archaeological evidence, the Egyptian evidence and the Bible story do not agree in some ways. List the main disagreements. If there were at least *two* groups of Hebrews, only one of which went to Egypt and then, under Moses' leadership, came out again, would all these disagreements disappear? Give reasons for your answer.

8 Make sketches of the scenes of Joshua's conquest of the Promised Land such as David or Solomon might have had carved in their palace in Jerusalem. Use the stories in the Bible as your guide (Joshua 6).

The Greeks

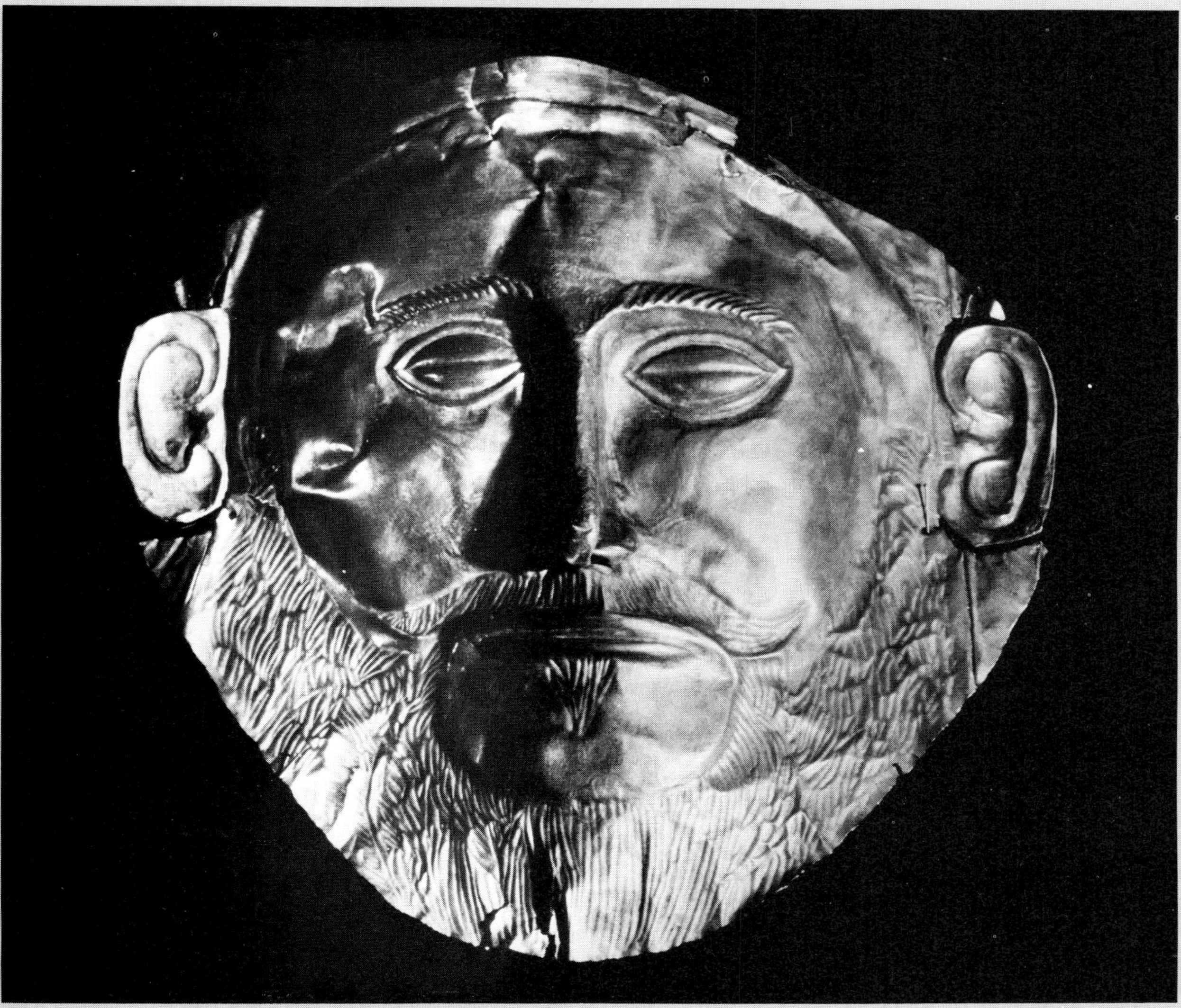

The island of Dia and the coast of northern Crete.

12 Crete

There is a mysterious king mentioned by the Greeks when they first began to write down their own history: Minos of Crete. About 700 BC Homer wrote:

Out in the dark blue sea there lies the island of Crete, a rich and lovely land, washed by waves on every side, densely populated and boasting ninety cities. . . . One of the ninety towns is Knossos and there, for nine years, King Minos ruled. . . .

About 410 BC Thucydides added a little more information.

Minos is the earliest ruler we know of who possessed a fleet and controlled most of what are now Greek waters. He ruled the Cyclades (the islands between Crete and the Greek mainland) and was the first coloniser of most of them, making his sons their governors. In all probability he cleared the sea of pirates.

Nothing more was known about this Cretan empire until Arthur Evans began to dig at Knossos in AD 1900.

Evans was fortunate. On the second day's dig, he found an ancient house with traces of pottery and wall-paintings within it. On the fourth day he came across a huge wall which had been badly damaged by fire. He had struck the edge of a vast palace. The uncovering of it was to take up the rest of his life. Evans realised the large and complex ruins were really of a palace and town combined.

In the centre is a great court 49 metres long and 27 metres wide. Grouped round it are the rest of the buildings, some once three or four

The palace of Knossos

storeys high, linked by many corridors and stairways. There are two large halls and a theatre. On the eastern side of the court lie the royal apartments and opposite, the holy area devoted to religious ceremonies. Farther to the west are many storerooms, mainly for corn and olive oil which would be kept in large pottery jars.

All over the ruins Evans found jewellery, pottery and wall-paintings, many of the latter containing vivid scenes of palace life. In addition he discovered clay tablets on which the palace scribes had written. Though he was unable to decipher this writing, Evans was in no doubt as to what he had found. It must be the palace of the great King Minos. So, to this ancient Cretan civilisation, he gave the name Minoan.

The palace of Phaestos: the theatre and marble staircase

Other archaeologists have been busy in Crete and elsewhere in the eastern Mediterranean. Further important discoveries have been made: great Minoan palaces at Phaestos, Mallia and Zakro; a Minoan town with a smaller palace within it at Gournia, and, on the islands of Kythera and Thera (Santorini), prosperous Minoan colonies. Minoan pottery and jewellery have also been found all over the eastern Mediterranean, especially at Mycenae on the Greek mainland. An Egyptian wall-painting probably shows Cretan traders at the pharaoh's palace.

The clay tablets found at Knossos proved the Cretans could write. But we only have clay tablets containing lists of names and stores; of the stories and beliefs of the Cretans we know nothing. Two types of writing are known but only one has yet been deciphered – Linear B. After much hard work a clever young archaeologist, Michael Ventris,

Linear B writing on a clay tablet found at Knossos. How would you have set about deciphering it?

discovered this was an early form of Greek. The other writing, Linear A, has proved more difficult to understand and still has to be deciphered.

Finally there is the famous legend of Theseus and the Minotaur which links Minos, the great king of Crete, with Theseus, the son of the king of Athens. What historical truth if any may be hidden inside this marvellous story is the subject of the Using the evidence section.

So we know about Crete from Greek historians like Thucydides, excavations such as those by Evans, Linear B clay tablets, and legends. Of these, excavations are much the most important.

Minoan cities and palaces

The first Cretans of whom we have clear evidence were farmers of the New Stone Age. They lived about 6000 BC in mud-brick houses with flat roofs. About 3000 BC another people came to the island from Asia Minor. These people knew how to use metal, copper, bronze, silver and gold. By 2000 BC they had developed their skills not only as craftsmen in metals but as potters and farmers. They traded all over the eastern

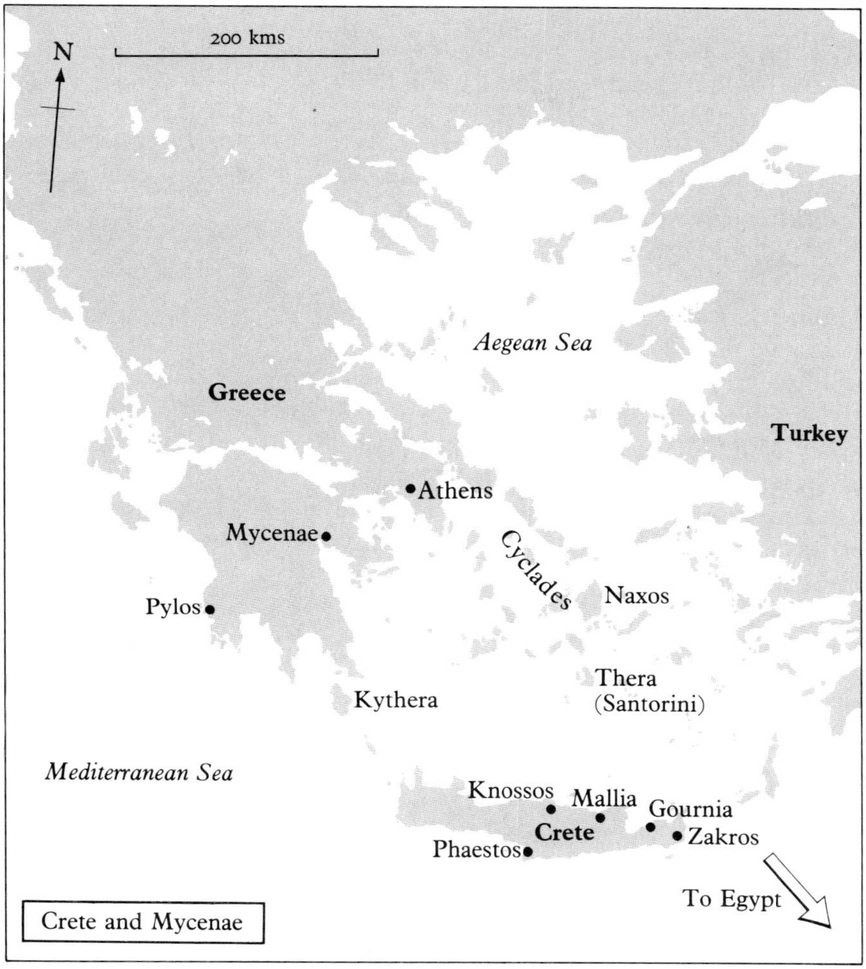

Mediterranean, making the wealth which in turn made the building of the great palaces possible. The first palaces were built about 2000 BC, and the kings and nobles were able to live most pleasant lives and encourage artistic work of very high standards.

Catastrophe, however, always lurked near Minoan life. About 1700 BC all the known palaces were destroyed, probably by a violent earthquake. The palaces were rebuilt almost at once on a grander, more luxurious scale. The Cretan empire now reached its peak. It is clear that Cretans traded with the Greek islands and the mainland. It is not yet clear whether the Cretans actually took control of any part of the mainland.

But about 1450 BC a second catastrophe struck. All the palaces and many other towns and villages were destroyed. Just how is not known for sure. Some archaeologists believe that the most likely cause was an extraordinary volcanic eruption which blew up the island of Thera, and sent huge waves pounding against the coasts of Crete flooding many parts. Tonnes of poisonous ash rained down on the eastern half of the island which, if that were not enough, was shaken again by further earthquakes. Of the palaces, only Knossos was rebuilt, a shadow of its former glory. And for at least a short time its rulers, so the Linear B tablets show, were Greeks from the mainland.

Within fifty years Knossos was burned down yet again – for the last time, perhaps by an earthquake, perhaps by other Greeks from the mainland, perhaps by sea-raiders. Minoan civilisation was dying. By 1000 BC it was dead, having disappeared with barely a trace beneath two further invasions from Greece.

Royal and important Cretan families had a pleasant life. The palaces were well designed and built, attractive to look at and comfortable to live in. They had piped water supplies, good drains, flushing water closets and plenty of baths. Food supplies were varied and abundant. Though they did not eat beef, they could choose from the following meats: pork, mutton, goat, deer, hare, duck, geese and partridge. Of countless fish, octopus and shellfish were popular, and among fruits, apples, pears, grapes, pomegranates, figs and dates. (The oranges and lemons which nowadays are found all over Crete were not grown in Minoan times.) Their usual vegetables were peas, lentils and olives; honey rather than sugar their main sweetener, and wine and herb tea their favourite drinks.

A junction in the Knossos drains

The throne-room of the palace of Knossos. The large basin was probably for religious ceremonies.

The ladies of Knossos – a wall-painting

The men dressed simply, in a belted loincloth or kilt and high leather boots. The women in contrast dressed up. Long pleated skirts with short-sleeved, tight-waisted bodices, which left their breasts bare, were fashionable. They wore their hair quite long in complicated hairstyles, painted their lips, used eye shadow and adorned themselves with beads and jewellery. By the standards of the Ancient World, the Minoan ladies who appear in the palace wall-paintings look unusually lively and confident. There seems good reason to believe they were less dominated by their menfolk than most!

Minoan Crete also appears to have been an unusually peaceful place. Archaeologists have found few traces of weapons or fortifications, and the favourite subjects of the painters and potters were not heroes and battles, but hunting, music and animals. With a powerful fleet and a strong king, the danger of war on land could not have seemed very real.

Their religion appears to have been closely connected with games and festivals. Of major importance were the bull-sports. Bulls were the most dangerous of all the animals of the island. They may well have seemed to the Minoans like the terrible earthquakes which out of the blue could bring such sudden destruction into their lives. When Evans experienced a small earthquake while working at Knossos, he noticed that a dull sound rose from the ground, like the muffled roar of an angry bull. At certain times of the year, the animals were brought either into the central courts of the palaces or to an open space close by. There, teams of young acrobats, female as well as male, would jump and somersault over the horns and backs of the charging beasts. A

A terracotta bath tub in the Queen's Chamber, Knossos

momentary misjudgement and the acrobat might be trampled underfoot or badly gored. When the sports were over the bulls would be sacrificed to the Mother Goddess by the Priest–King.

So extraordinary and so dangerous did this bull-jumping look that some archaeologists have refused to believe that the wall-paintings, which showed the acrobats jumping the bulls, could be picturing a real event. A similar sport with many of the risks removed does, however, exist to this day in the south of France. Bulls and acrobats appear very frequently in Cretan art. There seems no very good reason why we should not believe what we see. It must have been a thrilling sight, a bullfight and circus in one.

The Minoans buried their dead often knees-to-chin in a crouching position. Until about 1600 BC they made large round tombs which might contain several hundred bodies. Later they preferred smaller tombs cut out of the hillside and large enough for just two or three bodies. Like the Egyptians, but never with the same thoroughness, they would place useful possessions beside their bodies for the life to come. Terracotta bathtubs were often used for coffins.

Using the evidence: the legend of Theseus and the Minotaur

By the sixth century BC Athens was growing into one of the most important cities of Greece. A favourite story of the Athenians was the legend of Theseus and the Minotaur. It linked Theseus, believed to be one of the earliest and greatest kings of Athens, with Minos of Crete.

The Gods were angry with Minos, so the story went, because he had failed to sacrifice a particularly strong and handsome bull to them. As a punishment, his wife gave birth to a monster, part man, part bull, which fed off human flesh. This Minotaur grew to full size and was hidden away by Minos in a specially built maze or labyrinth. Meanwhile, Minos' eldest son had gone to Athens to take part in the Athenian games. There after winning many prizes, he was treacherously murdered by those whom he had defeated. The Cretan fleet sailed on Athens. Minos forced Aegeus, the Athenian king, to send to Crete every nine years, seven young men and seven young women, who were then imprisoned in the labyrinth until they were tracked down, killed and eaten by the terrible Minotaur.

Twice already, the Cretan ship had arrived to take the young Athenians to their deaths. On the third time however Aegeus' son, Theseus, volunteered to go. He would slay the Minotaur, he proudly boasted. Promising his sorrowing father that if he was successful he would change the sails of the returning ship from black to white, he set sail and was soon landing with the other young Athenians at the port of Knossos. Escorted by Minos' soldiers, he led his countrymen up towards the palace. His princely appearance much impressed the watching Cretans, among whom was Ariadne, the beautiful daughter of the Cretan king.

She fell instantly in love with Theseus and decided to do everything in her power to save him from the Minotaur.

That night, the Athenians slept in prison cells. At daybreak, their ordeal in the labyrinth would begin. During the night Ariadne managed to drug the soldiers who were guarding Theseus and armed him with two sharp swords, one short and the other long. She then led him to the entrance of the labyrinth. There she handed him a coil of long strong thread, with the help of which he would be able to find his way back through the maze. She unlocked the entrance and let him in.

Theseus made fast one end of the thread near the entrance and then crept silently through the dismal and confusing passages of the labyrinth. After what seemed hours he stumbled upon a pile of bones: some animal, some human. Realising that here the Minotaur must come to feed, he hid himself in the shadows of a passageway and waited. In the distance hungry roars could be heard echoing, first faintly then louder and louder. Listening intently, Theseus could make out the padding of bare human feet. Suddenly in the grey dawn light filtering into the labyrinth, a huge and monstrous shape loomed above the pile of bones.

Amnissos – the ancient port of Knossos. Did Theseus and the young Athenians first set foot on Crete here?

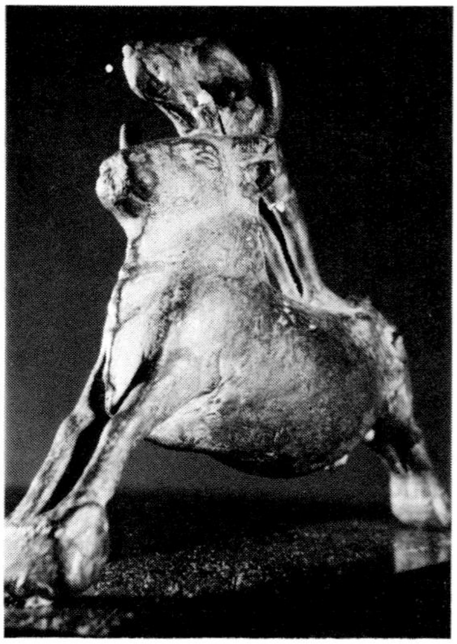

Is this how the legend began? A Minoan bronze statue, showing an acrobat about to somersault between a bull's horns.

A giant of a man to its shoulders, with a great bull's head, lion's teeth and an awful wild beast's roar, the Minotaur sniffed the air to trace where its next human meal was hiding.

Theseus did not hesitate. Darting from the passageway, he slashed at the back sinews of the monster's knees with his short sword and, as it collapsed in agony on its back, drove his long sword into its heart. It was dead before it could clutch hold of its attacker. After hacking off the Minotaur's head, he followed the thread back to the labyrinth entrance where Ariadne was anxiously waiting. He then strode to the throne room of King Minos and placed the bloodstained head at the king's feet. Amazed by such bravery, Minos not only freed the other Athenians and granted them free passage home, but agreed to Ariadne's request that she might return with Theseus to Athens to be his wife.

Theseus' triumph soon turned to tragedy, however. The voyage to Greece was long and stormy and, say some versions of the legend, Ariadne became ill and died in Theseus' arms on the island of Naxos. Other versions say that Theseus simply deserted her there. And he forgot his promise to his father. The sails of his ship were unchanged, black. His father, Aegeus, anxiously waiting for news from Crete had taken to pacing the cliff tops scouring the horizon for the first sight of those white sails. When they did at last appear and were black, his heart broke and he threw himself to his death in the sea below.

Many legends are fanciful stories woven round a historical event of great importance. From his study of the legends of the Trojan War the archaeologist Schliemann discovered the city of Troy. What historical event, if any, may be hidden inside the legend of Theseus?

Questions and further work

1 What part do the following persons or places play in the legend: (a) Minos; (b) Theseus; (c) Ariadne; (d) Knossos; (e) Athens; (f) Naxos; (g) Aegeus?

2 For which of these persons or places have we evidence that they existed, other than the legend? Note what the evidence is. Make sure that you study the map on page 125.

3 What does the legend tell us about the power of King Minos compared with the power of the kings of the Greek mainland? How does this fit with the archaeological evidence for:
(a) 1700–1450 BC ;
(b) 1350–1000 BC?
Explain your answer (see pages 124–6).

4 Draw a sketch of the labyrinth. Then draw a ground plan of the palace of Knossos using the picture above. Compare your two drawings. Do they suggest how the Greek storytellers may have got their idea for a labyrinth?

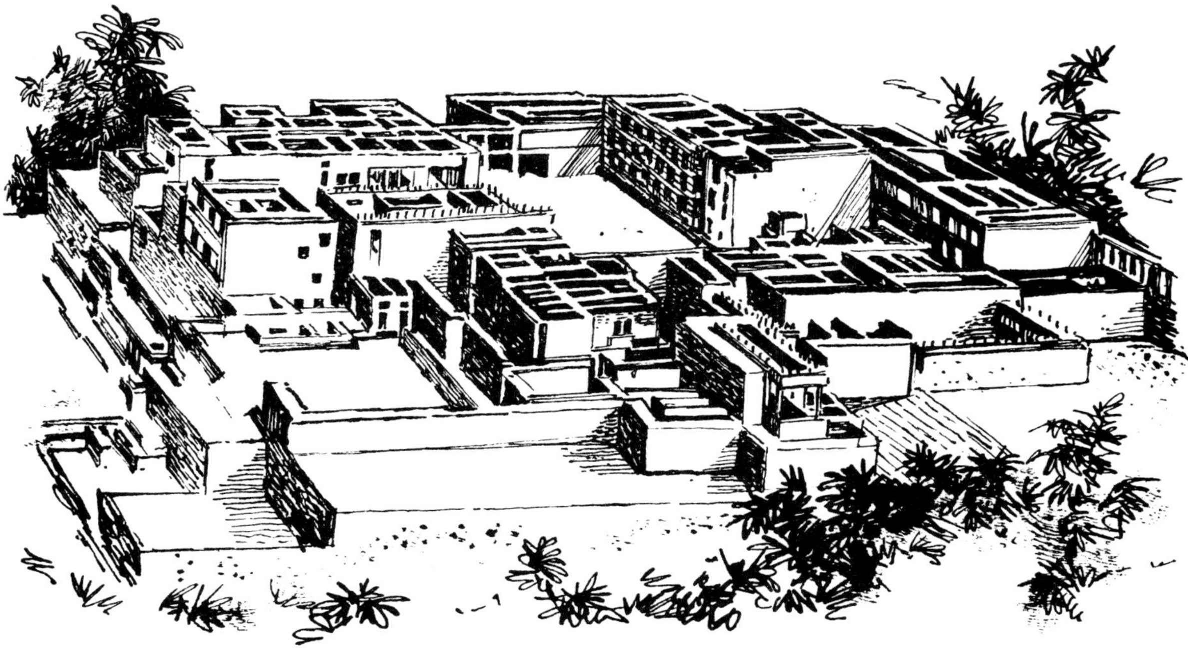

The palace of Knossos

5 Imagine that you are an Athenian sailor, shipwrecked on the Cretan coast in 1500 BC. While you are waiting for a ship to take you home, you stay in Knossos during the main religious festival of the year. Describe what you saw as you might have done to your family and friends. (Remember that in 1500 BC Athens would have been a small and backward place compared with Knossos.)

6 Is there any evidence that between 1500 BC and 1200 BC Greeks from the mainland visited and conquered Knossos? If so what is it (see page 126)?

7 Describe an event which could have happened which later storytellers might have built up into the legend of Theseus and the Minotaur and which fits the evidence known to you.

8 What kind of evidence might archaeologists find which would prove for sure that there was a Theseus, Prince of Athens, who came to Knossos to save his countrymen? (Remind yourself of the different kinds of evidence which Woolley used to solve the mystery of the three-metre band of clay, pages 53–4.)

13 Mainland Greece

How do we know about Ancient Greece?

The Olympic Games

In the Games of 516 BC the most exciting moment was the final of the men's wrestling. The defending champion was Milo of Croton. Even in his own lifetime, he was one of the most famous names in Olympic history. He had already won the wrestling six times and had thrilled the audience with spectacular feats of strength. On one occasion, he had carried a four-year-old bull round the stadium on his shoulders, on another a life-size marble statue of himself. He normally ate nine kilos of meat and of bread each day which he washed down with ten litres of wine. When he was not wrestling he was a soldier. He led his troops into battle wearing his Olympic crown of laurel and carrying a huge club such as the god Heracles was supposed to bear.

Myron's magnificent statue is one good piece of evidence for Greek athletics

His opponent in 516 BC was a much younger man, Timasitheus, who used newer methods. In this struggle of the younger generation against the older, youth triumphed. Milo's favourite tricks did not work against the new style of Timasitheus. We know about such contests from *writers* like Pausanias and the poet Pindar, some of whose best poems were in honour of the Olympic champions.

The beginnings of the Games are hidden away in *legend*. According to the story, Pelops, the grandson of the supreme god Zeus, wished to marry Hippodamia. Her father, Oenomaus, was king of the lands in which Olympia lay and a brilliant charioteer. Anyone who wished to marry his daughter must accept his challenge to a chariot race. Victory would win Hippodamia, defeat would mean death. Many had already accepted Oenomaus' challenge. They had all lost and died. Pelops, however, was aided by the gods. He defeated and killed Oenomaus, and made Hippodamia his wife. To commemorate his victory he ordered games to be held every four years at Olympia in honour of Zeus.

We also know about the Olympic Games through *archaeology* which uncovered these ruins at Olympia and through *inscriptions*.

Hippias, a citizen of Elis, the town which organised the Olympic Games every four years, made a list of inscriptions during the fifth century BC. From this list he was able to calculate that the first games must have been held in 776 BC.

This stone carving of wrestlers and this vase-painting of runners give us useful evidence too

Vase paintings also give us some idea of the methods Greek athletes would have used.

We know little about Ancient Greece before 700 BC beyond what *archaeology* and *legends* can tell us. After 700 BC *written* evidence becomes more and more important.

Olympia now – excavations by archaeologists have proved this corridor/archway was the athletes' entrance to the stadium

From the Mycenaeans to the Persian Wars

Helen, wife of King Menelaus of Sparta, and the most beautiful of Greek women, was taken from her home (so the legend of the Trojan Wars tells us) by Paris, son of the king of Troy. So Agamemnon of Mycenae, brother of Menelaus and overlord of all Greece, sailed with his brother and his fellow kings across the Aegean Sea. He would attack the proud and powerful city of Troy to win back Helen and revenge the terrible insult to his family.

The war was long and cruel. On both sides there were countless acts of skill and courage. Outstanding among the Greeks was the fearless and pitiless Achilles; among the Trojans, Priam's eldest son, the brave and generous Hector.

Left This carving from a Roman tomb shows one of the most famous stories from the Trojan War. The cruel Achilles (top right) drags the Trojan Hector, whom he has just slain in battle, past the walls of Troy.

Above The strong tower of the northern walls of Troy which Schliemann found

Several times the Trojans came near to victory. Once they even broke into the Greek camp and burned many ships. For the most part, however, the Greeks had the better of the fighting outside the city walls. Yet they could not break into the city.

Ten years passed. Achilles and Hector were dead and both sides exhausted. At last Odysseus, the most cunning of the Greek kings, hit on a plan to get inside the gates of Troy.

A huge and hollow wooden horse was built large enough to hold a handful of the finest Greek warriors. The rest of the Greeks set sail as if for home, fooling the Trojans who believed that the horse had been left behind by the defeated enemy, as an offering to the gods. The Trojans hauled the horse into the city and placed it beside their temples thinking that by so doing they would please the gods. Under cover of night, the Greek warriors slipped from the horse and opened the gates to let in the Greek army which had quietly made its return. The city of Troy was captured and burned to the ground, its people slain or taken into slavery.

The legend of the Trojan War is almost certainly based on a real war between the Greeks and the Trojans. It was first written down by the poet Homer, about 700 BC. It is certainly based on real places. While Mycenae overlooks the fertile plain of Argos, Troy stood on one of the more important trade routes of the eastern Mediterranean. Using the

Mycenae – the walls of the ancient city, which Schliemann also excavated, can be seen circling the central hill

Homeric legends as his guide, a German archaeologist, Heinrich Schliemann, discovered first (in 1870) the ruins of Troy and then (in 1876) those of Mycenae. In both he discovered marvellous treasures which he believed had belonged to Priam and to Agamemnon respectively. Later archaeologists have proved that the treasures come from a time much earlier than Schliemann had calculated. They have also discovered that Troy was certainly destroyed by fire and by violence rather later. The evidence suggests that Mycenae was a great power and may well have been involved in a long war with Troy about 1250 BC.

The centuries between 1200 BC and 800 BC are hidden in shadow. Most of the cities of Mycenaean Greece were destroyed or left empty. There may have been fighting between the cities, attacks by invaders by land and sea, or terrible famine. The eleventh century was a time of troubles all over the eastern Mediterranean and western Asia. Peoples were on the move across thousands of kilometres in search of new homes. New Greek-speaking peoples (the Dorians) moved into Greece forcing the existing inhabitants (the Ionians) into Asia Minor. The map shows the changes which took place between 1100 BC and 900 BC. Only in the eighth century BC did villages and towns begin to grow up again and normal life return.

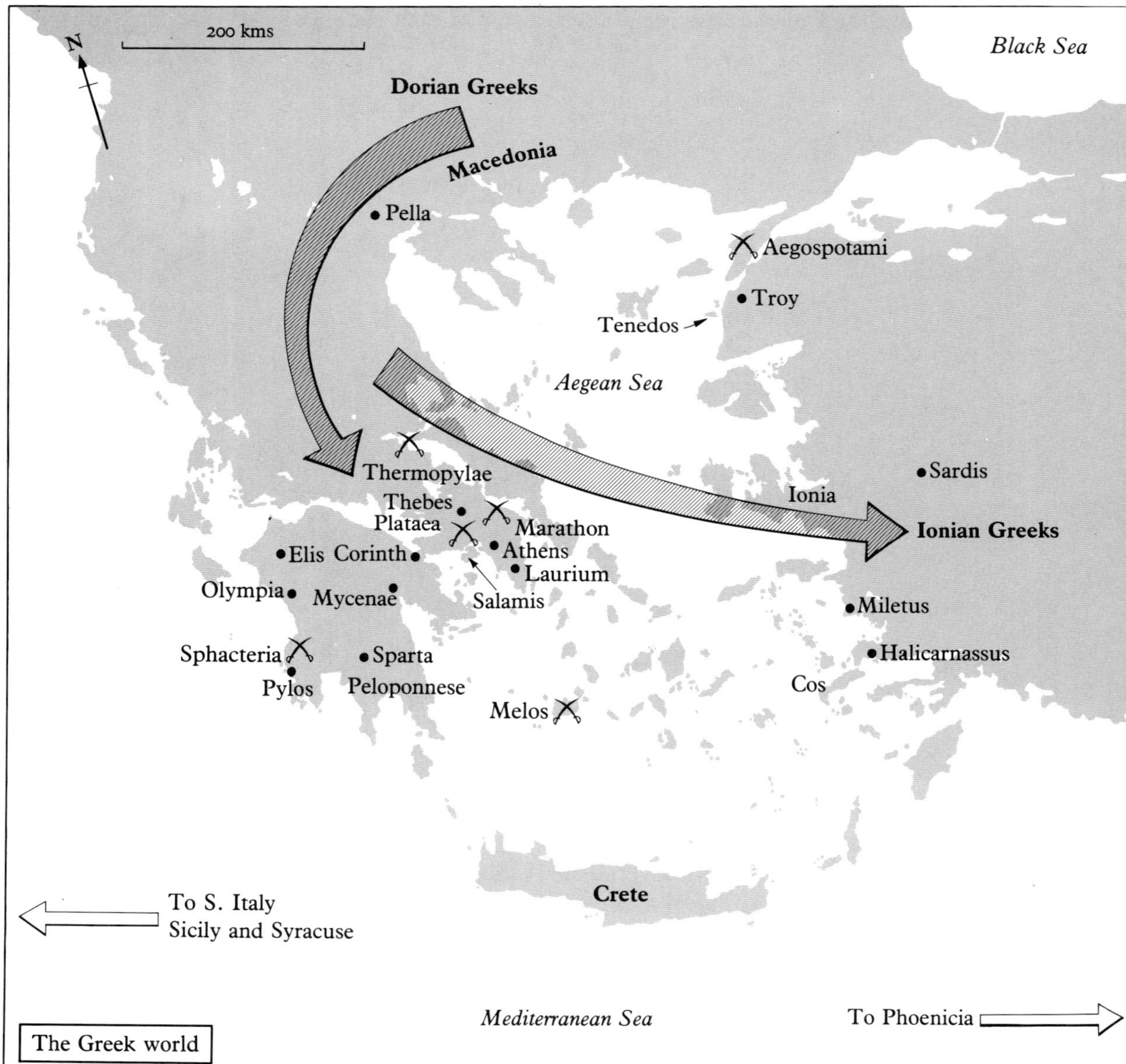

The Greek world

Nowhere in Greece is far from the sea and the new settlers, like the Mycenaean Greeks before them, made themselves fine sailors. The power of the Phoenicians (see chapter 10) was fading and the Greeks took their place. They traded all over the Mediterranean and founded colonies wherever the chances of successful trading and farming seemed good. Land shortages forced many families to move from their native cities. In search of a better life they came to these colonies which grew rapidly in size and number. To the west the most popular areas were southern Italy and Sicily, to the east the shores of the Black Sea.

Greece is also a land of high mountains, valleys and small plains. Movement by land was difficult. Many villages were small and isolated.

The high, bulky merchant ship on the left is about to be rammed by a fifty-oared pirate warship

There were no large kingdoms as in Egypt and Mesopotamia but rather a series of small city-states. Few of these were more than 1000 square kilometres in size with a single city at their centre. At first these city-states were ruled by kings and nobles but as time passed other classes demanded a say in the way their city-state was run. For a time in the fifth and fourth centuries BC some Greek city-states, notably Athens (see page 150) became democratic; i.e. all male citizens were able to vote and, if they wished, take part in the government. Whatever their type of government, the Greek city-states were fiercely independent. They disliked any kind of interference in their affairs and quarrelled continuously amongst themselves. Only once did they all unite, when their mighty neighbour, Persia, threatened them all.

The Persian Wars

The Persian Empire was the creation of Cyrus the Great who had captured Babylon in 539 BC. He and his successors had spread their power westwards and had forced the Greeks of Asia Minor (the Ionians) to accept their rule. In 499 BC the city of Miletus led an Ionian revolt, supported by the Athenians. Sardis, the capital of the province, was captured. Against the full might of the Persian army and navy, however, the Ionian Greeks stood little chance. The Athenians hurried home, Miletus was captured and destroyed. By 493 BC Persian rule had been fully restored.

The Persian Emperor, Darius, wished to revenge the insult which the Athenians had offered him by helping in the attack on Sardis. He sent messengers to the cities of mainland Greece with the demand that they should send to him earth and water, as signs that they were ready to obey him. When the Athenians not only refused but also murdered his messengers he sent his army and navy into action.

They planned to make the Greeks tremble. The Persian emperors Darius I (seated) and his son Xerxes.

The invasion of 490 BC and the Battle of Marathon

The Persian fleet struck directly across the Aegean Sea and landed the army without opposition at Marathon Bay (see below). Athens was in easy reach both by land and by sea. An Athenian army hurriedly barred the main road and Pheidippides, the best long-distance runner in Greece, set out for Sparta to seek aid. He covered the 225 kilometres in thirty-six hours but in vain. The Spartans were in the middle of their most important religious festival. They refused to take up arms until the next full moon which was still six days away. Only a small force from the nearby town of Plataea came to help the Athenians in this desperate hour.

The Greeks held the high ground overlooking Marathon and the sea. The Persian army, twice the size, was drawn up in the plain. The Persian army commander knew that if he could land part of his army round behind the Athenian position, Athens itself was defenceless, and he began to move the cavalry, the best section of the Persian army, on to his ships. At this moment Miltiades, the best if not the most senior of the Athenian generals, persuaded the others that the time for an attack had come. He cleverly strengthened the wings of the army, which charged at speed down the hill. The strengthened Greek wings smashed all before them then swung inwards to surround the Persian centre, which was driving back the weaker Greek centre. The Persians were defeated with heavy losses. However, the Persian fleet took off many

The Plain of Marathon. Athens lies behind the mountains in the background. The Persian ships were anchored off-shore (bottom left). The Greek army was drawn up on the mountain slopes. Almost exactly in the middle is a small mound. Here the victorious Greeks buried their dead, in the centre of where the battle had raged.

survivors and sailed south for Athens. They still hoped to get some troops ashore and capture the city before the victorious defending army could get back.

The exhausted Athenians hurried home. They arrived just before the Persians, who then retreated back to Asia Minor.

The invasion of Xerxes

Darius intended to attack Greece again, this time leading the army in person, but he died before his preparations were complete. In his place, in 480 BC, came his son Xerxes, young, proud and cruel. His army was huge and his finest regiment, the Immortals, magnificent. Crossing the Hellespont by a bridge of boats, he marched south towards Athens by the main coast road. At Thermopylae a small Greek force barred his way. It was commanded by Leonidas, one of the two kings of Sparta. This first sight of the enemy did not worry Xerxes in the least. The Greeks numbered only a few thousand and included just three hundred Spartans. In comparison with the Persians they were greatly outnumbered.

But try as they might the Persians could not break through. Leonidas had chosen his position carefully with steep hills on his left and the sea on his right. The Greeks with extraordinary skill and courage drove off every attack. For Xerxes, each day's delay was a setback and, with

Thermopylae – along this little valley (centre) the Persians slipped round behind the Spartan position. They were led by the traitor Ephialtes. The sea is just off the photo (bottom) and the main Persian army lay to the right. The Spartans made their final stand beside the low mound in the bottom centre.

mounting anger, he ordered assault after assault on the Greek position. Persian losses were very heavy yet still the Greeks held out.

Then a Greek traitor came to Xerxes and showed him a hidden path which ran through the hills round behind the Greek position. Picked troops found their way along this path. To guard it Leonidas had used Phocians, the least reliable of his troops. When they heard the sounds of the approaching Persians rustling the fallen leaves, they fled. The Greek position could not now be held. Leonidas ordered most of his army to retreat before they were cut off. Only he with his Spartans and the men of Thebes and Thespis held their ground and fought on in order to make safe their comrades' retreat. Anyway, no Spartan ever turned his back on the enemy. There they fought and died. Years later the Greeks put up a monument at Thermopylae in honour of Leonidas and his comrades. Herodotus saw it and copied down the inscription. 'Stranger, let those in Sparta know that here we lie, obedient to their laws.'

The Greek position was now most serious. The army, which was mainly Spartan, started to fall back towards the Peloponnese. The navy, which was mainly Athenian, also retreated after some minor skirmishes with the Persian fleet. The Greek leaders were unable to agree what they should do next. In these dangerous days one man stood out, Themistocles. In previous years he had made sure that Athens had a good fleet and now he was sure that it could prove its worth. But he agreed with the Spartans that Athens should not be defended and ordered the citizens to leave. They had to watch from a distance while the Persians set fire to their temples and houses.

Themistocles refused to allow the fleet to retire any further, however. The best chance of defeating the Persians, he was convinced, was to fight in the narrow waters near Salamis which the Athenians knew so well.

Autumn was now closing in and Xerxes was anxious to complete the conquest of Greece before winter. He ordered his fleet to attack the Greek position at Salamis. What actually happened there is not clear (see the Using the evidence section). But there is no doubt about the result. The Persian fleet was smashed beyond repair. With it Xerxes' hopes of a quick conquest disappeared. While Xerxes himself hurriedly retreated the way that he had come, what was left of his fleet sailed to the Hellespont to guard his crossing back into Asia.

None the less the war was still far from over as a formidable Persian army wintered in northern Greece. Under the capable command of Mardonius, the Persians marched south again in the summer of 479 BC. There followed the long, fierce and confused battle of Plataea. There the finest Persian and Spartan soldiers grappled together in bitter hand to hand conflict until Mardonius himself was killed. Then the Persians fled. On land and sea the Greeks had proved that when they were united they could defeat the world's most mighty empire. Never again, however, did they find such unity.

Using the evidence: how Salamis was won

There are two main sources of information about the Battle of Salamis; the *Histories* of Herodotus and a play by Aeschylus called *The Persians*. They do not completely agree and leave some vital points unclear. Modern historians are unable to agree either. See if you can work out how the Greeks won their famous victory from the two accounts which now follow. Answer the questions as you go along.

Introduction

Herodotus

We know something already about Herodotus' *Histories* (see pages 66–9) and will hear of them again (see page 153). Herodotus was a child of four when the battle was fought. In his home town of Halicarnassus he would have grown up hearing the stories about the daring Queen Artemisia who fought on the Persian side. He came to Athens about 450 BC and his account is based on the memories of the Athenians a generation or more after the battle had been fought.

The account of Aeschylus comes from his play *The Persians* and is spoken in the play by a Persian messenger. Aeschylus lived for most of his life in Athens and fought both at Marathon and at Salamis. *The Persians* was first performed in Athens eight years after Salamis to audiences many of whom would have known well what actually had happened at Salamis.

The night moves

Themistocles, the Athenian commander, sent a message to Xerxes with the false information that the Greek fleet was about to sail away and that if he were to attack the next day the Athenians would come over to his side, so disgusted were they with the chicken-hearted behaviour of the other Greeks.

Herodotus' account

The Persians believed (Themistocles) and proceeded to put ashore a large force on the islet of Psyttaleia, then, about midnight, they moved their western wing in an encircling movement upon Salamis, while at the same time they also blocked the whole channel as far as Munychia. . . . These tactical moves were carried out in silence to prevent the enemy from being aware of what was going on; they occupied the whole night, so that none of the men had time for sleep.

Aeschylus' account

Xerxes didn't realise he was being tricked . . . and at once gave orders to his captains. When darkness came they were to bring up the main body of ships sailing three abreast to block the exits and the sounding straits and station the ships in a circle round the island of Salamis. But with this warning: should the Greeks escape . . . every captain would lose his head. Our crews then prepared their evening meal while each sailor looped his oar about its thole pin so it fitted well. But when the night drew on, each master of an oar and each man versed in arms went on board. The long galleys cheered each other line by line and they held their course as each captain had been ordered. All through the night the commanders of the fleet kept their whole force cruising back and forth across the strait.

1 (a) In what ways do Herodotus and Aeschylus agree about the night moves of the Persian fleet?
(b) In what ways do they disagree? (Clue: find Munychia on the map on page 144.)

The beginning of the battle

Learning that they were trapped the Greeks now prepared for battle.

Ships like this fifty-oared penteconter fought at Salamis

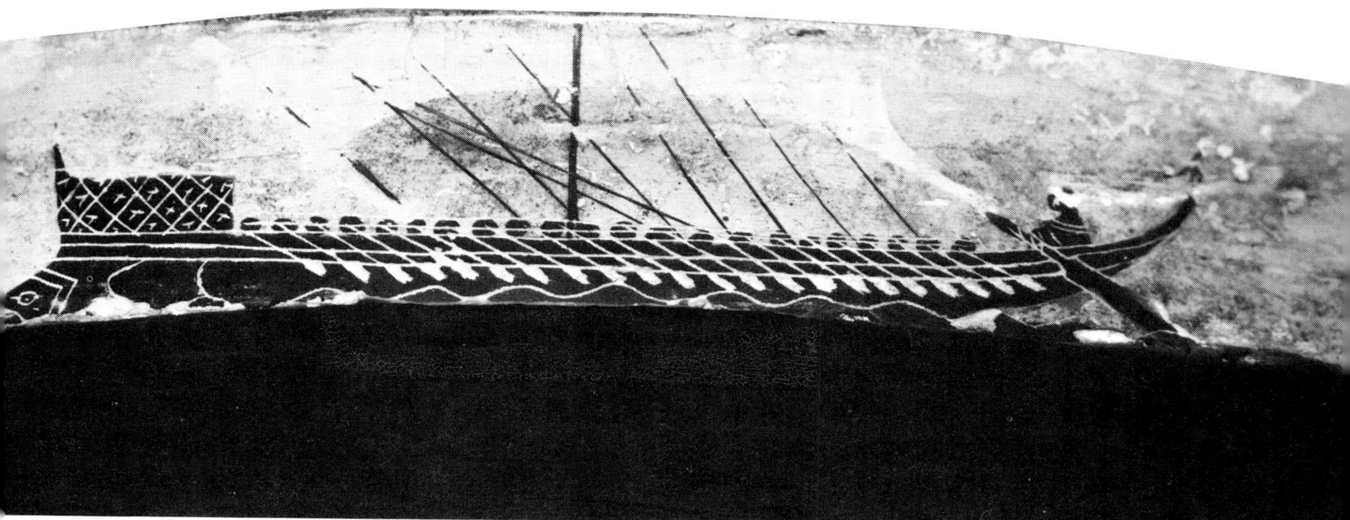

The whole fleet now got under way, and in a moment the Persians were on them. The Greeks checked their way and began to go back astern and they were on the point of running aground when an Athenian ship drove ahead and rammed an enemy vessel. Seeing the two ships locked together, the rest of the Greek fleet hurried to the Athenian's assistance and the general action began.... There is also a popular belief that the phantom shape of a woman appeared and, in a voice which could be heard by every man in the fleet, contemptuously cried out: 'Fools, how much further do you propose to go astern?'

The trumpet with its blast fired the Greek line. Instantly at the word of command with even strokes of their foaming oars they smote the briny deep. Swiftly they came into view. Their right wing was marshalled well and led their advance. Next their whole fleet came against us and a mighty shout greeted our ears. 'On ye Sons of Hellas! Free your native land, free your children and your wives, the temples of your fathers and the tombs of your ancestors. Now fight with all your worth.' It was a Greek ship which began the charge and sheered off the complete curved stem of a Phoenician galley.

2 (a) In what direction does Herodotus have the Greek fleet moving just before the fighting begins (see lines 17–18)?
(b) In what direction does Aeschylus have the Greek fleet moving just before the fighting begins (see lines 25–30)?

The battle itself

Herodotus' account

The Athenian squadron found itself facing the Phoenicians, who formed the Persian left wing on the western, Eleusis, end of the line; the Spartans faced the ships of Ionia, which were stationed on the Piraeus, or eastern, end. . . . The Persian fleet suffered severely in the battle. Since the Greek fleet worked together as a whole, while the Persians had lost formation and were no longer fighting on any plan, that was what was bound to happen. None the less they fought well that day.

. . . I must mention Artemisia (Queen of Halicarnassus). She was chased by an Athenian trireme. As her ship happened to be closest to the enemy and there were other friendly ships just ahead of her, escape was impossible. In this awkward situation she hit on a plan which turned out greatly to her advantage: with the Athenian close on her tail she drove ahead with all possible speed and rammed one of her friends. . . . The captain of the Athenian trireme, on seeing her ram an enemy, naturally supposed that her ship was a Greek one, so he abandoned the chase.

The greatest destruction took place when the ships that had been first engaged turned tail; for those astern fell foul of them in their attempt to press forward and do some service before the eyes of the king. . . .

Xerxes watched the course of the battle from the base of Mount Aegaleos, across the strait from Salamis. . . .

When the Persians were trying to get back to Phalerum, the ships of Aegina, which were waiting to catch them in the narrows, did memorable service. The enemy was in hopeless confusion; such ships as offered resistance or tried to escape were cut to pieces by the Athenians, while the Aeginetans caught those which attempted to get clear.

Aeschylus' account

Each Greek captain drove his ship against some other ship. At first the Persians held their own, but the mass of ships had been crowded in the narrows so that they were unable to help one another. Each ship crashed its bronze-headed beak against the next, breaking all its oars. The Greek galleys hemmed them in on every side. The hulks of our vessels rolled over and the sea was filled with wrecks and slaughtered men. The shores and rocks were crowded with our dead as if our men were tunnies or some haul of fish; the enemy kept striking and hacking them with broken oars and fragments from the wrecks; and groans and shrieks together filled the sea until night came.

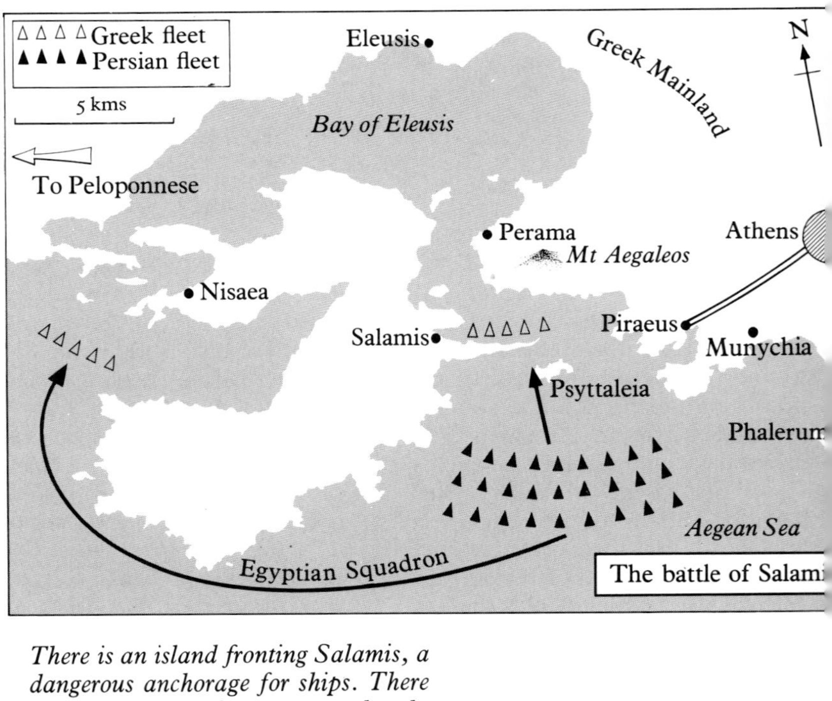

There is an island fronting Salamis, a dangerous anchorage for ships. There Xerxes placed his best troops to slaughter those Greeks who escaped the sea.

The battle of Salamis was fought in these waters. The island of Salamis is in the foreground. Psyttaleia is the long narrow island on the right. Mount Aegaleos where Xerxes sat is across the water, top left. Athens itself is top centre (behind the smoke).

Such of the Persian ships as escaped destruction made their way back to Phalerum. . . . During the confused struggle a valuable service was performed by the Athenian, Aristides. He took a number of the Athenian heavy infantry, who were posted along the coast of Salamis, across to Psyttaleia, where they killed every one of the Persian soldiers who had been landed there.

The victorious Greeks bounded from their ships and encircled the whole island so our men were at a loss which way to turn. They were struck down by stones and by arrows. At last the Greeks charging with a shout, smote them and hacked to pieces the limbs of the poor wretches until they had destroyed the life of all.

3 (a) What were the problems which faced the Persians once the battle had begun?
(b) How did the Greeks gain victory? How well do the writers agree about this?
4 What remarkable incident is mentioned by Herodotus and not by Aeschylus? Why might Aeschylus have left it out while Herodotus gives it a lot of space? (Clue: check the information about Herodotus on page 142.)
5 (a) Where is Psyttaleia?
(b) What were the Persians doing there?
(c) What happened to them?

The end of the battle

Herodotus' account

Xerxes laid his plans for escape; but at the same time in order to conceal his purpose both from the Greeks and from his own troops, he began to construct a causeway across the water towards Salamis, lashing together a number of ships to serve at once for bridge and breakwater.

Aeschylus' account

Xerxes groaned aloud when he saw the size of the disaster because he occupied a lofty spot hard by the open sea commanding a clear view of the battle-scene. Rending his robes and uttering a loud wail, he at once gave orders for his land forces to flee.

6 Where had the surviving Persian ships gone?
7 In what ways do Herodotus and Aeschylus disagree about Xerxes' actions at the end of the battle? Does anything strike you as at all odd about Herodotus' account here?

The battle as a whole

8 On two outline maps of the area draw diagrams with arrows (using the diagram on page 144 as your guide) to show:
(a) the course of the battle as described by Herodotus;
(b) as described by Aeschylus.
On each should also be marked the following: Athens, Piraeus, Munychia, Eleusis, Mount Aegaleos, the island of Salamis, the island of Psyttaleia, Phalerum.
9 Re-read the information on page 142 about Herodotus and Aeschylus. Whose account do you think is the more reliable? Give your reasons.
10 You are a Persian servant of Xerxes with him on the slopes of Mount Aegaleos on the day of the battle. Describe your experiences that day.
11 Choose an incident in the battle and sketch as vividly as you can how it might have been.
12 This account of the battle can be found in the *Encyclopaedia Britannica* (14th edition 1973):
(i) The first problem for the Greek command was to offset their smaller numbers by drawing the Persian fleet into the straits.
(ii) As dawn broke, the Greeks embarked at their bases half-way up the straits and rowed off northward out of sight.

(iii) The Persian fleet, seeing them disappear, thought they were in flight and rowed into the straits.
(iv) Then the Greeks returned in battle order to the narrowest part of the waters, maneuvered under oar to create favourable circumstances for ramming and went into the attack at the crucial moment.
(v) The Phoenician squadron, in the van, suffered heavy losses, and the leading files were driven back onto those that were still advancing.
(vi) Then the Greek ships, encircling the scene of confusion, rammed repeatedly with a sure aim until the Persian ships capsized and the sea was covered with wreckage and corpses.

Take each of these numbered sentences one by one. Each is based either: (a) directly on Herodotus; (b) directly on Aeschylus; (c) on intelligent guesswork only.
Say which sentences are based on (a) which on (b) and which on (c). Give line numbers from the extracts as evidence for your answers for (a) and (b).

14 The Greek achievement

A Spartan soldier

Sparta and Athens

During the Persian Wars, Sparta had provided the best army, Athens the best navy. Though only 160 kilometres apart as the crow flies, two cities could hardly have been more different.

Sparta lies in the southern Peloponnese, in the valley of the River Eurotas. The first Spartans were Dorian invaders (see page 136), who turned the previous inhabitants into their slaves (helots). To keep the helots under control and to defend themselves against their neighbours, their way of life was planned to make Spartan men above all fine soldiers. Overlooking the valley was Mount Taygettus. On its wild slopes weak babies were left to die. At the age of seven, all boys began a strict education which ended each year in difficult tests of discipline and endurance. The adult Spartan man spent most of his time in a completely male community. He lived, trained and relaxed in the company of other men only. Marriage was allowed but only men over thirty were allowed to sleep at home. Spartan women were encouraged to be physically fit so that they could be healthy mothers of healthy children. They enjoyed greater freedom and respect than in many Greek cities.

Sparta kept itself cut off from the rest of the world. It prided itself on being different. Trade was left to outsiders. When the rest of Greece changed to gold and silver coins, the Spartans still used iron bars; when the Greek fashion was for beards and moustaches, the Spartan government ruled that all the citizens must shave off their moustaches. The most powerful members of the government were the ephors who were elected each year by an assembly of all citizens. There were also two kings who led the army in wartime. Another assembly, made up of nobles over sixty years old, was the chief court of justice and guarded the ancient customs of the city.

Most farm work was done by the helots and most trade and commerce by foreigners. Consequently the Spartans had plenty of time and energy to spend on physical and military training. The result was as tough and as disciplined a city as the world has known. 'Be brave, fight and, if needs be, die but never tremble,' wrote the Spartan poet Tyrtaeus. At Thermopylae, Leonidas and the Three Hundred proved that in war the system worked. At all times, however, Sparta was a harsh and rough place. The helots, held in slavery by force, rose in revolt from time to time and were cruelly put down. Early Sparta was well known for its poetry and music but later it became a dull place. This was particularly noticeable when compared with the rest of Greece which was bursting with new developments in trade, commerce, art and ideas.

At the centre of these new developments was Athens, the other great city of Ancient Greece and in time Sparta's most dangerous military rival. Athens stands in the plain of Attica looking out over the Aegean Sea. The Athenians were traders from early on. The countryside could not produce enough food for a growing city. Corn was imported from the Black Sea; so too were iron, copper, timber and flax. In payment,

Athens: the Acropolis. On this strong rock the earliest town was built.

the Athenians exported olive oil, wine, pottery and luxury goods. Silver from the mines at Laurium was also exported. Not surprisingly the navy which defended the vital sea-routes was more important than the army. For fifty years after Salamis it ruled the waves of the eastern Mediterranean.

The careful housewife: an Athenian woman puts clothes away in a chest

Athenian democracy

In Athens in the fifth century BC all adult males, excluding slaves and foreigners, could play a part in government. They elected officials, served on juries in the law courts and voted in the assembly. Athens was a democracy, but not all city-states gave their citizens such freedom. In Sparta, for example, the two kings and the ephors took many of the decisions. But almost everywhere rule by one man was thought a bad thing. Such rulers were called tyrants whether they ruled well or badly. (What do we mean by tyrant today?) Rule by a few men, usually all belonging to noble families, was more common and more acceptable.

During the period of her greatest glory Athens was a democracy, but not always. In the sixth century there had been tyrants, like Pisistratus, who had ruled her many years. The Alcmaenids, a group of powerful nobles, also had a large say in the government at times. After the defeat of Athens by Sparta small groups of men, like the Council of Thirty, were temporarily able to seize power.

Not all Athenians enjoyed great freedom, even in the fifth century BC. Perhaps half the population were slaves. But not all slaves were as badly treated as those who worked in the silver mines at Laurium. The police force at Athens was formed of Scythians, who were themselves slaves!

Athenian women had far fewer chances to play a part in public life than their menfolk.

The Peloponnesian War 431 BC to 404 BC

This proud and ambitious city quarrelled with many cities of the Peloponnese and particularly with Sparta. War finally came in 431 BC. It was to last on and off for twenty years and became known as the Peloponnesian War. The chief reason for it was, in Thucydides' words, 'the growth of Athenian power and the fear which this caused in Sparta'.

The war was cruel and exhausting. Fortunes changed rapidly. Early on, the Athenian fleet blockaded towns in the Peloponnese while the Spartan army marched across Attica burning farms and villages. The country people took refuge between the long strong walls which ran from Athens to the sea. They were safe enough there from the Spartans. But many became victims of a dreadful plague which struck in 430 BC. Living in badly ventilated huts,

> . . . they died like flies. The bodies of the dying were heaped one on top of the other and half-dead creatures could be seen staggering about in the streets or flocking around the fountains in their desire for water . . .,

Thucydides wrote this (after he got the plague himself but somehow survived). About one-third of the population of Athens died from the plague. This national setback did not deter the Athenians but by 421 BC both sides were exhausted.

Permanent peace was impossible until one side was the clear winner. Soon Athenian forces were again on the move. The island of Melos, which wished to stay out of the struggle, was attacked and captured. Thucydides notes without comment that the Athenians then 'put to death all the men of military age and sold the women and children as slaves'.

Thucydides: historian of the Peloponnesian War

The following year a much more ambitious scheme was suggested in the Athenian Assembly. 'Let us attack Syracuse in the island of Sicily, the ally of our neighbour and deadly enemy Corinth. Successful at Syracuse we can then go on to conquer the whole island.' Most in favour of this plan was Alcibiades, a young man who, Thucydides tells us, was very much in the public eye. He was keen to win command of the army since 'success would bring him wealth and honour'. Wealth he needed because 'his enthusiasm for horse-breeding and other extravagances went beyond what his fortune could supply'. He succeeded in persuading Athens both to send an army and navy against Syracuse and to appoint him one of the commanders.

The expedition set sail from Athens in the midsummer of 415 BC to the cheers of a huge crowd. In the opinion of Thucydides it was 'by a long way the most expensive and finest-looking force ever to come from a single Greek city'.

Soon, however, things went badly wrong. Alcibiades was a good general 'but his way of life had made him much disliked as a person'. Back in Athens 'the people thought that he was aiming to make himself tyrant,' Thucydides explains, 'and turned against him'. Hardly had Alcibiades arrived in Sicily than he was ordered home. Since he was afraid to go back and stand trial with all the unfair feeling that was against him, he left his ship and went into hiding. He later joined the Spartans.

Nicias, the general remaining, was cautious and too slow at making up his mind in times of danger. The Syracusans were good fighters and the Spartans sent them useful support. The Athenian fleet met defeat in the Grand Harbour of Syracuse. The Athenian army marched in search of a safer position, was surrounded and forced to surrender. Nicias was put to death and the Athenian survivors imprisoned for ten weeks in stone quarries outside Syracuse. They were given only starvation rations. Those who survived were then sold as slaves. For the Athenians, Thucydides notes it was a terrible disaster: they were completely defeated; their sufferings were on an enormous scale; their losses were total; army, navy, everything was destroyed. Out of the many, only a few returned. So ended the events in Sicily.

Though the war lasted another nine years, Athens could not recover. The Spartans, now allied to the Persians, grew stronger both on land

and on sea. Ably led by Lysander, their fleet surprised and destroyed the remaining Athenian fleet at Aegospotami in 405 BC. Vital corn supplies no longer reached Athens. The following year the Spartans were able to blockade the city itself. Near to starvation the Athenians stopped fighting. They were then saved by the Spartans. The Peloponnesian allies demanded that Athens be destroyed and her citizens sold into slavery. Sparta, however, reminded them of the many achievements of Athens in the past, particularly during the Persian Wars. She saw to it that though Athens lost her empire, her fleet, and her Long Walls, the city itself survived and stayed free.

Terrible though the Peloponnesian War had been, it did not prevent further wars between the Greeks. Wars continued through the fourth century until first the Macedonians in 338 BC (see page 159) and then the Romans in 146 BC succeeded where the Persians had failed: Greece became part of a greater empire.

Science, History and Philosophy

Ancient Greece has a very special place in the history of man as a source of a remarkable number of ideas between 600 BC and 300 BC. Many of these ideas, on science, drama, poetry, philosophy and religion, for example, still influence our thoughts today.

Father of Science

Thales of Miletus is often called 'the Father of Science'. He was a man of wide interests. He is supposed to have successfully predicted the eclipse of 585 BC and to have discovered five geometric theorems (including the one that the angles of the base of an isosceles triangle are equal). He also applied his knowledge of geometry to improve navigation at sea. Most of all, Thales was fascinated by why and how the things of this world worked. He was not satisfied by describing everything which could not easily be explained as the work of 'the gods'. He decided that the whole universe was made up of different forms of a single substance, moisture.

Little is known for sure about Thales' life. There are many stories about him, though. He was the original absent-minded professor. Thinking so hard about the nature of the universe, he is said to have fallen down a well. But he also had the reputation of being a clever businessman when he wished. Observing in the spring signs that an excellent olive crop was on its way, he bought up all the local oil presses and made a fortune the following autumn.

Father of Medicine

Hippocrates was born on the island of Cos about 460 BC and founded a medical school there. He and his successors wrote much about the treatment of illnesses and on the responsibilities of doctors. Their *Hippocratic Collection* became an essential textbook for European doctors for the next two thousand years. Like Thales, Hippocrates was keen to discover the reasons for things; in his case why men suffered

Socrates

from diseases. He also refused to use 'the gods' to explain things not easily understood. Epilepsy in particular was believed to be a god-given disease but Hippocrates wrote 'this disease is no more sacred than any other. It is inherited and its cause lies in the brain'.

Father of History

Herodotus was born in Halicarnassus in Ionia about 484 BC. His *Histories* are not just an important source of written evidence (see pages 66–9), they are also the first surviving attempt to write history at all.

> I am giving the results of my inquiries so that the memory of what men have done shall not perish nor their achievements go unsung. They form my theme, and the reason why they went to war

he explains in the first sentences of the *Histories*.

Father of Philosophy

Socrates was born in Athens in 469 BC. He wrote no books of any kind, yet he is remembered as one of the greatest teachers the world has known, thanks to the writings of his pupils whom he deeply impressed. The son of a stone-cutter, he fought in the Athenian army and, like most Athenian citizens, played his part in politics. As he grew older, however, he took to going around barefoot and shabbily clad and spent most of his time discussing the nature and behaviour of mankind with the clever young men of Athens. His method of teaching was to ask questions. His first question would draw an answer from his pupil, his second would make clear the weakness of that answer. Then he would guide the pupil towards a better understanding by further carefully thought-out questions. Wisdom, he believed, lay in realising how little one really knew, and could best be gained by discussion. Great care must be taken by all involved in discussion to be as precise as possible with the meaning of words.

Most Athenians did not know what to make of Socrates. His odd appearance and way of life upset many. One of his best-known pupils, Alcibiades, became a traitor; another, Critias, tried to seize power by force. At a bad time for Athens (recently defeated by Sparta) the old man seemed a thoroughly undesirable influence. In 399 BC he was put on trial for 'introducing new gods' and 'corrupting the young'. These accusations were serious but Socrates could have avoided trouble by going into exile or paying a fine. Instead he treated them with the contempt he felt they deserved. He told his judges that they should be rewarding him for his services to Athens, not putting him on trial. Angrily they sentenced him to death. He spent his last days quite serenely talking to his pupils and refusing to consider any plans to escape. 'I am sure that it is better to die now and to be released from trouble,' were his words when the time came to take the poison hemlock.

His most gifted pupil was Plato whose writings are his best memorial.

1 *The Temple at Paestum (south Italy), sixth century* BC

2 *The Temple of Athena Niké (Athens), fifth century* BC

3 *The Temple of Zeus (Athens), second century* BC

4 *Euston railway arch (London), nineteenth century* AD

5 *The Royal Crescent (Bath), eighteenth century* AD

6 *St Paul's Cathedral (London), seventeenth century* AD

In an olive grove outside Athens, Plato founded a school, the Academy, which taught and developed Socratic and Platonic ideas. It became the most famous school in the Ancient World and continued to exist for more than nine hundred years.

In architecture, painting, sculpture, poetry and drama the Greeks also produced great masterpieces. Look, for example, at architecture.

Using the evidence: the influence of Greek architecture

This section shows how ideas first worked out by the Greeks between 600 BC and 300 BC have been used by later architects. Answer the questions as you go along.

1

2

4

5

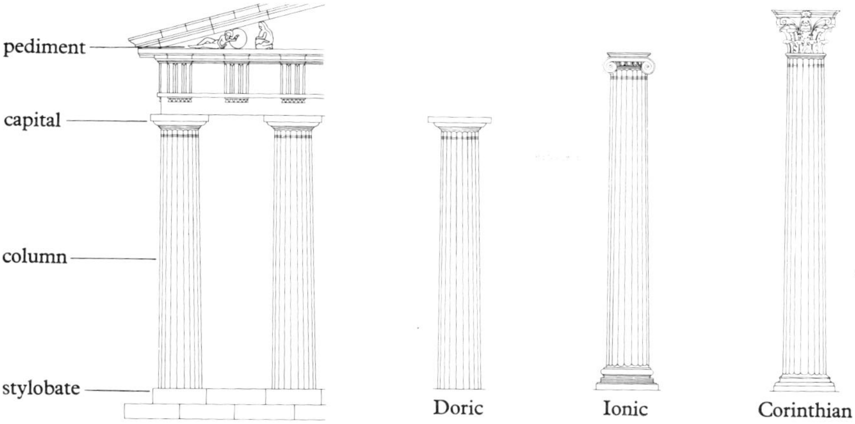

Greek architectural terms

3

6

1 What have each of these buildings in common?

2 (a) Sketch as accurately as you can the capital of each of these three styles.

(b) List the types of capital used in the buildings, figures 4–6.

Very few books on architecture have survived from Greek and Roman times. The most important, by a Roman, Vitruvius, and called simply *On Architecture* was first published about 27 BC. Vitruvius knew a great deal about buildings throughout the Roman Empire, especially in Greece and Italy. His views about what made buildings beautiful were based closely on Greek ideas. 'A temple design', he wrote, 'must be symmetrical. Without proportion and symmetry there can be no goodness in the design.' A symmetrical design is one that can be divided in half by a line so that each half is the same as the other.

3 Which of the figures 1–6 are symmetrical and which are not?

Proportion, i.e. how one part relates to the next, was most important to Greek and Roman architects. Vitruvius said:

Since nature has so designed the human body that its parts are in proportion to the whole frame, the ancients [the Greeks] had good reason for their rule that in perfect buildings, the different parts will be in exact proportions to the whole plan. If you measure the parts of the human body, you will discover the following proportions; from the top of the forehead to the chin is a tenth of the whole body, from the wrist to the top of the middle finger is a tenth, the foot is a sixth, the forearm is a quarter.

4 Measure yourself. Is Vitruvius correct?

Vitruvius goes on to explain the proportions which in a building give the most pleasing results.

7 Balance and proportion

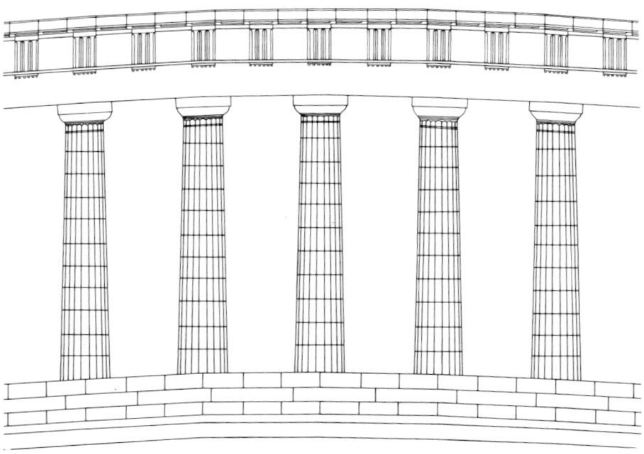

If a column is six to nine metres high, its width at the top should be six-sevenths of its width at the bottom. Columns twelve to sixteen metres high should be seven-eighths of the width of the bottom at the top. For the eye is always in search of beauty and without this thinning of the columns, the building will appear clumsy and awkward.

5 (a) Do the columns of buildings 1 and 2 thin?
(b) Measure them carefully. Do they thin in the proportions recommended by Vitruvius?

Vitruvius, who was an architect himself, knew the tricks of the Greek architects' trade. Here is one which they frequently used.

The level of the stylobate [the base from which the temple rises] must be increased in the centre by means of the builders' tools known as 'unequal levellers'. If it is laid perfectly level, then to the eye it will appear slightly hollow.

6 Look at figure 7. Did the architect use 'unequal levellers'? Explain your answer.

Under the Roman Empire and after, Greek influence on European architecture was strong. During the Middle Ages, however, the main style of buildings was Gothic which, as you can see from figure 9, was quite different.

After AD 1400 however, starting in Italy, there was an enthusiastic revival of Greek and Roman ideas, especially in architecture. Few people disagreed with the Italian architect, Serlio. 'Unless there is good reason otherwise, we must always follow the teaching of Vitruvius. As a guide, he never lets one down.' Palladio was another of the many European architects who knew Vitruvius backwards. Here is one of his most famous buildings, the Villa Rotonda, Vicenza.

8 *The Villa Rotonda (Vicenza, north Italy), sixteenth century AD*

7 Compare figures 8 and 9.
   (a) What are the main differences between them?
   (b) What Greek influence can you see in Palladio's design?
   (c) Which do you prefer and why?

Since then Greek ideas have been frequently used by architects the world over.

8 Describe and sketch some local buildings which show the influence of Greek architectural ideas.

9 *Salisbury Cathedral (Wiltshire), thirteenth century AD*

15 Alexander the Great

How do we know about Alexander?

Though much has been written about Alexander, modern historians still find it difficult to be sure what actually happened during his short and remarkable life or what kind of person he really was. Nothing written down during his lifetime now survives. The three best descriptions were written between two hundred and five hundred years after his death. They are based on accounts, now lost, which were first written near the time he lived. An important task of historians of Alexander's reign is to work out which parts of these three surviving accounts are most likely to be true. The Using the evidence section shows you some of the problems historians face in getting to the real Alexander.

Alexander's life and conquests

In the summer of 336 BC Philip, king of Macedon, celebrated the marriage of his daughter to his neighbour, the king of Epirus. The day after the wedding, games were to be held in an open air theatre. They began soon after dawn with a parade of statues of the gods which Philip intended to follow into the theatre with his son Alexander and his new son-in-law. He never reached the waiting audience. By the theatre entrance he was stabbed to death by a member of his bodyguard.

Pella, the Macedonian capital city

Why he was murdered is not known for certain. Possibly Olympias, Philip's ex-wife and mother of Alexander, planned the crime. She was a lady with a fiery temper, who had not taken kindly to being cast aside by Philip in favour of another woman. Whatever the true story, the person who gained most from Philip's death was Alexander. That same day he was proclaimed king by the Macedonian army.

Alexander was twenty, below average height, with long flowing hair. Unusually energetic, confident and ambitious, he was also moody with a terrible temper. Already he had shown himself to be someone out of the ordinary. At the age of ten, according to one famous story, he tamed a magnificent black stallion which the royal stablemen were quite unable to control. 'You will have to find another kingdom,' Philip is reported to have said on this occasion. 'Macedonia is not going to be big enough for you.' When he was still only fourteen, he took charge of Macedonia while his father was away fighting. Three years later when Philip finally smashed the resistance of the other Greek states at the great battle of Chaeronea, the move which won the battle was the cavalry charge led by Alexander.

The Lion of Chaeronea, built by the Thebans in honour of their dead. They were defeated here with the Athenians by Philip of Macedon.

The position which he had inherited from his father was a strong one. Philip had not only expanded Macedonia and forced the rest of Greece to accept his leadership, he had also made the Macedonian army the finest in the world. It was centred on the famous *phalanx*, heavily armed foot-soldiers marching sixteen rows deep. Each soldier carried a heavy spear four to four-and-a-half metres long. Beside the phalanx there were the less heavily armed, faster moving shield-bearers. The main attacking force was the cavalry and to support them were archers, javelin throwers and engineers with the most up-to-date siege equipment. Philip was so sure of his own and his army's abilities that at the time of his death, he was planning to attack the vast Persian Empire. He wished, he said, to revenge the wrongs done to Greece by Darius I and Xerxes during the Persian Wars (see pages 137–47).

The young Alexander was not going to give up this plan. But first he had to make it clear to the Macedonians and to the Greeks that he was to be feared just as much as his father had been. All possible rivals to the throne were murdered. One swift campaign made the Greek states accept him, as they had Philip, for their leader; a second forced barbarian tribes to leave his northern border alone; and a third, during which he marched his army nearly 900 kilometres through the Balkan mountains in less than a fortnight, ended a revolt by Thebes and Athens. He made an example of Thebes. Taken by storm, the city was completely destroyed except for its temples and the house of the great poet, Pindar. Six thousand Thebans were butchered on the spot. The rest were sold into slavery. Not surprisingly, the Greeks did as they were told from then on.

In 334 BC he crossed the Dardanelles with an army of fifty thousand men to attack an empire which could call on the services of a million soldiers. The most remarkable campaign in military history had begun.

Alexander and Bucephalus

During the next eleven years, he led his Macedonians nearly 28 000 kilometres across some of the world's roughest country, winning victory after victory and never halting for more than a few months. When he died in Babylon in 323 BC the Persian Empire had been destroyed for ever. In its place a Greek empire stretched from the River Danube to the River Indus. Of those eleven extraordinary years, here are some of the highlights.

The siege of Tyre 332 BC

Tyre was one of the most important ports of the Mediterranean and stood on a strongly fortified island and refused to surrender. How to capture Tyre was a difficult problem. A channel a kilometre wide and on average six metres deep divided the island from the mainland. Across this, Alexander ordered his engineers to construct a mole or causeway. Once it was close enough, wooden towers were built on it, from which the enemy could be bombarded with stones and arrows. The Tyrians resisted stubbornly and cleverly. Their ships harassed the

The campaigns of Alexander the Great

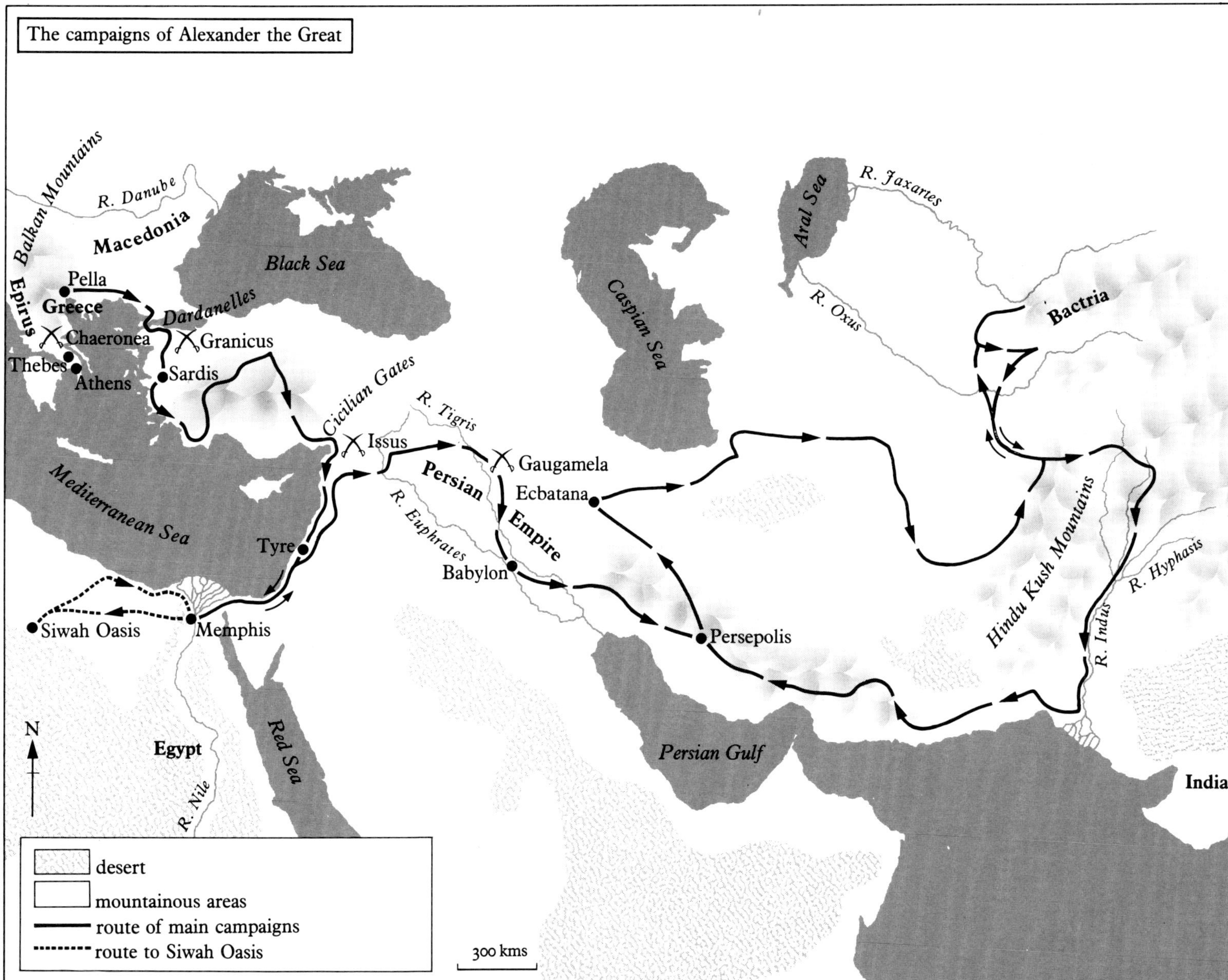

labourers on the mole and burnt down the towers. When Alexander launched floating platforms to attack the island from all sides, they hurled down rocks to prevent these platforms getting close in against the walls. When Alexander's ships tried to move these rocks, divers silently cut their anchors. When the mole at last reached the city walls and the Macedonians tried a direct attack, the Tyrians showered them with red-hot sand and gravel. This found its way between their armour and skin, causing horrible burns, and forced them to retreat.

At this point, however, part of the south-east wall collapsed from the continual bombardment. Alexander ordered a concentrated attack on this opening and, when driven back, a second from all sides. The defenders on the walls were overwhelmed. After savage street-fighting, Tyre was taken. The fury of the Macedonians building up during the seven months' siege was now let loose. Tyre, like Thebes, was razed to the ground. Several thousand men, women and children were slaughtered, thirty thousand made slaves and two thousand men of military age crucified.

The journey to the Siwah Oasis: spring 331 BC

The Egyptians were wise enough not to resist Alexander. He had himself crowned pharaoh in Memphis and then disappeared with a

handful of followers into the desert. His destination was the Siwah Oasis where the oracle of Zeus-Amon stood, a place specially holy to both Egyptians and Greeks. It was believed that the priests and priestesses of oracles could speak directly with the gods, so their advice was greatly valued. Alexander lost his way, and almost his life, in the desert but was delighted with the result of his visit. He never told anyone what he asked the Siwah oracle nor the answer he got. All he said was that he had 'been told what his heart desired'. Most of his friends believed (and most historians agree with them) that he had been told that he was the son of a god.

The Battle of Issus: the first battle in which Darius and Alexander met face to face. The bare-headed Alexander tries to force his way through to attack the Persian King, whose charioteer struggles to get clear of the battlefield. This is a Roman copy of a Greek painting.

The Battle of Gaugamela: late summer 331 BC

The Persian Emperor, Darius III, was trying to revenge the defeats which he had already suffered at Alexander's hands. He laid his plans most carefully and when the armies finally met near the River Tigris by the village of Gaugamela, a Persian victory seemed certain. Darius' army was far larger. Moreover he was fighting on a battlefield which he himself had chosen. Gaugamela stood on a wide, flat, treeless plain which would allow the Persians to make the fullest use of their advantage in numbers; also of their most dangerous attacking force, the regiment of chariots with sharp scythes fixed to their wheels. Alexander made a careful inspection of the battlefield and then sat up late into the night alone in his tent making his plans. He slept so soundly that the next morning his senior general, Parmenio, had to shake him awake. The army was breakfasted and ready to move. Yet the generals did not yet know what the battle plans were!

The plain was so dry that once the fighting started, those taking part were hidden from each other by clouds of dust. It was not easy, therefore, to be sure how exactly the battle went. Somehow the Persians were completely defeated.

Gaugamela was the most important victory for Alexander. Darius was finished. Within a year he had been murdered by one of his former followers. There was no one left around whom the Persians could rally. Alexander was now the unchallenged master of the Persian Empire.

The murder of Cleitus the Black: summer 328 BC

Tempers were rising among the Macedonian soldiers. They had spent a tiresome summer trying, without much success, to bring the wild tribesmen in the north-east of the Persian Empire under control. Alexander was making matters worse by seeming to favour the Persians who had recently joined the army and by becoming more Persian himself. He started wearing Persian clothes, and tried to insist that everyone who came into his presence should touch the floor with their forehead as a sign of their respect. The Macedonians thought this ridiculous and an insult to them as free men.

One evening Alexander held a party at which he and many of his guests became very drunk. He started boasting about his skill as a commander. This was too much for Cleitus (nicknamed the Black to distinguish him from another commander, Cleitus the White). He was a tough old Macedonian warrior who had once saved Alexander's life.

'It is by the blood of Macedonians and by these wounds of ours,' he said, 'that you have risen so high.' He then added, 'And you reject your real father Philip of Macedon and claim the god Amon as your father.'

This criticism of his claims to be a god further angered Alexander, who made some sneering remark about Macedonian stupidity aside to one of his companions.

'Say what you mean openly,' roared Cleitus, 'or stop dining with men who are free and speak their minds. Content yourself rather with slaves and barbarian creatures who will lie flat on the floor in front of you in your white robe and Persian sash.'

Members of his bodyguard tried to hold back Alexander, who was now wild with rage, but breaking free, he seized a spear from a guard and ran Cleitus through, killing him instantly.

The next few days showed what an astonishing hold he had on his men. Perhaps genuinely horrified by what he had done, perhaps just pretending, Alexander took to his tent. For three days he refused to eat or drink. It seemed that he might starve to death leaving the army leaderless in the middle of nowhere. His Macedonians came to him.

Cleitus, they said, had been fairly punished. Alexander started eating again and when he led them off again on the next stage of their journey, they followed him without hesitation.

The army will go no farther: summer 326 BC

Two years later, however, they could take no more. In that time Alexander had marched them over the Hindu Kush mountains and down into the Indus valley where they met their fiercest enemy to date. He kept them going through the damp and heat of the Indian monsoon until they reached the River Hyphasis (the modern Beas), which they refused to cross. It was swollen and dangerous and farther on, they were told, were other rivers just as dangerous. There were ferocious tribes, too, one of whose kings could put at least four thousand fighting elephants into battle against them. One of the few things that really scared the Macedonians was the elephant. Would they ever see Macedonia again, more and more of them asked themselves. First Alexander threatened them, then he pleaded with them. It made no difference. 'Sire,' said one of his oldest generals, 'if there is one thing a successful man should know, it is when to stop.' Alexander tried sulking in his tent. This time it had no effect. He had no choice but to turn for home.

How much farther will he go? The River Jaxartes, 4000 kilometres from Greece, deep in central Asia.

The death of Alexander: June 323 BC

He was never to see Macedonia again. Back in Babylon, he took a boat trip through the Euphrates marshes to inspect some irrigation canals. It seems likely that he picked up an infection (possibly malaria) which he made worse by heavy drinking on his return. When they heard that he was dying, his soldiers demanded that they all should see him. A second door was knocked through his bedroom wall so that they could file silently by to pay their last respects. He was then so weak, he could scarcely raise his head. When asked by his closest friends who should rule the empire when he was gone, his only answer was 'the strongest'. He died on 10 June 323 BC when he was still only thirty-two.

The palace of Persepolis: what Alexander and time have left of it

Alexander's achievement

Most of his short life was spent as an army commander. As such he was one of the greatest the world has ever known. The loyalty which he won from his men has seldom been equalled. As a ruler his ability is hard to measure since he had so little time. His empire fell apart on his death, various of his generals seizing parts of it for themselves. None the less, shortlived though he and his empire were, his life was a turning-point. Where once had stretched the immense lands of the Persian emperors, first Greeks then Romans came to rule. More important, however, was the spread of the Greek language and Greek ideas. Unlike Alexander and his soldiers, these came to stay.

Using the evidence: the burning of Persepolis

Two different accounts of this event have survived from ancient times. The first is by Arrian.

He [Alexander] burnt the palace against the advice of Parmenio who suggested that he should spare it, mainly because it was hardly wise to destroy what was now his own property and because the Asians would, in his opinion, be less ready to support him if he seemed only to be passing through their country as a conqueror rather than ruling it securely as a king. Alexander's answer was that he wished to punish the Persians for their invasion of Greece, for the destruction of Athens, the burning of the temples and for all the other crimes against the Greeks. My own view is that this was bad policy; moreover it could hardly be considered as punishment of Persians long since dead and gone.

The second is by Diodorus Siculus.

A farewell party was held in Xerxes' palace. When the company was full of good cheer, many became very drunk. Then one of the women present, an Athenian by the name of Thaïs, announced that the finest deed Alexander could do in Asia would be to lead them in a triumphal procession round the palace and then set fire to it. These words excited the younger men, already very drunk, and someone shouted out to lead on, snatch up torches and revenge the wicked deeds of the Persians against the temples of the Greeks. Others took up the cry, saying that this deed was worthy of Alexander alone.

The king took fire at their words and all leapt up from their drinking to make a procession. Flares were collected and with women singing and playing flutes and pipes Thaïs followed Alexander in throwing her blazing torch into the palace. The others did the same and the whole building rapidly took flame. So it was that the wicked act of Xerxes, king of the Persians, against the Acropolis of Athens, was revenged in kind and in spirit many years afterwards by one woman, a fellow-citizen of those who had suffered.

Questions and further work

1 Reread the extract from Arrian, then answer these questions:
(a) Alexander and Parmenio disagree about what should be done with the palace. In your own words:
(i) explain why Alexander wished to destroy it;
(ii) explain why Parmenio wished to spare it.
(b) About what invasion of Greece is Alexander talking? How many years previously did it take place? (If you are not sure, you will find the answer on page 139.)
(c) What was Arrian's opinion of the destruction of the palace?
(d) What reasons does he give for this opinion?

2 Reread the extract from Diodorus Siculus, comparing it with Arrian's. Then answer these questions:
(a) Who is Thaïs? What part does she play in the events leading up to the destruction of the palace?
(b) Why do you think that Diodorus specially refers to the fact that she is an Athenian?
(c) What part of Diodorus' account suggests that it was the excitement of the party rather than a carefully thought-out decision that persuaded Alexander to burn the palace?

3 In which account does Alexander come out better? Explain your answer.

4 To this day, historians cannot agree over which of these accounts is the more likely to be true. Here are some of the points which they have considered.
(i) The closer a historian lives to the time about which he is writing, the less likely is his information to have been muddled in the passing of time.
(ii) No account of the reign of Alexander which we can read today was written while Alexander was still alive.
(iii) Diodorus lived in the first century BC. We do not know where he got his information and he seems to have copied it down without considering it very carefully.
(iv) Arrian lived from about AD 96–180. He has the reputation of being the most reliable of the historians of Alexander's reign and he tells us his information comes from the accounts of two of Alexander's generals, including one very close to Alexander, called Ptolemy.
(v) Ptolemy later married Thaïs. If Diodorus' account is true, do you

think Ptolemy would have included it in his section on Persepolis or not?

(vi) Cleitarchus of Alexandria writing only a generation after the death of Alexander states that Thaïs was the cause of the burning of the palace. But he has proved unreliable on other matters.

(vii) Alexander had previously carried out spectacular acts of destruction to leave people in no doubt that he was master (e.g. Thebes and Tyre).

(viii) Alexander was a heavy drinker and quite capable of violent acts while drunk which he later regretted (e.g. the murder of Cleitus who had once saved his life).

List those points which seem to you to show (a) that Diodorus is likely to be true and give your reasons, (b) that Arrian's account is true and give your reasons.

5 Which account of the burning of Persepolis do you believe to be the more accurate? Give reasons for your choice.

6 You are a survivor of *one* of the following: the destruction of Tyre in 332 BC; the Persian army defeated at Gaugamela in 331 BC; the Macedonian army which fought in India in 326 BC. Describe your experiences of that year either in words or in pictures.

The burning of Persepolis

The Romans

16 Early Rome and the Republic

The earliest Romans

Archaeologists believe that the ancestors of the Romans moved into the fertile Tiber valley from the north-east about 1000 BC. They and other groups spoke the language which was later to develop into Latin. Simple peasant farmers, they lived in villages of wattle huts. A bridge was built across the Tiber over which one of the main trade routes of Italy passed. As trade improved, the villages grew into a town on the slopes of what are now the Palatine and Capitoline hills. In Roman legend, the city was founded by Romulus in the year which, by our methods of dating, is 753 BC. (The Romans used the foundation of the city as the starting point of their method of dating in the same way as we use the birth of Christ.) With the help of another Roman legend we can glimpse something of early Rome.

Tarquin the Etruscan

In his *Early History of Rome*, Livy tells how the Romans had driven out their hated king, Tarquin the Proud. Tarquin, an Etruscan, gained the help of Lars Porsenna, king of Etruscan Clusium, and marched back to gain his revenge. He caught the Romans by surprise. They fled in panic leaving the wooden bridge across the Tiber undefended. If the

Beneath growling leopards, Etruscans wine and dine. This painting is in a tomb near Tarquinia.

Etruscans got across the bridge, Rome must fall. Just one Roman noble stood firm, Horatius. In Livy's words: 'he proudly took his stand at the outer end of the bridge . . . sword and shield ready for action, one man against an army. The advancing enemy paused in astonishment at his reckless courage'. Two other Roman heroes sprang to his side and together they fought off the attackers while behind them others rapidly demolished the bridge. Ordering his comrades to retire to safety, Horatius fought on until he heard the bridge collapse behind him. Then 'with a prayer to Father Tiber . . . he plunged fully armed into the water and swam through missiles which fell thick about him to the other side where his friends were waiting to receive him'. So Tarquin the Etruscan was foiled.

Archaeological evidence backs up this legend in important ways. From about 800 BC to 450 BC the Etruscans were the strongest and most civilised people in northern Italy. They controlled Rome for two or three generations during which time the town grew fast as a trading centre. We also know that Etruscan power was declining between 520 BC and 500 BC. The legendary Roman date for the end of Tarquin's rule, 510 BC, makes sense. Certainly from this time onwards to the time of the first emperor, Rome was proud to be a republic, i.e. a state without a king. Instead the state was governed by two consuls, elected each year, and the Senate, which was made up of the heads of the leading Roman families.

A Roman legionary soldier ready for battle (a modern model)

Between 509 BC and 264 BC Rome grew stronger. From being one of many small Etruscan-ruled cities it became the most powerful city in Italy.

A remarkable army was the key to this success. It was a citizen army. Every Roman between the ages of seventeen to forty-six might be called upon to fight in the field, and up to the age of sixty to man the city walls. This meant that in times of crisis it could be a very large army. At the height of the war against Hannibal, the Romans may have had more than a hundred thousand men under arms. By about 350 BC the main units were the legions of between four thousand and six thousand men divided into maniples of 120. They were well trained, well armed, and well disciplined. Usually the legions were well led, and in military methods they were almost always far in advance of their rivals.

Defeating first the Etruscans, then the Samnites, the Romans won control of central Italy. Disaster followed in 390 BC. An army of Gauls raiding south from the valley of the Po crushed the Roman army on the banks of the River Allia. They occupied and burnt most of the city. The Gauls were paid to leave and new, stronger fortifications built. Then the expansion of Roman power began once more, this time southwards towards the Greek colonies of southern Italy and Sicily. The Greek cities were wealthy but they were no match for the Roman army. Only when Tarentum asked for help from Pyrrhus, king of Epirus, did the Romans have a real struggle on their hands. Eventually they won and, by 266 BC, the whole Italian mainland south of the River Po was Roman.

The Roman army in action

Setting up camp. Though there is a tent in the background, the camp walls are being built of solid brick.

Attacking an enemy fort. The legionaries make a 'tortoise' of their shields as they near the wall.

After the battle, the wounded are cared for. Standard-bearers can also be seen. (These three scenes are on the Column of the Emperor Trajan which still stands in Rome.)

The Punic Wars

Temptingly close to the toe of the Italian mainland lay the island of Sicily, rich in corn and commerce. Much of Sicily, however, was ruled by Carthage, the great trading city founded by the Phoenicians on the north African coast. With an excellent fleet and a large hired army, Carthage was the most dangerous enemy the Romans had yet faced. The winner of any war between Rome and Carthage would have the whole of the western Mediterranean as a prize. War came in 264 BC when the Romans broke a treaty of friendship with Carthage and invaded Sicily. During this First Punic War (so named because the Romans called the Carthaginians *Poeni* or Phoenicians) the Romans did well on land but at first, being inexperienced sailors, suffered disaster after disaster at sea. Typically, they learned from their mistakes. They designed ships which, instead of ramming the enemy like the Carthaginian ships, could be grappled or hooked to the side of the enemy. This provided a firm platform from which the soldiers on the Roman ships could attack. However, storms destroyed two fleets and the government ran out of money. Still the Romans refused to give up. Wealthy citizens clubbed together to raise money for a new fleet of two hundred ships, which won a great victory at the Battle of Aegates. The Carthaginians had had enough after twenty-three years of war. They agreed to leave Sicily and to pay Rome 3300 talents of silver.

Hannibal

In this war, the most formidable of the Carthaginian generals had been Hamilcar Barca. He led the Carthaginian army to Spain, quickly conquered a large area there and, with Spanish silver, paid off the money still owing to Rome. He is said to have forced his eldest son, Hannibal, when he was only a boy of nine, to swear undying hatred of Rome. By the time he was twenty-six, this Hannibal was commander of the Carthaginian armies and enlarging his father's conquests in Spain. In 219 BC the Romans ordered Carthage to surrender a city Hannibal had captured. They were also to hand over Hannibal. The next thing the Romans knew, Hannibal was marching on Italy and the Second Punic War had begun. Moving very fast, Hannibal took a dangerous route through the Alps (see the Using the evidence section), dodged the Roman armies defending the approaches into Italy and descended into the Po valley. Under his brilliant leadership, the Carthaginian army savaged the Roman armies time and time again. Victory on the River Trebia opened the way into central Italy. Consul Flaminius marched north to meet him. The armies met on the shores of Lake Trasimene. By skilful marching, Hannibal had Flaminius totally confused.

A Carthaginian coin showing the head of Hannibal

As soon as he had him penned in by the mountains and surrounded from the front, rear and flank, he gave the orders for a simultaneous attack. Down they came from the hills, taking the Romans completely unprepared. The unexpectedness of the attack was increased by the morning mist.

So Livy described the opening of the Battle of Lake Trasimene, which ended with the destruction of most of the Roman army, including Flaminius, in the marshes between the lake and the surrounding hills.

The Carthaginians were now within three days' march of Rome. In this crisis, the Senate placed Fabius in command of the war. He realised that the only way to deal with Hannibal was to wear him out by time and patience, to trust Rome's fortifications and to avoid open battle, since Hannibal lacked the siege engines necessary for an assault on Rome's walls. Fabius was right but his methods were too slow for the mood of the Romans in 216 BC. Two new consuls marched against Hannibal and to disaster once again. At Cannae, they were trapped and destroyed. Panic gripped Rome. The gods must be angry was the cry. To please the gods two Gauls and two Greeks, a man and a woman of each race, were buried alive. Hannibal's commanders urged him to ride directly against Rome. Hannibal refused. 'You know how to win a battle, Hannibal,' said his cousin, Maharbal, in despair, 'but you do not know how to use a victory.'

Hannibal moved instead into southern Italy to get food and supplies for his army and to persuade other cities to end their alliances with Rome and to join him. The Romans had time to recover. Their army in Sicily captured Syracuse and their fleet did well at sea. Suddenly Hannibal appeared out of the blue beneath the walls of Rome. The terrified citizens saw him clearly riding up and down on his coal-black stallion. Then he was gone as suddenly as he had come. The walls were too strong for an assault and his army too small for a siege.

The year 207 BC decided the war. Hasdrubal, Hannibal's brother, entered Italy from the north bringing much-needed reinforcements. He sent messengers to Hannibal, still in the south, to fix a meeting place. The messengers got lost and were captured by the Romans. Claudius Nero, the Roman consul, went into action straight away. He led north his army which had been watching Hannibal, joined up with a second Roman army, found Hasdrubal on the banks of the River Metaurus and attacked at once. After a hard-fought battle, the Carthaginians were defeated. When Hasdrubal realised all was lost, he rode into the thick of the fighting and was killed. The first news Hannibal had of this defeat was his brother's head tossed down outside his camp. 'Now at last I see the destiny of Carthage plain,' were his despairing words when he realised his brother was dead and the chance of complete victory gone.

Hannibal's conqueror, Scipio Africanus

Victory for Rome

Though Hannibal remained unbeaten in Italy for another three years, Roman armies were victorious everywhere else. Their best general, Scipio, first conquered Spain and then invaded north Africa. Hannibal left Italy to defend his homeland and, at Zama in 202 BC met Scipio and, for the first and only time in his life, defeat. Carthage asked for peace. She lost her empire and her fleet. Hannibal fled into exile and, rather than face captivity in Rome, committed suicide.

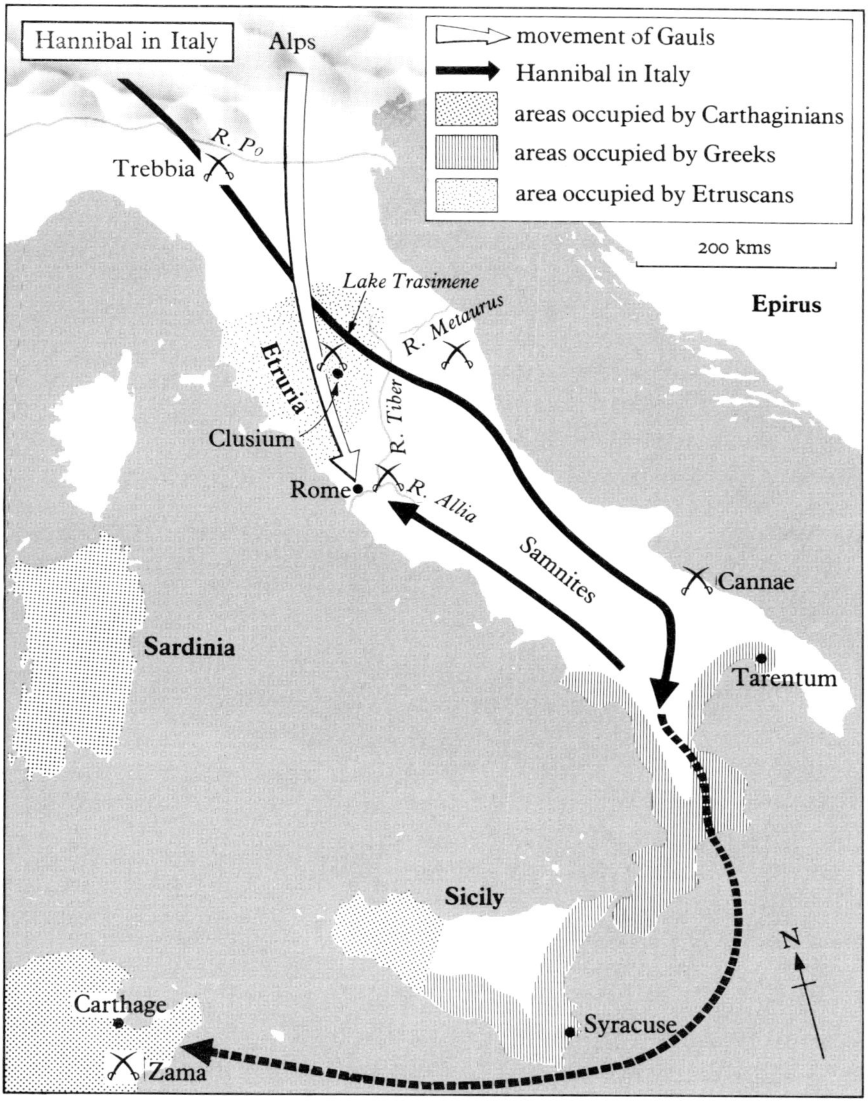

Just how the Romans managed in the end to win this extraordinary war, during which they lost so many battles, tells us much about the Romans themselves. They were obstinate, patient and determined. Though scared stiff by Hannibal, they never seriously considered peace without victory. They were able to put army after army into the field to replace their losses. They chose leaders like Fabius, who was wise, and generals like Scipio, who was brilliant. And perhaps most important of all, they never lost the support of most of the Italian cities even though many of them had been enemies, conquered in war only a few generations earlier. Italy had learned already that Roman rule had many advantages and stayed loyal through these dangerous and destructive years.

Carthage defeated, no other Mediterranean power could match the

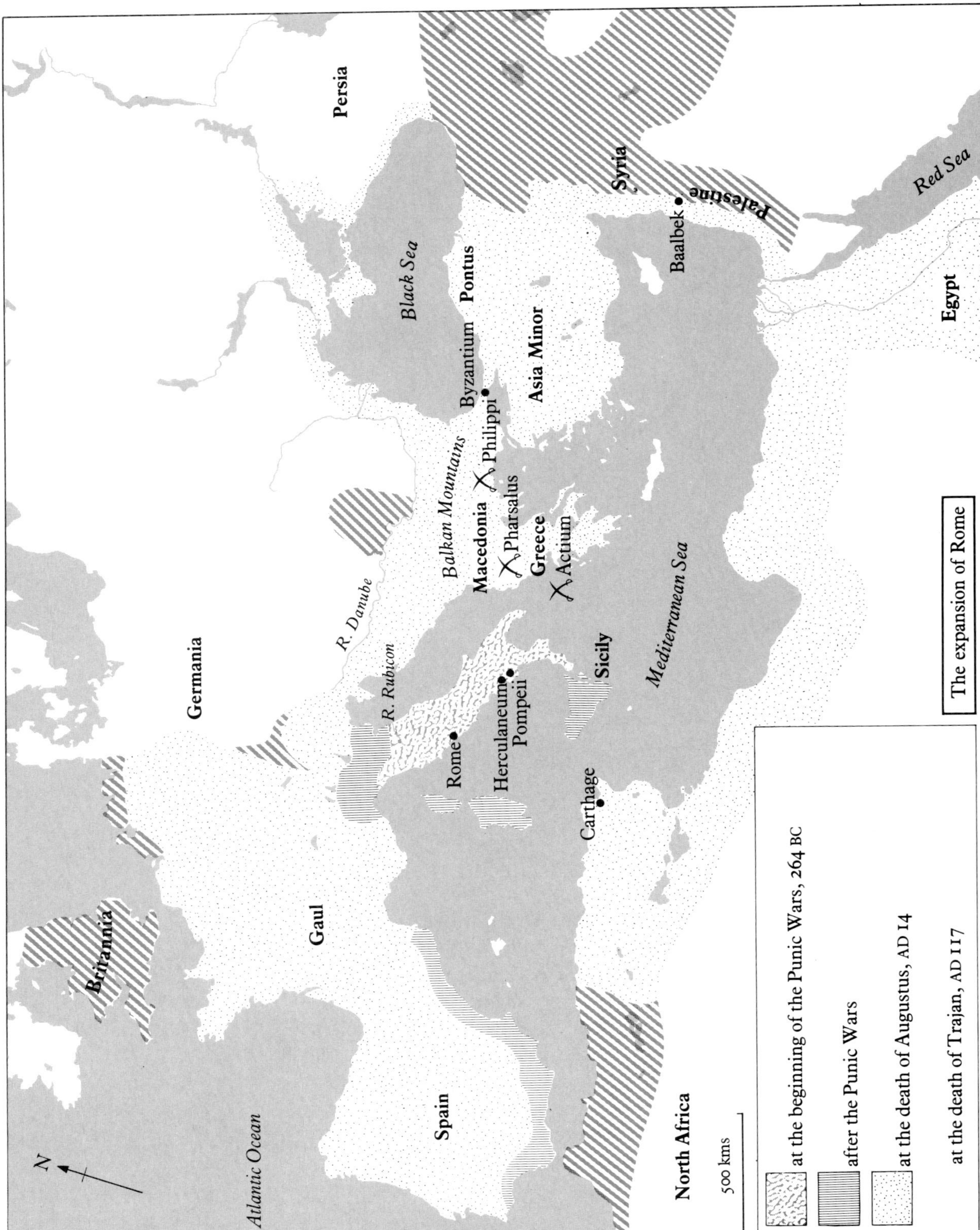

The expansion of Rome

might of Rome. First Macedonia, then Greece, Asia Minor, Syria, Palestine and Egypt fell to her generals. By the middle of the first century BC the Mediterranean was a Roman sea.

At home, Roman society was changing fast. The Punic Wars had been won by the citizen armies. Most of the soldiers were peasant farmers when they were not at war. A hundred years later they had been replaced by paid full-time professional soldiers who were loyal first to their generals, only then to Rome. The Italian countryside had suffered terribly during the Second Punic War. Peasant farming was replaced by ranch-type farms often managed by stewards while the owners lived elsewhere. The victorious armies brought back hundreds of thousands of slaves from their campaigns who were used increasingly for labour both in the country and in the cities. In the past, Romans had prided themselves on their simple life and willingness to work hard. Now they were able to enjoy luxuries and were ready to live off the work of others.

A slave rests with his load

Slavery

Like most ancient peoples, the Romans took slavery for granted. They used slaves especially as farm workers, household servants, clerical assistants in business and as mine workers. In times of war, slaves were made from prisoners, in times of peace they were bred from existing slaves. Some owners made fortunes as slave breeders. During the later Empire, both Christian and non-Christian writers criticised slavery as evil and the number of slaves grew less.

The Republic threatened

There had been many serious disagreements over how Rome should be governed since the Republic had been set up. On the one hand was the Senate representing the nobility, on the other the Assembly which spoke for the ordinary people. During the Punic Wars, the Senate had made most of the major decisions. In the second century BC however, its powers were called into question by the brothers Tiberius and Gaius Gracchus. Tiberius, backed by the Assembly, tried to change the way land was distributed in order that the poorer citizens might gain. The Senate opposed him since the nobility were the main landowners. During serious rioting in 133 BC, Tiberius and three hundred of his supporters were clubbed to death. Ten years later Gaius Gracchus, again supported by the Assembly, planned further changes which the Senate hated. He too was murdered, with three thousand supporters. The murders of the two brothers showed how far members of the Roman nobility were ready to go to keep their wealth and their privileges. They marked the beginning of a hundred years of wars, plots, assassination and mass murder where ambitious, unscrupulous and violent men struggled to win control of Rome and, through Rome, of most of the known world.

There was a pattern to the careers of these men. Through ability or luck or the influence of their friends and relations, they gained command of an army. With this army they won victories and plenty of loot for their soldiers and themselves. They returned in triumph to Rome to the cheers of the mob and made themselves powerful in politics by getting rid of their rivals by fair means or foul.

An early example was Marius (157 BC to 86 BC). He defeated Jugurtha, a powerful north African king; drove away Celtic tribes, who invaded northern Italy; and crushed a revolt of Italian cities. He, more than anyone, turned the Roman army into a professional paid force and showed how useful it could be to ambitious generals. He was consul seven times, the last time after he had led his army into Rome and murdered many of his opponents.

Another such general was Sulla, Marius' second-in-command during the African wars. He won a great victory over Mithridates, king of Pontus, (see the map, page 176) which made him and his soldiers rich. On his return to Italy, he marched on Rome. He murdered 1640 of his opponents, whose property he took for himself, his family and friends. He kept all power in his own hands until he retired a year before his death. The inscription which he wrote for his tomb read: 'No man ever did more good to his friends and more harm to his enemies.' He knew himself well.

A third was Pompey, who had been one of Sulla's commanders. He helped suppress a revolt in Spain and then ended the pirate menace which was threatening the city's food supplies. Between 66 BC and 63 BC he conquered a large area of western Asia, defeated Mithridates once and for all and returned to Rome laden with treasure.

Julius Caesar

Pompey, though a brilliant soldier, was a poorer politician than his great rival, Julius Caesar. Caesar was unusually ambitious, clever, energetic, confident and brave. We have a good idea of his personality from the time when, aged twenty-three, he was captured by pirates. They wanted a ransom of twenty talents. 'You do not know whom you have caught,' Caesar declared. 'I am worth at least fifty.' He sent off one of his companions to raise this huge sum. When the money was paid and the pirates set him free, his parting words were to promise that he would track them down, recover his money and crucify them all; which is exactly what he did.

To begin with he took care to be friendly with Pompey, and used his friendship to get command of an army. He took this army to conquer Gaul (58 BC to 50 BC) and to raid Britain (55 BC to 54 BC). At the same time, he was careful to keep plenty of supporters in Rome since his friendship with Pompey was cooling. By 49 BC it was clear that the Roman world was not big enough for the two of them. In December, Caesar's army stood beside the Rubicon stream, which was the most southern boundary of the area in which the law allowed him to lead an army. If he crossed it, there must be a war. For one of the few times in his life he hesitated and stood in the chilly night discussing with his

Julius Caesar

Pompey

companions what to do. Suddenly he broke away from the group. 'The die is cast,' he said and strode across the bridge. The Civil War had begun.

Pompey and the senatorial party had the larger army but Caesar, clear about his aims, moved more quickly. Italy was his before Pompey had time to get organised and the main fighting took place in Greece. At the decisive battle of Pharsalus (48 BC) Caesar's infantry dealt with Pompey's dangerous cavalry by jabbing their spears directly into their faces. Pompey fled to Egypt, where government officials had him murdered as he stepped ashore and sent his head to Caesar.

For the next five years, Caesar was master of Rome and made no attempt to hide the fact. He had an ivory statue of himself carried in procession round the city. In public he wore a purple gown and a laurel wreath. He sat in a gilded chair and abandoned the custom of rising to his feet when speaking to other senators. In 44 BC coins bearing his head started to appear. Led by Brutus and by Cassius, a group of senators were convinced that he was intending to make himself king. To save the Republic they decided that they must assassinate him. On the Ides of March (15 March) the Senate met in Pompey's theatre. At the foot of Pompey's statue, they attacked Caesar with daggers. According to Suetonius, he struggled to escape until he saw Brutus coming at him with dagger raised. He had a special affection for Brutus, who may have been his natural son. 'You too, my child,' was all he said and, covering his head with his toga, died.

The end of the Republic

The assassins had no clear idea what to do next. While they dithered, Antony, Caesar's leading supporter and Octavian, his nephew, gathered their forces. In Rome they murdered 2300 of their enemies, real and imagined, and at Philippi in Greece in 42 BC destroyed the army of Brutus and Cassius, both of whom committed suicide. Octavian and Antony then agreed to divide the Roman world between them. Octavian knew that a final conflict between the two of them must come and typically got on with his preparations. Antony for his part enjoyed life with Cleopatra, the beautiful but scheming queen of Egypt. The final conflict was not long delayed. Agrippa won the naval battle of Actium (31 BC), off the coast of western Greece, for Octavian. Back in Egypt first Antony, then Cleopatra, committed suicide.

Octavian was now master of the Roman world. However, he was careful to avoid using the hated title 'king'. He made the Senate feel that it still mattered, and continued the Republic in name at least. But in all important matters, power lay in the hands of one man. He took the name Augustus and on his death his power passed to his stepson Tiberius. The Roman Republic was dead. In its place had come the Roman Empire.

gustus rebuilt much of Rome and later perors followed his example. Here you see the Forum Romanum, the heart the ancient city. The ruins of public ildings, temples and arches spread over arge area. In the background lies a ge oval amphitheatre, the Colosseum. y to imagine how it looked in Roman es.

The reverse side of the coin on page 173

Using the evidence: Hannibal's crossing of the Alps, 218 BC

Answer the questions as you go along.

Leaving Spain behind, Hannibal marched swiftly across what is now southern France. A Roman army, led by Scipio, guarded the coast road into Italy and so Hannibal decided to cross the River Rhône well inland, about four days' march from the sea. However, he found his way across the river blocked by a barbarian tribe. Keeping the main force with him, he sent Hanno upriver with a smaller force which, having crossed without opposition, came back along the opposite bank. Polybius now takes up the story:

Hannibal got his soldiers ready. He filled the boats with the light cavalry and the canoes with the lightest infantry. The large boats were placed highest upstream to take the full force of the current. Some horses were towed swimming behind the boats. One man on each side of the stern guided the horses so a large number got across with the first batch. Sure that they could easily prevent the Carthaginians from landing, the barbarians poured out of their camp scattered and in no order. . . . Hannibal knew that Hanno's force was near at hand from a pre-arranged smoke-signal. As Hannibal's army crossed the river, the Carthaginians on the far bank attacked suddenly and unexpectedly. With everything turning out as he had planned, Hannibal led the attack on the barbarians and put them to flight.

1 (a) In your own words explain Hannibal's plan.
(b) What was the job of Hanno's force?
(c) Why do you think Hannibal insisted that the bigger boats take the full force of the current?

Hannibal's elephants cross the Rhône. How well does this modern picture fit in with the evidence of Polybius?

The next problem was to get the elephants across. Most were moved safely on great rafts piled high with earth and grass to make them look like land. Polybius continues:

Some however were so frightened that they threw themselves into the river half-way across. Their riders were all drowned but the elephants were saved since, owing to the length of their trunks, they kept them above water and breathed through them.

The Carthaginians then advanced up the east bank of the River Rhône. After a four-day march, they reached the 'island', a fertile triangle of land made by the Rhône and one of its tributary rivers on two sides and a range of mountains on the third. Hannibal then marched for ten days, a distance of eight hundred stades (130 kilometres) along the tributary river and began to climb the Alps.

He now faced great difficulties. The local chieftain of the Allobrogians got a large army into a strong position overlooking the Carthaginians' route. Hannibal made camp and learned from his scouts that at night the enemy returned to their town nearby. He therefore ordered fires to be lit in his camp and, leaving most of his army there, led his best soldiers by night and lightly armed through the rough hills and took the position which the enemy had left.

The next morning he charged down on the approaching Allobrogians and drove them off.

2 (a) What mistake did the Allobrogians make?
(b) Why did Hannibal order that the camp fires be left burning?
(c) What was daring about Hannibal's actions that night?

Four days farther on he was again in the greatest danger. His treacherous native guides led him into an ambush in a narrow and precipitous gorge. The army was temporarily split in two and suffered heavy losses. Fortunately the natives were terrified of the elephants and kept their distance. After a nine days' climb, Hannibal reached the summit. There he halted to wait for the stragglers.

As it was now near to the setting of the Pleiades [November], snow was already gathering on the summit. Hannibal saw that the men were in low spirits since they had already suffered much and expected worse to come. To cheer them up he called them together and pointed out Italy to them which lay close beneath these mountains. He showed them the Po valley, reminded them that the Gauls were friendly and to some extent raised their spirits.

The descending path was very narrow and steep. Neither men nor beasts could tell on what they were treading because of the snow and all those who stepped wide of the path or stumbled were dashed down the precipice. The going was made even more slippery as new snow was falling on ice from the year before. They then reached a place where it was impossible for the elephants and pack animals to pass, a land-slip having carried away about one-and-a-half stades (several hundred metres) of the mountain side.

Hannibal first tried a detour but a fresh fall of snow made this impossible.

So he camped on a ridge and set his soldiers the most difficult task of cutting a path out of the mountainside. After a day, the passage was wide enough for the pack-animals and horses. It took three days to get the elephants through. By then they were in a wretched condition from hunger.

He continued his descent with all his forces and after three days march from the precipice reached flat country. The whole march had taken five months and the crossing of the Alps fifteen days. Now as he boldly entered the plain of the Po and the land of the Insubres, his surviving army numbered twelve thousand African and eight thousand Spanish infantry and six thousand cavalry.

The rough, cold Alps. Up a valley such as this the Carthaginians marched.

3 (a) List the main dangers of the descent into Italy.
(b) How did Hannibal solve the problem of the path carried away in a land-slip?

Hannibal as a leader

4 There were several occasions when Hannibal's army faced disaster. Describe briefly when these were and how Hannibal won through.
5 Hannibal was a cunning general. Give examples of his cunning.
6 In what other ways was Hannibal a good leader?
7 Sketch as excitingly as you can either the crossing of the Rhône or the descent of the Alps. Make sure what you draw fits Polybius' account.
8 Imagine that you were one of the elephant riders on this journey from Spain to Italy. Describe your experiences.

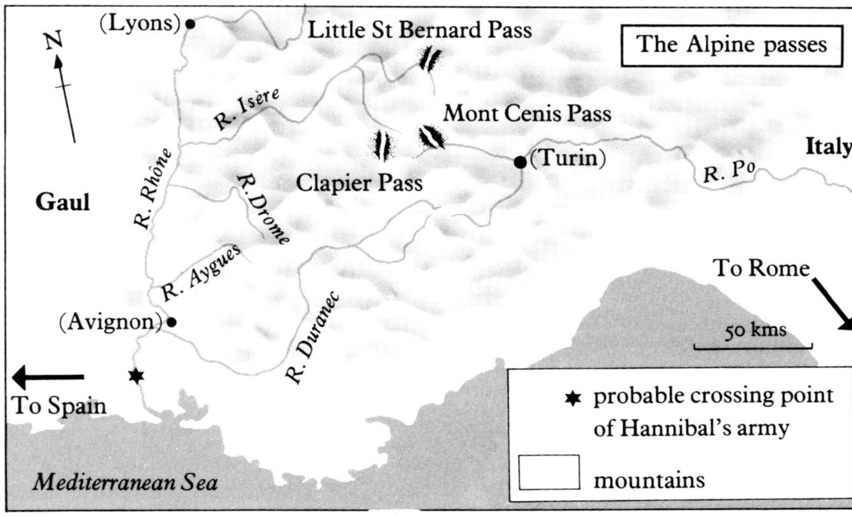

Which route did he take?

Historians disagree over which route Hannibal actually took across the Alps. Study the map above and re-read the extracts from Polybius on pages 181–2.

The 'island' and the rivers

9 (a) There are two possible places where the 'island' might be. Where?
(b) According to Polybius the Carthaginians marched 130 kilometres along the tributary river which runs into the Rhône beside the 'island'. Which is the more likely, the River Isère or the River Aygues? Explain your answer.

The passes into Italy

If he went along the Isère valley, the three passes it is most likely Hannibal would choose from are the Little St Bernard, the Mont Cenis and the Clapier.

Little St Bernard	2179 metres	No view of Italy	Moderate descent
Mont Cenis	2078 metres	Good view	Easy descent
Clapier	2491 metres	Good view	Difficult descent

Only at 2286 metres and higher is snow likely to remain from the previous year.

10 Which of these three passes best fits Polybius' description? Explain your answer.

Show which way Hannibal went

11 Copy the outline map above. On it mark Hannibal's route. Clearly marked should be the Rhône, the Alps, the Po Valley, the 'island', the tributary river and the pass across the Alps.

17 The Roman Empire

How do we know about Ancient Rome?

Let us take as our example Nero, one of the less pleasant men who became Roman emperor.

We can get a good idea of what he looked like from coins and statues, and of events of his reign and their dates from inscriptions on tombs and monuments. Nero was interested in art and architecture and had built for himself a luxurious palace, usually known as the Golden House. We know of this palace from archaeological excavations and from written descriptions. Tacitus, one of Rome's greatest historians, wrote:

> He built himself a palace remarkable not so much for its gold and silver as for its meadows, lakes and artificial wildernesses now of woods and now of views and open spaces.

Tacitus also tells us much about Nero and his doings but the most lively account is that of Suetonius who included Nero in his *Lives of the Caesars*, which were written in AD 125 about sixty years after Nero died. Here are some extracts.

His appearance

> He was about average height, his body marked with spots and smelly, his hair light-blond, his face regular rather than handsome, his eyes blue and rather weak, his neck too thick, his belly noticeable and his legs very slender.

His love of popularity

> His worst vice was to be carried away by a craze for popularity and he was jealous of anyone who stirred the feelings of the mob. His great ambition

Nero

Perhaps Nero chose the design of this wall-decoration which was once part of his 'Golden House'

was to compete in the Olympics for he was always practising wrestling and attending gymnastic competitions.

Nero on a coin with his mother Agrippina

His treatment of his mother Agrippina

He was keen to get rid of his mother because she disliked his mistress, Poppaea. (He was already married to Octavia whom he later divorced and murdered!)

After three times attempting to murder her by poison and finding that she had made herself immune by antidotes, he had the ceiling of her bedroom so engineered that it would collapse upon her while she slept. When news of this came out, he had a collapsible boat constructed to destroy her by shipwreck or by the collapse of her cabin.

(This failed too because though the boat did collapse as planned, Agrippina, a strong swimmer, made it to the shore!)

On learning that everything had gone wrong, he had a dagger thrown down beside her messenger and accused her of plotting to kill the Emperor. He had her killed and told the world that she had committed suicide knowing that she was guilty of treason.

His death

Nero fled from Rome after a successful revolt against his rule. As his enemies closed in on him, he cut his throat; according to Suetonius his dying words were: 'What an artist the world is losing.'

How do we know?

An elegant Roman lady

We know about Nero from writers like Tacitus and Suetonius, from archaeology, from inscriptions, from coins and statues. These are the main kinds of evidence for all periods of Roman history though the importance of each varies. Archaeological evidence is always important as the Using the evidence sections on Pompeii and Herculaneum (pages 192–5) and on Roman Cirencester (pages 202–207) show. It is also vital for the very early history of Rome to about 220 BC. The written evidence, including the famous legends of Romulus and Remus and of Aeneas fleeing from burning Troy to settle eventually in Italy, is extremely unreliable. It improves after 220 BC thanks to historians like Polybius (see pages 181–3). It remains patchy, however. We know far more about Julius Caesar and Pompey, for example, than we know about the Gracchi brothers, simply because more that was written about them has survived. We also know much more about the years AD 353 to 378 than about any other twenty-five years of the later Roman Empire because the last great Roman historian, Ammianus Marcellinus, concentrated on those few years. As always the surviving written evidence needs to be read with the greatest care. The Using the evidence section on the conversion of the Emperor Constantine to Christianity shows this (see pages 215–18).

Rome triumphant

Edward Gibbon, whose *Decline and Fall of the Roman Empire* is among the most famous histories of the Roman Empire, thought the hundred years leading up to the death of the Emperor Marcus Aurelius in AD 180 'the period in the history of the world during which the condition of the human race was most happy and prosperous'. Many other historians have agreed with him and they echo what many Romans themselves thought. Here, for example, is what Aetius Aristides, a Greek who was also a Roman citizen, wrote about AD 150.

Greek and barbarian with his possessions or without them can go wherever he likes ... to be safe it is enough to be a Roman or a subject of Rome.... You [Rome] have measured the whole world, spanned rivers with bridges, cut through mountains to make level roads for traffic, filled desolate places with farms and made life easier by supplying its necessities amid law and order. Everywhere are gymnasia, fountains, gateways, temples, factories and schools. The world which from its beginnings has been labouring in illness has now been made healthy. Cities are radiant in their splendour and the whole earth is as trim as a garden.

The Forum Romanum at the height of the Roman Empire. Compare this modern model with the photo on page 180.

This marvellous world has not disappeared completely. The best way to get the feel of Roman life is to walk through the streets of Pompeii and Herculaneum in southern Italy. Pompeii was a bustling trading town of about twenty thousand inhabitants; Herculaneum smaller, quieter and more residential. Both lay on the shores of the Bay of Naples, one of the richest and most fashionable areas of Roman Italy. Both lay near the volcano Vesuvius and on 24 August AD 79 a huge eruption buried them suddenly, swiftly and completely along with many of their inhabitants (see the Using the evidence section). But though buried, they were not destroyed. In the last two hundred years much of both cities has been uncovered and can now be visited.

We enter Pompeii through the Marine Gate which is set in the town walls overlooking the sea. There were two sets of parallel walls each nine metres thick with towers evenly spread along them. They had been built in the centuries before the Romans finally took control of Pompeii in 89 BC. Now with all Italy at peace they were not needed. The street rises steeply and leads us directly among temples and other public buildings. On our left is the Temple of

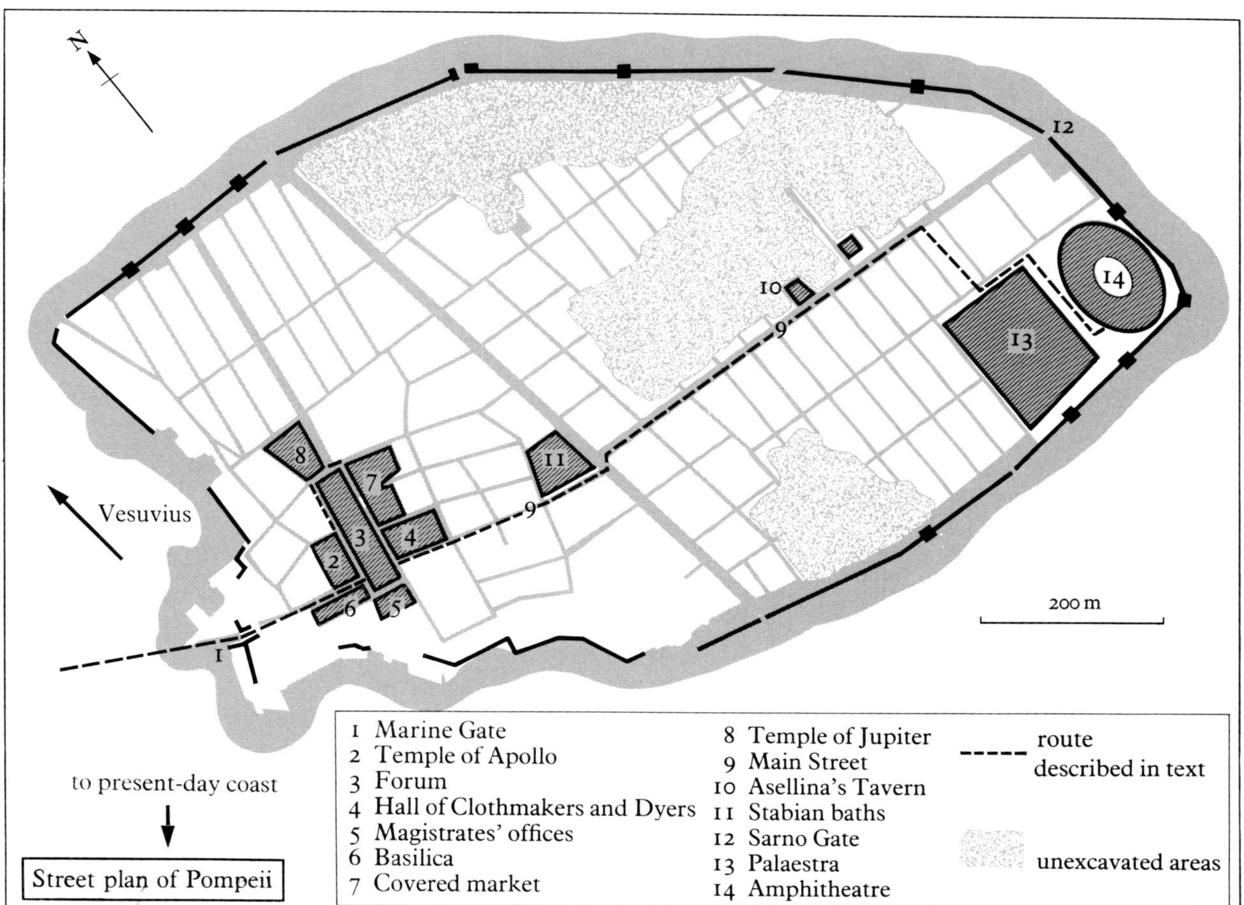

Street plan of Pompeii

Apollo. In its central courtyard, lined by forty-eight columns, stands a statue of the god. His hands once held a bow.

Past this temple lies the forum. This great rectangular space was forbidden to traffic. It was the centre of business, of justice and law. Its walls were covered with advertisements and public notices. A number of important buildings opened on to the forum. Opposite to us as we enter from the Marine Gate is the Hall of the Clothmakers and Dyers. They were one of the most important groups of workers in Pompeii, the wool for their trade coming from the hills of southern Italy. Their hall was beautifully decorated with statues and wall-paintings. On the short south side of the forum were the magistrates' offices and next to them across the road from the Temple of Apollo was the basilica.

Pompeii: the Forum. Looking southwards away from Vesuvius towards the magistrates' offices at the far end. To their right is the Temple of Apollo. In the right foreground is the Temple of Jupiter.

In a Roman town the basilica was a law-court, a trading centre, a place where business men could meet to discuss affairs and where those with nothing better to do could pass the time. (Many carved bits of poetry on the marble!) The Pompeian basilica was large for a town of twenty thousand and old, dating from about 130 BC. At the opposite north-east end of the forum was a covered market which included a small temple, a money-changer's booth and an auction room. The most impressive building of all, the Temple of Jupiter, filled the whole of the northern side. It stood on a marble platform three metres high and guarding the steps leading up to its columned entrance stood two marble horsemen.

We leave the forum by the exit next to the Clothworkers Hall. We are now in one of Pompeii's busiest streets. The ruts in the paving stones show how much traffic there must have been. The paving stones were for the convenience of pedestrians. In the torrential downpours of this part of Italy they would otherwise have got their feet both soaking and filthy. Along this street were luxury shops and offices. There were also taverns, like Asellina's, which sold wine both hot and cold. When it was first excavated, wine jars, cups and the stove were all in place.

The tavern was well-placed for business since the public baths, a

Pompeii: Asellina's Tavern

Pompeii: the main street. The shops were set well back from the roadway. The stepping stones and ruts left by chariot wheels can be seen clearly.

most important centre of Roman social life, was just along the street. This one, the Stabian Baths, was the oldest in Pompeii, there was another near the forum and a third was being built. They were like a modern sports centre, sauna bath and social club combined. The Romans, especially the men, spent hours there both by day and by night. At the Stabian Baths even the toilet seats were finished in marble and so arranged that those using them could chat together in comfort.

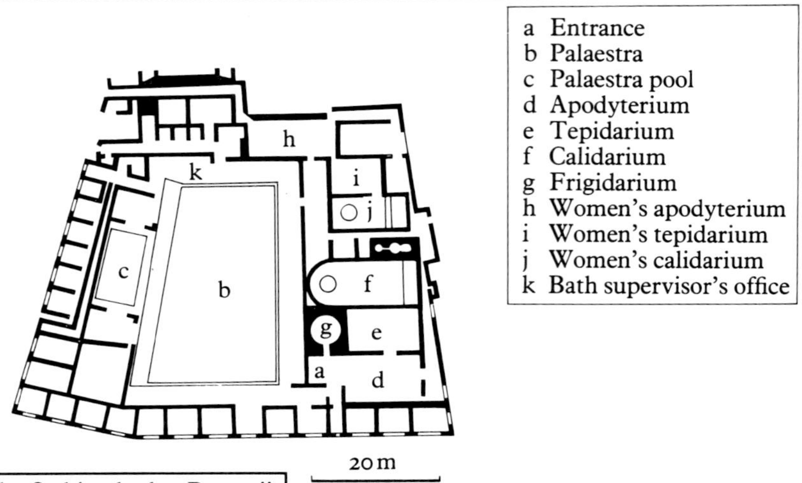

The Stabian baths, Pompeii

Pompeii: the tepidarium *or lukewarm bath. (This one was in the Forum baths.)*

A visit to the baths might go like this (see the plan). The visitor would enter at (a). He would take some exercise in the *palaestra* or games area (b). Bowls, boxing, wrestling, running, throwing the discus and weightlifting were all available. A cool dip in the palaestra pool would be followed by a rub-down and a massage. He would then enter the baths proper. Leaving his clothes in the care of an attendant in the *apodyterium* (d) he would first bathe in the *tepidarium* or lukewarm pool (e) before entering the *calidarium* or hot bath (f) where he could either sit in hot air or plunge into hot water. Either was bearable for a few minutes only; then back to the tepidarium for a massage and good scrape with strigils. The final stage was a quick plunge in the *frigidarium* or cold bath (g). All sections of the baths were brilliantly decorated with mosaics and wall-paintings.

The Stabian Baths stood at one of the town's main crossroads. We keep straight across and continue eastwards towards the Sarno Gate. The Pompeians were great scribblers and the walls of the shops and houses were covered with messages, as often as not about

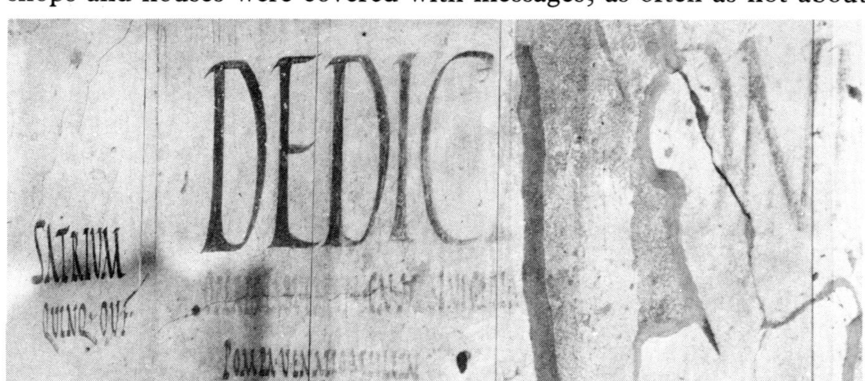

Pompeii: wall messages

politics or love. 'All the fruitsellers with Helvius Vestalis support the election of M. Holconius Priscus as duovir', reads one. 'Have you ever seen Venus?' wrote one happy lover. 'Just look at my fair one, she is as beautiful.' Livia, however, had quarrelled with her boyfriend Isidore. 'What do I care whether your health is good or bad', was her crushing message. 'Do you think that I would care if you dropped dead tomorrow?'

As we near the Sarno Gate, a turn to the right takes us into the area of the palaestra and the amphitheatre.

The amphitheatre was large enough to seat most of Pompeii's adult population. The most popular acts were men killing animals or each other or animals killing animals. For example a bull and panther would be tied together to see which one would first kill the other. The crowd often got wildly excited. One 'games' ended in a riot in which some visitors from the neighbouring town of Nucera were killed. As a punishment the Emperor closed the amphitheatre

Pompeii: the amphitheatre

for ten years! The stars were the gladiators. By fighting for his life to entertain the crowd, a slave might win his freedom and a debtor pay off his debts. Wall messages tell us that at Pompeii, Severus won fifty-six victories and Auctus fifty, but on 6 November Officiosus ran away from his enemy. Two gladiators whose names are unknown to us had for some reason been chained up in the prison of the gladiators' barracks on the day of the eruption. In the panic they were left behind and buried alive.

To see the best-preserved shops and homes we must go to Herculaneum. One shop sold beans, chick peas, hot food and drink. The containers for the peas and wines are still in place. The shop-

Herculaneum: the bakery of Sextus Patuculus Felix, showing the main ovens, and, beyond, a large millstone for grinding corn into flour

keeper was doing well. His home, which can be entered through the shop, is beautifully decorated with mosaics. This bakery looked out on to the Herculaneum palaestra. It was a large shop. A millstone stood in the front section while in the rear baking pans hung on the wall. Carbonised rolls have been dug up with SP, the initials of this baker, Sextus Patuculus Felix, stamped upon them.

Herculaneum was marvellously situated overlooking the Bay of Naples. The House of the Mosaic Atrium enjoyed one of the best positions. It stood on the southern edge of the town and its sun terrace looked out over the sea. From the street you enter the *atrium* or main hall at the opposite side of which is the *tablinum* or dining-room, which in older Roman homes was one of the main reception rooms. In this more modern and spacious home the main living rooms lie off to the right and are connected by a windowed 'cloister' which runs round a rectangular garden. The main reception room, the *triclinium*, is between the garden and the sun terrace. On either side are rooms for sleep or relaxation.

Finer houses still were built outside the town. In fact the most magnificent of all Roman houses known to us other than the palaces of the emperors is just outside Herculaneum along the coast towards Naples. It lies underneath twenty-four metres of volcanic rubble to this day. It was discovered in the eighteenth century by tunnellers working for a local prince. Because they found so many treasures inside it they explored it quite thoroughly before danger from poisonous gases and falling rock forced them to leave it and seal up the tunnels. Its front was 230 metres long and faced the sea. It had a long garden running down the hillside to its own small harbour. From excavations we know that the main living rooms were linked by a number of courtyards and gardens, which were full of magnificent bronze and marble statues. The owner also had a library full of papyrus rolls some of which though badly singed have been unrolled and their contents read. They were mainly works of philosophy and literature. This magnificent house is now usually known as the Villa of the Papyri and historians believe that it may well have been the home of Lucius Calpurnius Piso, father-in-law of Julius Caesar.

Using the evidence: the eruption of Vesuvius 24 August AD *79*

An intelligent young Roman, the Younger Pliny, was staying at Misenum on the bay of Naples with his uncle at the time of the eruption. Two of his letters to the historian Tacitus survive. The first tells how his uncle, the Elder Pliny, died during the eruption and the second describes his own experiences.

Pompeii: the plaster-cast of a young woman's body found where she fell beside the Sarno Gate

The death of the Elder Pliny

My uncle was stationed at Misenum, in active command of the fleet. On 24 August, in the early afternoon, my mother drew his attention to a cloud of unusual size and appearance. [It resembled] an umbrella pine, for it rose to a great height on a sort of trunk and then split off into branches.

As he was leaving the house he was handed a message from Rectina, wife of Tascus whose house was at the foot of the mountain, so that escape was impossible except by boat. She was terrified by the danger threatening her and implored him to rescue her. He gave orders for the warships to be launched and went on board himself with the intention of bringing help to many more people besides Rectina, for this lovely stretch of coast was

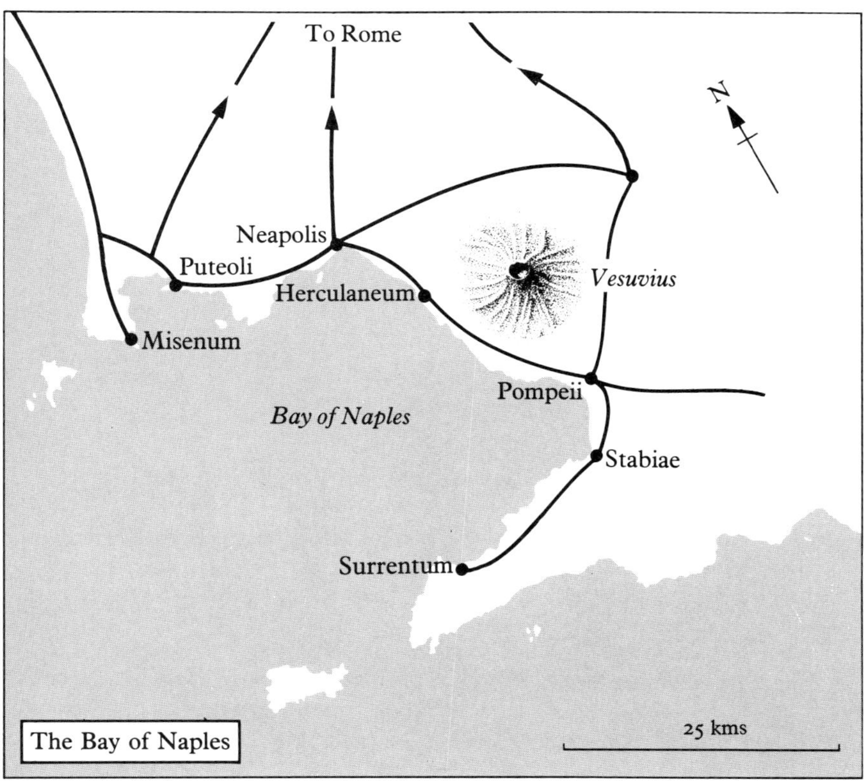

The Bay of Naples

thickly populated. . . . Ashes were already falling, hotter and thicker as the ships drew near, followed by bits of pumice and blackened stones, charred and cracked by the flames: then suddenly they were in shallow water, and the shore was blocked by the debris from the mountain. For a moment my uncle wondered whether to turn back, but when the helmsman advised this he refused, telling him that Fortune stood by the courageous and they must make for Pomponianus at Stabiae.

The winds were against them so the Elder Pliny had a meal and a nap. Then he joined Pomponianus and the rest of the household. As a protection against falling objects, they tied pillows on their heads.

Elsewhere there was daylight by this time, but they were still in darkness, blacker and denser than any ordinary night. My uncle decided to go down to the shore and investigate on the spot the possibility of any escape by sea, but he found the waves still wild and dangerous. A sheet was spread on the ground for him to lie down, and he repeatedly asked for cold water to drink. Then the flames and smell of sulphur roused him to stand up. He stood leaning on two slaves and then suddenly collapsed, I imagine because the dense fumes choked his breathing by blocking his windpipe which was constitutionally weak and narrow.

The experiences of the Younger Pliny

He and his mother were caught up in a crowd of fugitives.

The buildings round us were already tottering, and the open space we were in was too small for us not to be in danger if the house collapsed. This finally decided us to leave the town. Once beyond the buildings we stopped, and there we had some extraordinary experiences which thoroughly alarmed us.

Herculaneum: the baths. The volcanic stone, now solid, seems to squeeze through the doorway.

We saw the sea sucked away and apparently forced back by the earthquake: quantities of sea creatures were left stranded on dry sand. On the landward side a fearful black cloud parted to reveal great tongues of fire, like flashes of lightning magnified in size.

Ashes were already falling, not as yet very thickly. I looked round: a dense black cloud was coming up behind us, spreading over the earth like a flood. 'Let us leave the road while we can still see,' I said, 'or we shall be knocked down and trampled underfoot in the dark by the crowd behind.' We had scarcely sat down to rest when darkness fell, not the dark of a moonless or cloudy night, but as if the lamp had been put out in a closed room. You could hear the shrieks of women, the wailing of infants, and the shouting of men. Ashes began to fall again, this time in heavy showers. We rose from time to time and shook them off, otherwise we should have been buried and crushed beneath their weight.... At last the darkness thinned and dispersed into smoke or cloud; then there was genuine daylight, and the sun actually shone out, but yellowish as it is during an eclipse. We were terrified to see everything changed, buried deep in ashes like snowdrifts.

Questions and further work

1 What did the eruption look like from Misenum?

2 (a) Where did the Elder Pliny sail in order to save Pomponianus?
(b) How close did he get to Pompeii and Herculaneum?

3 What was the main danger at Stabiae?

4 How did the Elder Pliny die?

5 What were the main dangers which persuaded the Younger Pliny to leave Misenum with his mother?

6 What were conditions like in the Misenum area?
(Pompeii was hit in the same way as Pliny describes the situation at Stabiae, only much more heavily since it was closer to the mountain.)

7 Red-hot volcanic stone and ash fell on Pompeii to an average height of three-and-a-half metres. What effect would you expect this to have on the buildings?
(Herculaneum was buried differently by a vast torrent of hot liquid volcanic matter which flooded through the town and then solidified into volcanic rock eleven to eighteen metres thick.)

8 How did rock (in the picture opposite) get into the baths?

9 Would you expect the upper stories of buildings to be better preserved in Pompeii or in Herculaneum? Explain your answer.

10 Which would you expect to be harder to excavate? Explain your answer.

11 Imagine you are *one* of the following: Asellina, the Pompeian innkeeper; Sextus Patuculus Felix, the Herculaneum baker; one of the quarrelling lovers, Livia or Isidore. Describe your experiences on 24 August AD 79.

12 Draw as realistically as you can the eruption of Vesuvius as it would have appeared from Misenum.

18 Roman Britain

Britain lay on the edge of the Roman world. It was the largest of the islands known to the Romans but a distant and unattractive place. The historian Tacitus includes a description in his *Life of Agricola*, first published about fifty years after the successful invasion of AD 43. He gives a good idea of the Roman attitude. Britain is remote, wild and tossed by storms. The sea surrounding it is strange and 'heavy to the oar, it does not rise as do other seas even in high wind.' Yet the tides are tremendous, affecting the rivers deep inland. 'The climate is wretched with its frequent rain and mists but there is no extreme cold. The day is longer than in our part of the world.' Like the Gauls, whom they resemble closely in dress and appearance, the British 'are barbarians. But they show more spirit than the Gauls who have been made lazy by a long peace.' Though some of them fight from chariots, 'their strength is their infantry. It is but seldom, however, that two or three states combine to drive off a common danger. Thus, fighting in separate groups all are conquered.'

The Romans were neither the first nor the last invaders to enter and settle Britain. After the Neolithic peoples who brought farming with them about 3500 BC came the Beaker people from the Rhine valley about 1800 BC. Though they are named after their special kind of pottery, they were also skilled craftsmen in metal, particularly copper, bronze and gold. Further invasions came before the Romans. Between

A fine example of British craftsmanship: a gold and silver neckband from the Snettisham Treasure

the fourth and first centuries BC came tribes with iron tools and weapons who built large impressive-looking hill forts. Skilled and artistic metalworkers, they had close links with northern Gaul, receiving many fugitives fleeing from Caesar's conquering legions. Partly to punish the Britons for helping the Gauls and partly to win further glory for himself, Caesar raided southern Britain in 55 BC and again the following year. His second expedition swept in a wide circle round the site of London (see the map) and secured the submission of the local chiefs. Yet this was far from being a thorough or permanent conquest.

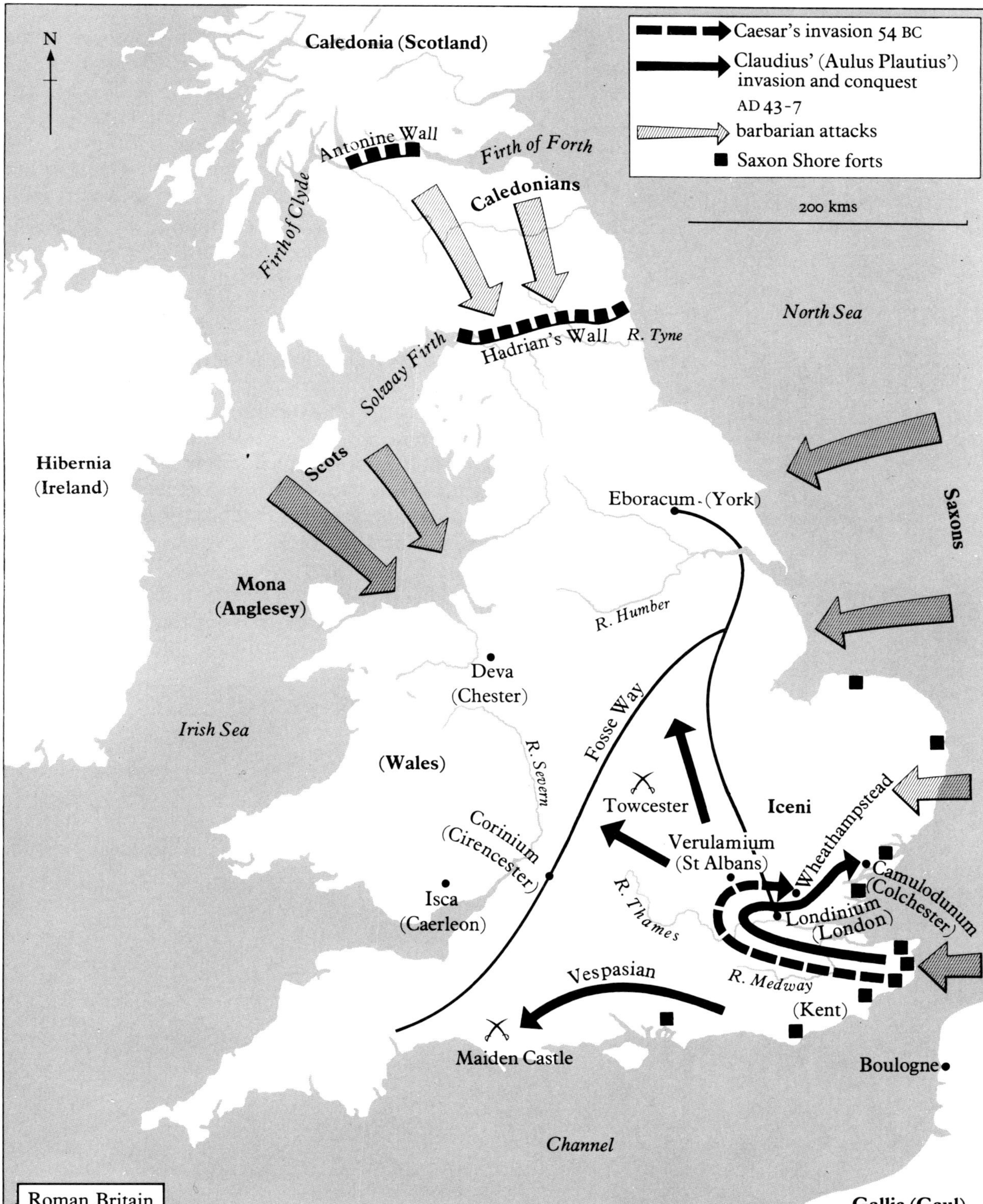

Roman Britain

The conquest

A proper invasion of this large and misty island with its quarrelsome chiefs was discussed many times. In AD 43 during the reign of the Emperor Claudius, it began. A British king, suffering at the hands of the ambitious Caractacus, king of the powerful Catuvellauni tribe, asked the Romans for help. This Claudius was happy to give. Like Caesar a hundred years before, he was anxious for glory. The invasion was well planned and led by Aulus Plautius. Forty thousand men crossed the Channel in three groups. After landing safely without opposition on the Kent coast they advanced eastwards. Caractacus with his brother, Togidumnus, and a large British army held a strong position along the banks of the River Medway (see the map). Two days of furious fighting and all the skill and discipline of the legionaries were needed before the Britons broke and fled. With the Thames crossing secure, the Emperor Claudius now arrived to lead his victorious army to capture the main settlement of the Catuvellauni, Camulodunum (modern Colchester). This was done within a few days, and he returned to Rome where poems and inscriptions greeted him as a returning hero. He called his son Britannicus in honour of the conquest.

Aulus Plautius got on with the hard work. Three armies moved out from the south-east in different directions. One went north and east, a second into the midlands. The third, commanded by the future emperor, Vespasian, marched to the south-west and then north to the valley of the River Severn. We know most about the southern campaign. According to Suetonius, the British retreated into their hill forts.

Buried beside Maiden Castle – a British spine with a Roman arrowhead still wedged in it

Maiden Castle from the air. The Romans attacked the far end.

Vespasian had to assault and capture at least twenty of these. One of the strongest was Maiden Castle in Dorset. Excavations have made clear how the attack went. Vespasian concentrated on the less massive eastern entrance. He softened up the defenders by an intense catapult barrage and then his legionaries stormed the entrance. They broke through, causing heavy casualties among the British. Once resistance ended, Vespasian allowed the survivors to bury their dead just outside the fortifications.

By AD 47 all Britain south and east of a line which runs from the Severn to the Humber and is marked to this day by the Fosse Way road, was under Roman control. But the next thirty years were more difficult for the Romans. Though the courageous Caractacus was again defeated and then betrayed to the Romans by Queen Cartimandua, in whose lands he had sought refuge, the hill tribes of the north and west were hard to crush. In AD 60 the tribes of eastern Britain led by Boudicca, queen of the Iceni, rose in furious revolt. 'They hunted down Roman troops in their scattered posts,' Tacitus wrote, 'they stormed the forts and there was no form of savage cruelty which they did not use.' Londinium, Verulamium (St Albans) and Camulodunum were burnt to the ground. Their inhabitants, Britons and Romans alike, were butchered. Only the swift, decisive action of the Roman governor, Paulinus,

whose cruel rule had helped to cause the revolt in the first place, saved the province for Rome. Though heavily outnumbered, he chose a strong defensive position, which was probably near Towcester. There he stood his ground. Once again the disciplined legions were too much for the excitable and unorganised British. They fled in all directions. Soon Boudicca was dead, probably by suicide, and Paulinus and his legions laid waste the lands of those tribes which had supported her.

There then followed a number of able generals including Agricola. Roman control over Wales and the north was strengthened. Agricola fought his way deep into Caledonia (Scotland) and was planning to conquer Hibernia (Ireland) too when he was recalled to Rome. Caledonia was never completely conquered. The Emperor Hadrian decided that the northern limit of the Roman Empire should be the line from the Tyne to the Solway and had built the magnificent wall which still bears his name. Twenty years later the Emperor Antoninus pushed the frontier farther north to the shorter line from the Clyde to the Forth.

Richborough Castle: a Saxon Shore for

Hadrian's Wall: Housesteads Fort as it probably once was

This Antonine Wall was built largely of turf. A frontier so far north proved difficult to hold with the troops available. In AD 211 it was finally abandoned in favour of Hadrian's Wall which remained the frontier as long as Roman rule continued. Legions for the defence of the north and west were stationed at Eboracum (York), Deva (Chester) and Isca (Caerleon).

The occupation

After Boudicca's revolt the southern and eastern parts of Britain settled down to enjoy the benefits of Roman rule. They were helped by a number of tactful governors. Tacitus shows how Agricola took care to get the British:

> ... used to a life of peace and quiet by providing them with amenities. He encouraged the building of temples, public squares and good houses. He educated the sons of chiefs ... and said that he preferred the British ways to those of Gaul. Instead of hating the Latin language they became eager to speak it well. In the same way our national dress came into favour and the toga was everywhere to be seen. So the population were led to enjoy arcades, baths and banquets and to give up thoughts of war.

Though most of the population continued as peasant farmers living in simple wooden huts, towns grew, noble estates (based around villas) were developed (see the Using the evidence section) and trade with the rest of the Roman Empire increased. British lead, iron, tin, gold, silver and hunting dogs were always in demand and, especially in the fourth century AD, wheat and wool also. The centre for foreign trade and of the road network was Londinium, by far the largest city of the island.

After two centuries of peace the weaknesses which were beginning to show all over the Roman Empire were felt in Britain too. In AD 286 a mutinous admiral, Carausius, set himself up in Britain which he ruled, calling himself emperor, until murdered by his second in command. Not until AD 296 was the Emperor of Rome back in control. Other dangers threatened, from all directions. From the north the Picts menaced Hadrian's Wall, and the Scots raided the western shores. Most serious of all, Saxon pirates from across the North Sea brought terror to the eastern coast. The Roman government took firm action to meet these dangers. Special forts were built along the eastern shore and a single commander, the Count of the Saxon Shore, made responsible for their defence. Light, fast scout ships, camouflaged sea-green and driven by twenty oarsmen, kept watch for the raiders and rapidly raised the alarm when they were sighted. In the west a new naval base was built on the island of Mona (Anglesey).

For some years these defences worked. The fourth century was a time of considerable prosperity for many parts of Britain. Then, in AD 367 all the enemies managed to combine in a simultaneous attack. The Picts came over the Wall helped, it seems, by traitors within the defending garrisons. Surging south they seized and ransacked Eboracum and Deva. The Saxons overwhelmed the forts of the Saxon Shore, whose

Count was killed in a hopeless attempt to save them. To the undefended north-west came the Scots. Together they plundered southwards, eventually reaching as far as Kent. Only the fortified cities were able to hold out against them. To their amazement and horror the citizens of Londinium found themselves besieged. From Gaul, however, came a Roman army led by the capable Theodosius. The invaders had split up into groups since their main interest was plunder and they were no match for a disciplined army. Londinium was relieved and Theodosius speedily cleared the whole province. In revenge he marched far into Caledonia, spreading death and destruction as he went. The damaged fortifications were repaired.

This was, however, the last time that we hear of military aid being sent to Roman Britain. The Roman emperors had problems nearer home and they could no longer spare any troops. In AD 383, the Emperor Maximus took troops from Britain. They never returned. When in AD 410, the British cities wrote to the Emperor Honorius asking for aid, he answered in irritation (hardly surprisingly since the barbarians were at the gates of Rome): those in Britain must look after their own defences.

A Corinium tombstone (now in the Cirencester Museum)

What happened after this date is far from clear. Both written and archaeological evidence is scanty. Barbarian attacks across northern Gaul cut Britain off from Rome. No doubt the Romano-British did defend themselves but the Saxon attacks from the east grew heavier and more frequent. And they were coming not just to plunder but to settle. Before the fifth century was over, the Romano-British had been driven from the eastern half of the island. In the west their resistance may well have been tougher and better led. Certainly the pace of the Saxon advance slowed – perhaps as a result of victories by the legendary King Arthur. From AD 550, however, the Saxons were advancing once again. By AD 580 they were into the Severn valley and the Romano-British pushed into the hills of Wales and the far west. Their villas and towns, left empty by the Saxon conquerors, crumbled into decay.

Using the evidence: the southern Cotswolds under Roman rule

Cirencester in Roman times

Cirencester in Gloucestershire is a small, attractive market town. Nowadays it is best known for its lovely medieval church and for the polo played in the park nearby. Though a pleasant place to live in, it is not one of the major cities of modern Britain.

As the modern town has grown and new offices, shops, houses and roads have been built, many remains of a Roman town have been found. It was called Corinium. Archaeologists are now in no doubt that it was one of the main cities of Roman Britain, and the centre of one of the most civilised and prosperous parts of the province. Here are some of the kinds of evidence which they have used. Study each piece carefully and answer the questions as you go along.

Notes (See Map A)
Bagendon was the main British settlement in the area. The Fosse Way was the boundary between the Romans and British at the end of the first phase of conquest (AD 47).

1 There are at least three good reasons why the Romans should have had a settlement at Corinium. Work out from the map what they were.

Notes (See Map B)
A is the first legionary fort, built about AD 44 for 3000 soldiers.
B is a smaller fort built between AD 49 and 70.
C is a settlement of British from Bagendon. The former British settlement to the north of Corinium lost all its inhabitants between AD 43 and 60. There is no evidence of fighting nor of death from illness or starvation.

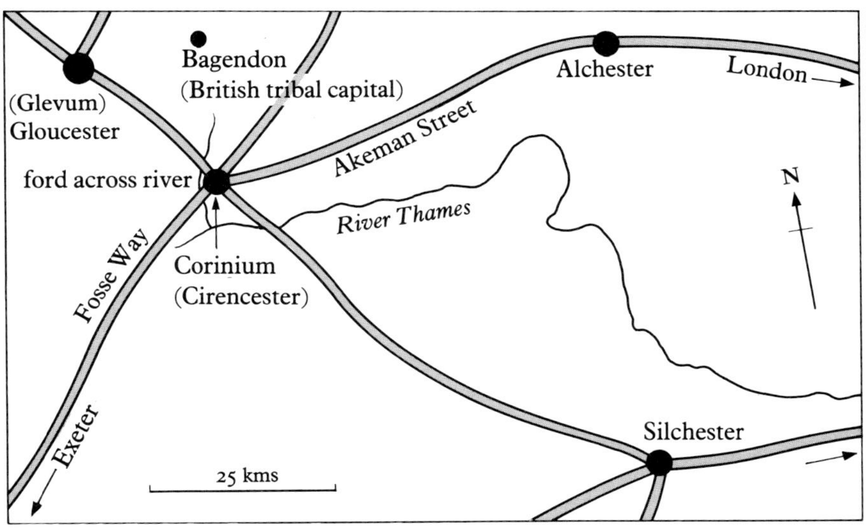

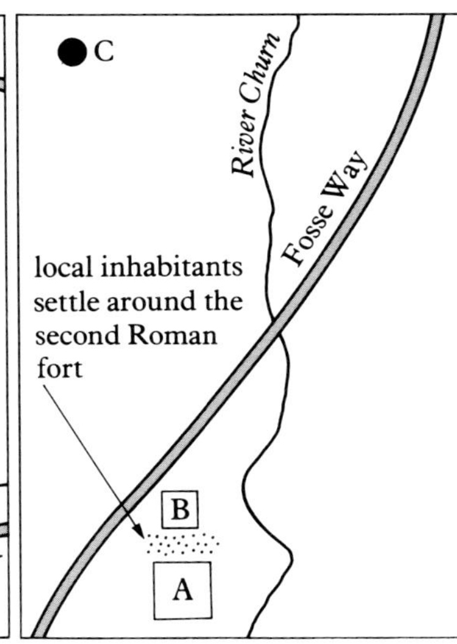

Look at the picture opposite. The inscription reads:

Sextus Valerius Genialis, Trooper of the cavalry regiment of Thracians, a Frisian tribesman, from the troop of Genialis, aged 40, of 20 years service, lies buried here. His heir set this up.

2 (a) Describe the first fort built at Corinium. Who may well have been the commander of the legion which built it? (Clue: re-read pages 198–9.) Explain your answer.
(b) The second fort is smaller. Why do you think that was?
(c) What does the tombstone (which dates from between AD 103 and 150) tell you about its soldiers? Thrace is in Greece, Frisia in Holland.

3 Where have the British from Bagendon got to? (Clue: re-read Tacitus' account of Agricola's acts as governor on page 201.)

The completed city

4 (a) These are what you can see at 1. What do you think they are the remains of? Explain your answer.

(b) In the centre of the city were found the remains of a paved courtyard (2) surrounded by columns on three sides and a hall (3) eighty-four metres long on the fourth. From your knowledge of other Roman towns such as Pompeii (see pages 187–92), what do you think 2 and 3 were?

(c) This is what 4 looks like now. It lay just outside the Roman walls. What do you think it was? Explain your answer.

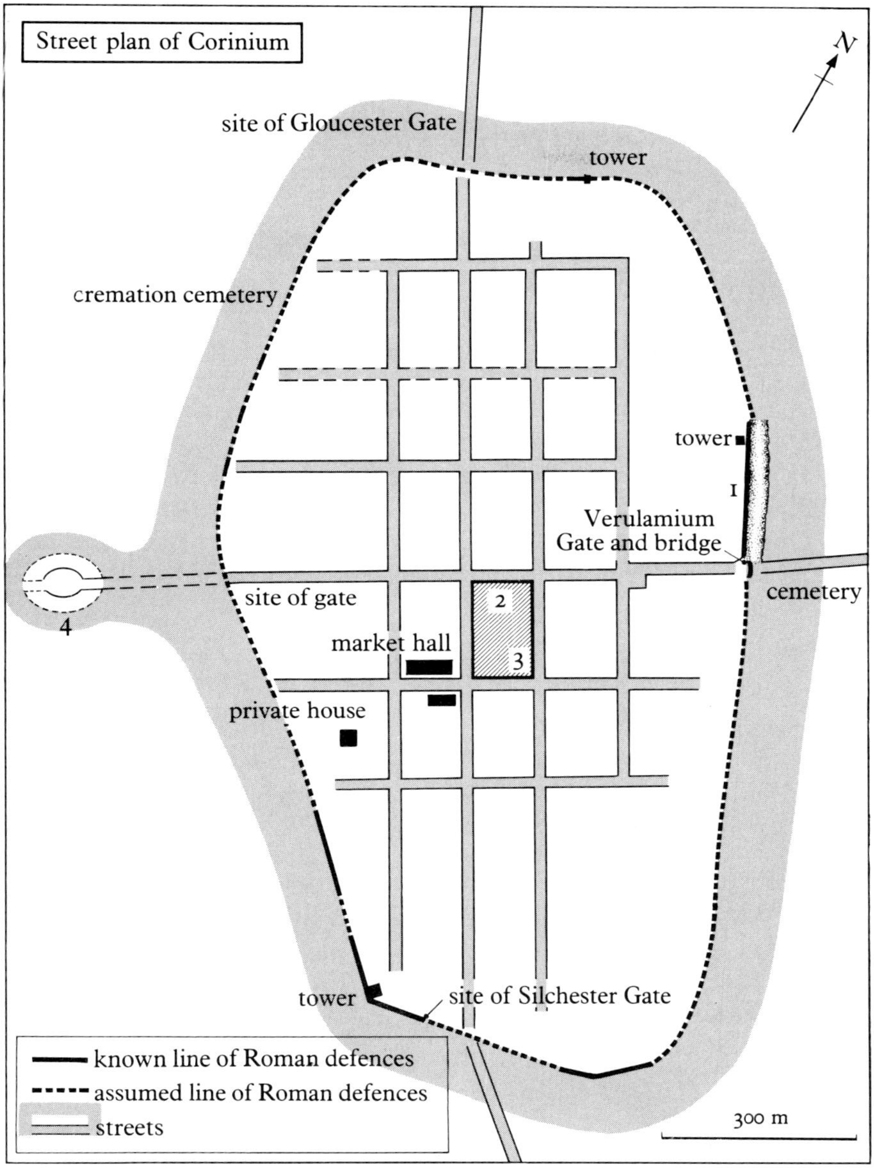

(d) These are all the public buildings found so far in Corinium. What other public buildings would you expect to find? Again using Pompeii as your guide, whereabouts on the Roman street plan would you expect them to be?

Corinium in the fourth century AD

Here is some further evidence about Corinium.

(i) In the fourth century, Corinium grew to become the second largest city in Britain. Only Londinium was larger.

(ii) Turrets were added to the walls. Many houses, previously built of wood, were rebuilt in stone.

The Great Pavement, Woodchester: part of a rich villa about twenty kilometres to the west of Corinium

The base of the column (now in Cirencester Museum). It reads:
SEPTIMIVS RENOVAT
Septimius rebuilt
PRIMAE PROVINCIAE
of the First Province
RECTOR
Governor

(iii) A firm specialising in mosaic pavements such as this did good business locally.
(iv) In the fourth century Britain was divided into four provinces. Corinium was the largest town in the province of Britannia Prima.
(v) This column was found near the forum. The inscription tells how Lucius Septimius, ruler of Britannia Prima, restored this monument in the honour of Jupiter, chief of the gods.

5 (a) What do these various pieces of evidence tell us about Corinium in the fourth century?
(b) Can one say for sure that Corinium was the provincial capital of Britannia Prima? Or is it merely likely? Give reasons for your answer.

Chedworth Villa: the warm-air heating system

Corinium and the south Cotswolds

The Cotswolds have always been good farmland, particularly suited to grazing sheep.

There were many villa estates in the Corinium area, the best preserved being at Chedworth. Near the forum in Corinium there was a large market hall for the butchers.

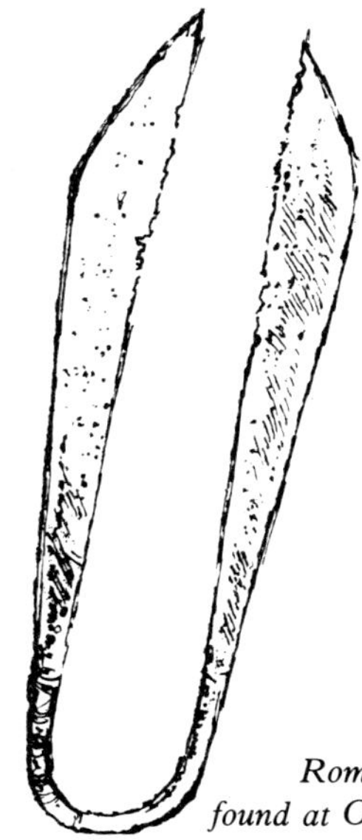

Roman shears found at Chedworth

6 (a) What evidence is there that the owner of Chedworth was rich?
(b) What evidence is there that the Chedworth estate raised sheep?
(c) What evidence is there that Corinium was an important sheep market?
(d) How well does this evidence fit in with what you already know about British trade in the fourth century (see page 201)?

The decline of Corinium

Roman soldiers were withdrawn from Britain between AD 383 and 410. Here is a cross-section of a Corinium street. A is silt from traffic dust. B is silt from rotting grass and weeds.

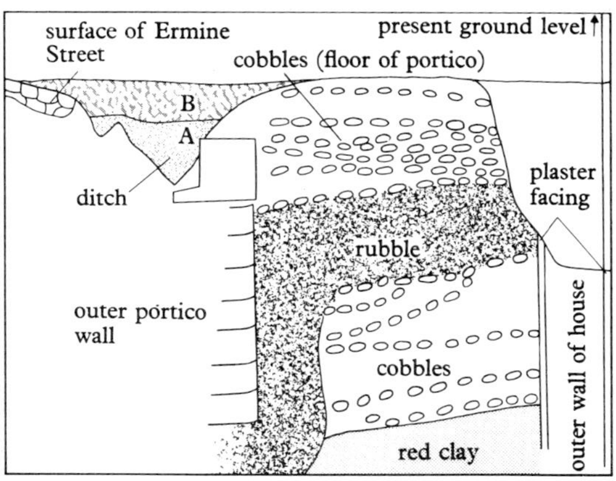

Cross-section of a Corinium street

Worn paving stones in the forum are not replaced. Two skeletons are found unburied in a ditch beside Ermine Street. A terrible plague sweeps through Europe in AD 443. The only mention which we have of Cirencester/Corinium in writing is in the *Anglo-Saxon Chronicle* for the year AD 577:

Cuthwine and Ceawlin [Saxon Chiefs] fought against the Britons and killed three of their kings . . . at a place which is called Dyrham and captured three of their cities, Gloucester, Cirencester and Bath.

7 (a) What conclusions can you draw from: (i) the worn paving stones in the forum; (ii) the street cross-section; (iii) the unburied skeletons?
(b) Imagine that you were born in Corinium in AD 400, the son or daughter of a mosaic craftsman. You live to at least the year AD 460. Describe the changes that come to the town and the surrounding countryside, making sure that your description fits in with the evidence above.

19 The decline of the Western Empire

The Emperor Commodus

Commodus succeeded his father Marcus Aurelius as emperor in AD 180. It was the beginning of a hundred years of bad government. The main interests of Commodus were chariot racing and lion baiting. According to Dio Cassius who lived at the same time, 'He was a greater curse to the Romans than any epidemic or crime.' After twelve years of incapable yet cruel rule he was assassinated. He was followed by many other wicked or weak emperors. They were usually chosen by the army whose main desire was to make money. Julianus, who succeeded Commodus, did so simply because he offered more money per soldier than his rival. The auction took place at an army camp in Rome! The importance of the army was well understood by Severus, who got rid of Julianus and made himself emperor instead. 'Make the army rich', was his motto, 'and don't bother about anyone else.'

Between AD 235 and 285 there were more than twenty emperors. They reigned on average two-and-a-half years and almost all died violently. Civil wars were frequent and on the borders of the Empire dangerous enemies gathered. In the east, the Persians threatened Syria and Egypt, the Franks and the Alemanni raided deep into Gaul and the prosperous cities of Africa were attacked by desert tribesmen. If this were not enough, economic conditions within the Empire worsened.

Prices rocketed. By the end of the third century wheat was two hundred times as expensive as it had been at the beginning. Heavier and heavier taxes were demanded by the emperors, desperate for money to pay their soldiers. Roman citizens once so proud to hold office in their city now did their best to avoid doing so in order that to someone else would fall the hated task of collecting in the taxes. Some villages in Asia Minor complained to the emperor in the middle of the third century.

> We are most terribly oppressed and squeezed by those whose duty it is to protect us. . . . Officers, soldiers, magistrates and imperial agents come to our villages, take us away from our work and make off with our oxen. They take what is not owed and we suffer outrageous injustice and misfortune.

The Arch of Septimius Severus, Rome

Modern citizens of the town of Split (Yugoslavia) relax against a pillar of Diocletian's palace. It was so large that a small town later grew up within its walls.

The western half of the Empire grew poorer and its population fell.

This sorry story of disaster and decay was stopped for a time by Diocletian (AD 284–305) and Constantine I (AD 306–37). Diocletian improved the army and refortified the frontiers. He also made sure that soldiers, who since the time of Severus had played a large part in governing the Empire, stuck in future to their job of defending it. To provide more effective rule, he appointed a co-emperor to rule with him. Each emperor had a second-in-command, who was given the title Caesar. Diocletian took the eastern half, Maximian, his co-emperor, the western. Great efforts were made to solve the economic problems. Diocletian had careful records made of all the citizens in the Empire and of their possessions. On the basis of this information he then worked out how much tax they should pay. He then forbade anyone to change his job or sell their farmland. If anyone moved from their land, the government took it over. You could get a better job if you could get a permit from the government but better jobs meant higher taxes. Most people preferred to stay where they were. Diocletian also tried and failed to bring down rising prices. His method was simple; to fix a maximum price on every article bought and sold within the Empire. The snag was that traders were so worried about the situation that they did not put their goods on sale. Consequently most things were in short supply and prices, instead of coming down, went up even faster. There were no easy solutions to the problems facing the Empire.

Diocletian retired in 305 and Constantine eventually won the lengthy and bitter struggle to succeed him. Constantine took two important decisions. He decided to move his capital east from Rome to a new city which he had built round the ancient harbour town of Byzantium (see page 214), and he made Christianity the official religion of the Empire.

Though the Western Empire crumbled away less than 150 years after his death, the Eastern Empire round Byzantium (Constantinople) was to last another 1016 years. As for Christianity, it survived and flourished to become and remain one of the world's major religions. Within the Christian Church much of Roman civilisation – the language, literature and laws – survived also.

Roman religion and the rise of Christianity

The first Romans were shepherds and farmers. Like many peoples in the Ancient World they believed that the natural things about them like rocks, woods, lakes, seas, clouds and thunder had gods within them. They could do good or harm, depending on how they were treated. It

Religious sacrifices. In the upper carving a bull, a sheep and a pig are being led to the altar where their throats will be cut by the priest. In the lower carving, a slaughtered bull (left) lies on its back and the priest cuts open its stomach. From the way its heart, liver, kidneys and other innards look he will decide whether the gods are pleased or angry.

was important to show them respect, build shrines or statues in their honour, and sacrifice to them at the right time of year. The Romans also believed in household gods; the Lares who guarded the home and its lands, and the Penates who took care of the larder. Many houses had special shrines where at meal times small pieces of food were burnt in bronze containers. The Romans borrowed many of their other religious ideas from the Etruscans and the Greeks. Some of their most popular gods, e.g. Jupiter, Venus and Minerva were Etruscan or Greek with Roman names. Like the Greeks they were great believers in oracles and in omens. During the First Punic War, Claudius Pulcher, the commander of the Roman fleet, sailed with a flock of sacred chickens with him. According to the way they pecked their food, he and his priests would be able to tell whether the time was right to fight the Carthaginians. The chickens, however, would not eat. Pulcher lost his temper and threw them overboard, shouting, 'drink then if you won't eat'. He then fought with the enemy and was heavily defeated. When he

The Persian warrior-god Mithras

got back to Rome, he was put on trial and fined for the way in which he had treated the unfortunate chickens. He had angered the gods, who then made sure that he lost the battle.

As the Roman armies spread Roman power round the Mediterranean, links with other parts of the world increased through trade, and eastern religions became popular among the Romans, especially the poorer and least educated. In Pompeii there was a temple to the Egyptian goddess, Isis. The Persian god, Mithras, was very popular with soldiers. With the creation of the Empire by Augustus, temples were built in honour of Rome and the emperor; the worship of the emperor as a god was officially encouraged to link together the various peoples of the farflung Empire. All citizens were supposed to show their loyalty by regularly burning incense in front of a statue of the emperor.

Jesus Christ was a Jewish carpenter. In AD 30 he was crucified by the Roman governor of Palestine at the request of the Jewish religious leaders, who strongly disapproved of his religious teaching. His followers were convinced that he was the Son of God, that he had risen from the dead. As the Messiah foretold by the Hebrew prophets, he would soon come again to destroy the wicked and save the good. Led by St Paul, they spread his ideas first in Asia Minor then in Greece and Italy. Christian ideas quickly proved attractive to many poorer townspeople. By AD 64 the Christians had made themselves unpopular with the government by their refusal to worship the emperor as the law required. The Roman mob was equally hostile, since the Christians set themselves apart and were very ready to point out the wickedness of the world which they saw round about them. When Rome went up in flames, the Emperor Nero blamed the Christians and let loose the first of the persecutions. 'Their executions became sporting entertainment,' noted Tacitus. 'They were covered with wild animal skins and torn apart by dogs.' Other persecutions followed.

In the second century AD these were usually local and short-lived but during the third century persecutions grew more severe. The emperors became more worried lest the Empire break up. At a time when citizens needed to be both united and warlike in spirit, the Christians, whose numbers were increasing and now included the well-educated, seemed a tightly knit group loyal only to itself and also hopelessly peaceful in outlook. Diocletian was a fierce persecutor of the Christians. First he forbade them the privileges of Roman citizenship. He then ordered their sacred books to be destroyed, their priests to be imprisoned and forced by torture to worship the official gods. Many individual Christians suffered greatly but the Church survived. Within a generation Diocletian's approach had been reversed. In 313 Constantine ordered that Christians should be allowed complete freedom of worship throughout the Empire. For the rest of his life he showered the Christian leaders with gifts of land, churches and privileges. Finally on his deathbed, he was himself baptised.

Christianity victorious – what was once the cool room (tepidarium) *of Diocletian's giant baths in Rome is now the church of St Mary of the Angels*

The collapse of the Empire in the west

In other ways Constantine followed thc example of Diocletian. He tried to solve the economic problems of the Empire by government regulations but with no more success. He reformed the army. His main achievement was to create a crack, fast-moving cavalry army, which could strike hard and fast wherever it was needed in support of the hard-pressed frontier armies. In the long run, however, the effect of this change was to make the frontier armies think of themselves as second-rate. Situated in garrison towns for long periods, these troops became less reliable and were of little use for actual fighting. The armies were finally unable to cope with the endless attacks which pounded the Empire in the years after Constantine's death.

These attacks, which finally destroyed the Western Empire, were part of a massive movement of peoples which was set in motion about AD 360 by the Huns. These nomadic horsemen, who had for centuries plagued the Chinese Empire, suddenly shifted towards the west, forcing westwards and southwards other tribes like the Alans, Ostrogoths, Visigoths and Vandals. Against such pressure the imperial defences gave way. Attempts to win the aid of some of these barbarian groups, so that they would fight against the others either by giving them land in which to settle or by paying them, only made matters worse. In AD 376 the Visigoths crossed the Danube; in AD 406 the Alans and Vandals broke into Gaul; and in AD 410 Alaric, king of the Visigoths, sacked Rome itself. The Emperor, whose empire had almost completely disappeared, hung on in Ravenna (see below). In AD 451 the Huns, led by

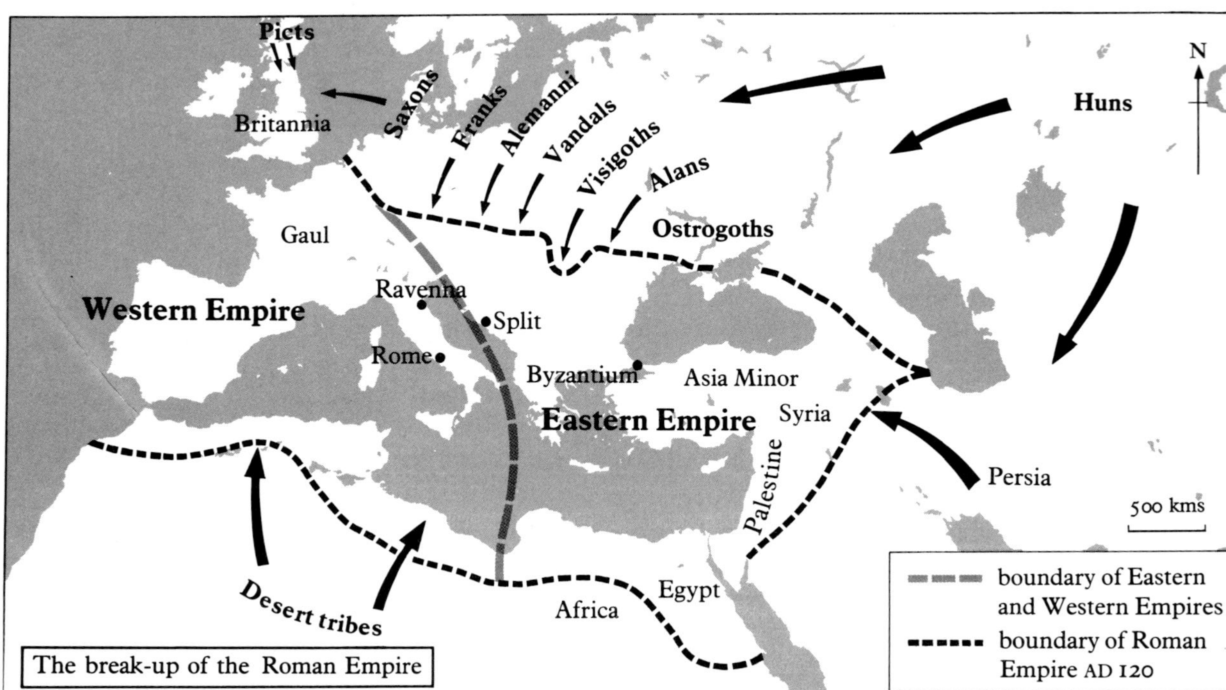

The break-up of the Roman Empire

the terrifying Attila, crossed the Rhine, plundered Gaul and, though defeated by a combined Roman and Visigoth army, were able to enter Italy. There Attila died and his followers made off into the Balkans to harass the Eastern Empire. In the west there was no revival. Rome was plundered again this time by the Vandals. The Western Roman Empire had already ceased to exist in reality when Odoacer, leader of an army made up of a number of barbarian tribes, ended it in name as well by dethroning the last emperor, Romulus Augustulus, in AD 476.

Using the evidence: why Constantine became a Christian

In AD 312 Constantine advanced on Rome with an army of ninety thousand men. He was ready for a fight to the finish with his great enemy, Maxentius. However, he was 'convinced that he needed more powerful aid than his troops alone could give him, because of the wicked magic being so busily practised by the tyrant Maxentius; so he began to seek help from heaven'. At any rate this was what Eusebius wrote in his *Life of Constantine* in AD 336 just before the emperor died. (Constantine remembered that while other emperors had worshipped many gods and been defeated, his father, Constantius, had always worshipped one god whom he called simply the Supreme God, and had

Constantine, the first Christian emperor: the head, one arm and a kneecap are all that remain of a colossal statue made in Rome after his victory at the Milvian Bridge

done well. So he decided to honour no other god but the god of his father.) Eusebius continues:

Accordingly he called to God in earnest prayer that He would reveal to him who He was and help him in his present difficulties. While he was praying, a most marvellous sign appeared from Heaven, the account of which would be hard to believe had it been told to me by any other person. But since the victorious person declared it to the writer of this history . . . and confirmed his statement on oath who can doubt its truth? He said that about mid-day . . . he saw with his own eyes a cross of light in the heavens above the sun and the words 'Conquer by this'. He was struck with amazement at this sight and his whole army with him witnessed the miracle.

He said moreover that he was not at all sure what this sign could mean and having pondered it deep into the night, in his dreams the Christ of God appeared to him with the same signs that he had seen in the heavens, and commanded him to have made a standard in the likeness of that sign, and use it as a safeguard against his enemies.

At dawn he arose and told the secret to his friends. He then called together the workers in gold and precious stones and explained to them the shape of the sign which he had seen so that they could begin to make it. This I have had the opportunity of seeing for myself. . . . Now the banner is made like this. A long spear, overlaid with gold formed the figure of a cross by means of a piece laid across it. On the top of the whole was fixed a crown of gold and precious stones to which were added the two (Greek) letters which begin the name of Christ,

the letter P being intersected exactly at its centre by X. . . . From the piece crossing the spear was hung a streamer of purple cloth covered with embroidery of gold and precious stones . . . this banner was of square shape and the upright staff, which was very tall, bore a half-length portrait of the emperor and his children on the upper part, beneath the trophy of the cross and immediately above the embroidered streamer.

The Emperor constantly used this sign as a safeguard against all his enemies and ordered that others similar to it should be carried at the head of all his armies. . . . Being amazed by his extraordinary vision he decided to worship no other god than He who had appeared to him. . . .

On 28 October AD 312 the armies of Constantine and Maxentius met. They fought just to the north of the Milvian Bridge which crossed the Tiber about five kilometres from the walls of Rome. As Constantine's army began to circle round the enemy position, Maxentius tried to retreat in an organised way. But his bridge of boats broke and in panic the troops fought each other to get back across the Milvian Bridge, which was far too narrow to take them all. Maxentius, with hundreds of others, was thrown into the river. In his heavy armour he drowned. Constantine entered Rome in triumph with Maxentius' head carried before him on a spear.

The Battle of the Milvian Bridge: the dark, bearded Maxentius tries to flee across the river. The Italian painter of this fresco put the soldiers into armour of his own time (the fifteenth century AD).

Questions and further work

Eusebius' explanation

1 (a) From which book do these extracts come?
(b) How many years after the events which it describes was it written?
(c) From whom has Eusebius got a lot of his information?

2 (a) Why did Constantine feel the need to find out the truth about the gods?
(b) What gods did his father believe in?

3 Describe the two happenings which convinced him that the one Supreme God must be the god of the Christians.

4 Draw as accurately as you can the *Labarum*, the Standard of the Cross as described by Eusebius.

The reliability of Eusebius

5 What parts of this story do you find hard to believe?

6 In what way does Eusebius himself show that he himself expects his readers to find the story hard to believe?

7 What arguments does he then use to convince his readers that the story must be true? Are you convinced? Explain your answer.

8 Read carefully through the following points. Taking the points one by one, say whether you think they make Eusebius' account reliable evidence or not.
(i) He does not mention the Vision of the Heavenly Cross in his *Church History* which was written soon after AD 312 and describes

the events leading up to the Battle of the Milvian Bridge.
(ii) No other historian of the same generation mentions the Vision of the Heavenly Cross.
(iii) Constantine's sons were born after the Battle of the Milvian Bridge.
(iv) Crosses of light are sometimes seen in the area of the Alps as a result of ice-crystals falling across the rays of the sun.
(v) Of all the historians of the time, Eusebius knew Constantine best.
(vi) Eusebius was a Christian bishop and can be relied on to tell the truth.
(vii) Eusebius, lived at a time when Christians were recovering from the persecutions of Diocletian, and so might put things in such a way as to favour Christianity.
(viii) It was a most superstitious age. Both Constantine and Eusebius were quite likely to have convinced themselves that Constantine's remarkable successes were due to a miracle, whether or not that miracle actually happened.

9 Look carefully at the picture on page 216, which shows how an Italian painter imagined the battle. Imagine you are one of the soldiers at the Milvian Bridge. Describe your experiences.

Glossary

alliance an agreement between two or more groups of people, or countries
amphitheatre a stadium (usually oval or circular) for sporting events and other entertainments
ancestor an earlier member of a family, who has been dead for a long time, e.g. a great-grandfather
antechamber a small room leading to a main room
antidote a cure for poison
aqueduct a channel for carrying water
archaeologist someone who seeks the truth about the past using the evidence of objects discovered, usually by digging
architecture the design and planning of buildings

barbarians the Greek word for foreigners, which came also to mean backward or savage people
barrage a large number of arrows or stones thrown through the air at the same time
barter to exchange one thing for another, e.g. pigs for bronze axes
besiege to surround a town or fortress with the aim of forcing it to give in
blockade to cut off every approach to a place occupied by the enemy

campaign a series of troop movements against the enemy, possibly including a number of battles
capital (1) the chief city of a country or province
(2) the top part of a column
caravan a group of people travelling together across the desert
cartouche hieroglyphic letters surrounded by an oval line, spelling the name of a pharaoh
caste a social level or grade in Indian society
causeway a raised roadway across marsh or land liable to flooding
cavalry soldiers on horseback
civil war when people in the same country or city fight against each other
closet a small room
colony an area of land settled by people from overseas (e.g. the Greek colonies in southern Italy)
column a pillar of stone supporting the roof of a building
community a group of people living in close contact with each other
conclusion (1) the end
(2) a judgement made after you hear all the evidence
conquer to attack and take over someone else's country
consuls officials elected each year to rule Rome
crisis a serious situation which if not handled carefully may end in disaster (e.g. war)
crucifixion death by nailing to a wooden cross
cuneiform Mesopotamian wedge-shaped writing

decipher to work out the meaning of a language or a code
decree a written order or instruction of a ruler
democracy a state where all adults take part in or elect their government
detour the route followed (e.g. by an army) to get round an obstacle
domestic at home, homely
domesticated tamed

economic to do with money and business
emmer a type of corn
emperor ruler of an empire, a most powerful ruler
empire lands ruled by an emperor
ephors Spartan officials
epilepsy a disease which causes fits
evidence information which can be used to show that something is likely to be true or false

excavations careful digging by archaeologists in search of evidence about the past
exile someone forced to live outside his own homeland
export to sell goods to people outside your country
extinct no longer living today

fermentation a process in brewing beer (for example)
fertile good for growing crops
flank the side of an army
flint a type of stone (found in chalk) which can easily be chipped to a sharp edge
formal according to the rules
fortifications building works to help defend a house, village or city
fossils the remains of ancient animals or plants, turned to stone by chemical action
fugitives people fleeing from their homes in search of safety

galley a warship
generation people born at much the same time
geologist an expert on the history and structure of the earth's crust
gladiators men who fought for their lives to entertain the Roman crowd
granary a building for storing grain

halberd a combined spear and battle-axe
hieratic a form of Egyptian writing, quicker to write than hieroglyphics
hieroglyphics ancient Egyptian writing

import to buy goods made in another country, when in one's own country
incense herbs burnt (often in temples) to give a pleasant smell
independence self-rule
infantry foot-soldiers
inscriptions writing (e.g. on a tomb or gravestone)
irrigation methods of bringing water to land otherwise too dry to grow crops

jade a semi-precious stone much valued in China

labyrinth a building with many corners and corridors, a maze
legion the main unit of the Roman army (4000–6000 men)
lichen a type of moss
literature good writing, including poetry and plays

megaliths great stones put in position in Neolithic times
merket a tool for measuring the position of stars
Messiah a God-sent leader expected by the Hebrews
missile something thrown by hand, intended to hurt
mortar a stone container for grinding corn
mortuary a place for dead bodies
mosaic patterned floors or walls made from small coloured squares of baked clay
mummification an Egyptian method of preserving bodies after death
mutiny when soldiers or sailors refuse to obey orders

Neanderthal Man an early type of man, who died out about 30 000 BC
Neolithic Man New Stone Age Man, living from about 8000 BC
nomadic on the move from one grazing land to the next

obelisk a tall stone column with a pyramid top
omen a sign (e.g. a black cat crossing the road) which means good or bad news in the future

Palaeolithic Man Old Stone Age Man, living before 8000 BC
palaestra the games and exercise area in a Roman town
palette a wooden board for mixing ink or paints on
papyrus a writing surface made from the papyrus reed
pass where a road goes through a mountainous area
penteconter a fifty-oared Greek warship
persecute to treat badly
pestle a tool for pounding grain into flour in a mortar
phalanx a section of the Macedonian army
philosophy the study of wisdom
plague a highly infectious disease
politics the business of ruling a country
prehistory the study of men who lived before the invention of writing
profit money gained by buying and selling
prosecute to try to prove someone guilty at a trial
provision making arrangements for something which may happen in the future

radio-carbon dating a modern method of dating ancient remains, using the traces of carbon left in them
reform changes intended to improve things
regiment part of an army
reinforcements extra soldiers brought in to strengthen an army

relief a scene or pattern carved on a flat surface
reservoir a place where water is stored
revenge harming someone because of harm they have done you
revolt when people join together to try to get rid of their rulers
ritual a special kind of religious act

sacrifice killing animals, or people, to please the gods
sanitation methods of keeping towns and houses clean
sarcophagus a stone container for the remains of a dead person
scholar a person who knows a great deal, as a result of study
scout someone who goes in front of an army to spy out the land
scribe a person whose job was writing (especially letters and records)
selective breeding mating only the best animals in a flock or herd to improve its quality
shrine a small holy place
sickle a curved tool for cutting crops
siege when a town or castle is surrounded by an enemy who intends to capture it
silt mud left behind by a flood
skirmish a very small battle
strait a narrow stretch of sea between two areas of land
stratum a layer in an excavation
strigil a curved metal scraper used on the body in Roman baths
submit to agree to the rule of another king
successor someone who follows (or succeeds) another as ruler
superstitious ready to believe in magic, ghosts and such things
suppress to use force to prevent people getting their way
symbol a sign with a special meaning

talent a Roman measure of money
tavern an inn, pub
technical terms special words used by experts in a subject
tender a small boat which follows a larger one
terra cotta a type of pottery
toga a long robe worn by Roman men
trade routes the routes (by land or sea) followed by men buying and selling goods
traitor someone who gives secrets to the enemy
trawl a type of fishing net
treasury a store for the king's money
tributary a small river which runs into a larger one
tribute money paid by a conquered people to their conqueror
trireme a ship with three rows (or banks) of oars
tyrant a man who becomes ruler of a country, but has no legal right to hold power

villa the country house of a Roman noble

wattle building material made from willow branches woven together
whim a sudden idea, not well thought-out
wings (of an army) the sections at either end of a battle-line of soldiers

ziggurat a Mesopotamian step-shaped pyramid

Index

Acknowledgements

The author and publishers wish to thank the following who have kindly given permission for the use of copyright material:

Wm. Collins Sons & Co. Limited for short extracts from *Leakey's Luck* by Sonia Cole;

Encyclopaedia Britannica for an extract from 'Greece' contained in the 14th Edition 1973, 10:798;

The Loeb Classical Library (published by William Heinemann Limited and Harvard University Press) for quotations from the Loeb Editions of Polybius, Suetonius, Arrian, Diodorus Siculus and Aeschylus;

Metropolitan Museum of Art for an extract from *Models of Daily Life in Ancient Egypt from the Tomb of Meket-Re at Thebes* by H. E. Winlock, Egyptian Expedition Vol. XVIII;

Penguin Books Limited for extracts from *The Letters of the Younger Pliny* translated by Betty Radice from Penguin Classics 1969, Copyright © Betty Radice, 1963 and 1969, and *Herodotus: The Histories* translated by Aubrey de Selincourt from Penguin Classics, Revised Edition 1972, Copyright © 1954, The Estate of Aubrey de Selincourt.

The author and publishers wish to acknowledge the following photograph sources:

Aerofilms, pp. 65, 199.
Hallam Ashley, p. 32.
Ashmolean Museum, p. 73.
Barnaby's Picture Library, p.30.
Janet Bord, p. 36.
Trustees of the British Museum, pp. 16 middle right, 33, 42, 50 top, 51, 53, 57 bottom left, 61, 62, 63, 132 bottom, 137, 148, 173, 181 top, 196.
Trustees of the British Museum (Natural History), pp. 18, 20, 26 top left and right.
British Tourist Authority, p. 155 bottom.
Cambridge University Collection, pp. 31, 204.
Camera Press, pp. 12, 103, 182, 183.
Museo Capitolini, p. 185 bottom.
J. Allan Cash Ltd., p. 154 top right.
Peter Clayton, pp. 16 top left, 21 top, 38, 39, 43, 49, 52, 58 bottom, 69, 70, 72, 74, 75, 77, 79, 83 bottom, 88/89 bottom, 90 right, 91 bottom, 184 right.
Corinium Museum, Glos., pp. 202, 206 right.
Crown Copyright reproduced with permission of the Controller of Her Majesty's Stationery Office, pp. 200, 201.
Crown Copyright – National Monuments Records, p. 206 top.
Devizes Museum, p. 29.
Dorset Museum, p. 198.
Fototeca Unione, pp. 180 top, 186, 213.
Giraudon, pp. 143, 177.
Glyptotek, Copenhagen, p. 179 right.
Sonia Halliday title page, pp. 169, 188.
Robert Harding Associates, pp. 104/105, 105 right.
Photo Hinz, Basel, title page, p. 95.
M. Holford, p. 111 top, cover
India Office Library, p. 15.
Dame Kathleen Kenyon, p. 26 bottom.
A. F. Kersting, pp. 154 bottom right, 157 bottom, 206 bottom.
London Midland Region (B.R.), p. 154 bottom left.
Louvre Museum, p. 211.
Mansell Collection, pp. 134 right, 135, 152/153, 157 top, 159, 160, 162/163, 170, 171, 174, 184 left, 208, 216, 217.
Leonard Von Matt, p. 150.
The Metropolitan Museum of Art, Photo by Egyptian Expedition, pp. 88, 90 left, 91 top, 93.
The Metropolitan Museum of Art, Excavations 1919–20, Rogers Fund Supplemented by contribution of Edward S. Harkness, pp. 89, 92.
The Metropolitan Museum of Art, Rogers Fund 1914, p. 133 top.
Novosti Press Agency, p. 165.
Popperfoto, pp. 21 bottom, 48.
J. Powell, pp. 97, 98.
Press Assoc., p. 13.
Public Records Office, p. 16 middle left.
Radio Times Hulton Picture Library, p. 57 top left.
Science Museum title page, p. 17.
Rev. Prof. V. Schoder, S.J., pp. 139, 140, 145.
R. Sheridan title page, pp. 37, 45, 55, 56, 57 top right, 58 top, 60 top, 71, 80, 81, 82, 83 top, 86, 87, 108, 110, 111 bottom, 114, 115, 116, 117, 118, 121, 122, 123, 124, 126, 127, 128, 129, 130, 132 top, 134 left, 138, 142, 151, 154 top left, 155 top, 172, 185 top, 189, 190, 191, 192, 193, 194, 209, 210, 212.
Society of Antiquities of London, p. 16 bottom.
Snark International, p. 64.
Staatliche Museum Zu Berlin, pp. 66, 68.
Taken from the publication 'Sumer' Andre Parrot, p. 47.
The Times, p. 102.
N. A. Tombazi, p. 158.
John Topham Picture Library, p. 25.
Roger Viollet, p. 133 bottom.
By Permission of the Wellcome Trust, p. 60 bottom.
Werner Forman Archive, pp. 100, 101.
Roger Wood, pp. 40, 41, 166, 167.

The publishers have made every effort to trace the copyright holders, but if they have inadvertently overlooked any, they will be pleased to make the necessary arrangements at the earliest opportunity.